LITTLE KARL

13

Praise for *Dear Bob . . .*

"Bob Hope, the legendary Hollywood entertainer began doing USO shows in 1941 and continued supporting and encouraging troops for the next fifty years. He became the figurehead of tribute from an entire grateful nation, setting the bar very high in his fifty years of entertaining and supporting our troops. The correspondence in *Dear Bob . . .* is further proof of his absolute and unwavering commitment to the American G.I."
—GARY SINISE, actor, veterans advocate, and author of *Grateful American: A Journey from Self to Service*

"During World War II, Bob Hope saw firsthand the efforts of the American Red Cross to support military service members. He worked alongside us to build morale and raise the spirit of those who served, and he witnessed how we connected military members with their loved ones back home through emergency messages. He saw our Red Cross volunteers hand out comfort kits and care to the wounded in hospitals. It was through Bob Hope's compassion, commitment, and voice that the American Red Cross was able to make an even greater impact helping US service members during WWII."
—GAIL J. McGOVERN, president and chief executive officer of the American Red Cross

"*Dear Bob . . .* gets you in your gut, your heart, your soul. Timing is everything, as Bob Hope would attest. 'Timely' is this important, deeply moving publication. Martha and Linda hit it! This should be required reading in our schools. It's a labor of love—a treasured memorial to a true American and human being!"
—JUDITH B. FELDMAN, former personal assistant/secretary to Bob Hope

"During World War II, Bob Hope dedicated himself to live performances that brought his show to troops in the field where he saw the power of comedy lift the human spirit even in the most desperate of times. Hope's unique and powerful connection with those serving our nation is beautifully illustrated in the words of those servicemen in letters to Hope. Likewise, his replies demonstrate the energy and care he gave to the US troops in World War II and the decades beyond."
—STEPHEN WATSON, president and CEO, World War II Museum

"For a half century, Bob Hope entertained our men and women serving in uniform across the globe, bringing laughter, joy, and a bit of home to those standing the watch and safeguarding our American ideals. The Coast Guard is forever grateful for his service."
—ADMIRAL KARL SCHULTZ, 26th Commandant of the US Coast Guard

"College history profs take notice—you don't become 'the entertainer of the century' without depth of character and love for others. *Dear Bob . . .* will prove that and make history live for your students. *Dear Bob . . .* will move you between laughter and tears as you read letters sent by service members Bob entertained over five decades. When they heard him, they knew they could connect with him personally. *Dear Bob . . .* opens a window into their lives, our quiet national heroes, as they open their hearts to the man who had proven he cared about them. This glimpse into an unheralded facet of Bob Hope's care for others completes the picture of an amazing man."
—JAMES R. LYTLE, president, Clarks Summit University

"Of the twenty-seven Bob Hope shows in which I participated, the most heart-warming and powerful ones were those spent entertaining the men and women of our armed forces. We traveled all over the globe, and Bob never stopped entertaining. We were his sidekicks, performing spontaneous skits and singing songs whenever and wherever we were greeted by a group of servicemen and women. We would deplane the C-130 Fat Albert or land atop an aircraft carrier and begin cracking our rehearsed jokes, customizing them to the current location. Bob even risked sneaking out to the front lines alone, via a SEAL boat at the crack of dawn to visit and share a laugh with those who missed our shows. The love and appreciation Bob expressed energized our entourage and filled us with a beautiful sense of purpose."
—BROOKE SHIELDS

"Martha Bolton and Linda Hope remind us why people across the globe loved Bob Hope. He loved freedom and the men and women in uniform who worked to preserve and expand it. What a delightful and uplifting read!"
—MARSHA BLACKBURN, US Senator

"Bob Hope lit up the stage as our Oscars host nineteen times. He is the gold standard! We remember him not only as one of the world's greatest entertainers, but also among the most giving in our industry."
—DAWN HUDSON, CEO, Academy of Motion Picture Arts and Sciences

"It was said of Britain's inspirational wartime prime minister, Winston Churchill, that he marshaled words and sent them into battle. Thanks to the painstaking research efforts of Bob Hope writer Martha Bolton, with assistance from his daughter and producer Linda Hope, we are now privy to the words of some who participated in battle. Bob Hope not only praised America's military, he put his suitcase where his mouth was by traveling thousands of miles over the years to entertain troops in numerous theaters of war. We know about these classic and historic shows, but until this book we have not known, in their own words, about the bonds forged between this iconic entertainer and many of those who went in harm's way in service to our country. How Hope not only eased their sacrifice with laughter but touched their hearts in enduring ways is beautifully presented in this treasure trove of history."
—DOUG GAMBLE, member of the Bob Hope writing team from 1983–93 and writer of humor for Presidents Ronald Reagan and George H. W. Bush

"My dad, Jerry Colonna, was on a lot of these tours and was impressed with Bob's interest in the personal lives of the servicemen he spoke to. Jerry said that years later a guy in civvies might come up and introduce himself, and Bob would say something like, 'Okinawa! Hey, did that boy of yours make it into law school?' One of a kind."
—ROBERT COLONNA

"This story is not just about Hope but about all those individuals and groups he sought out and who relied on him to visit them. It is this sense of reciprocity that makes *Dear Bob* . . . a moving and essential volume."
—CARL ROLLYSON, biographer

"I was honored and privileged to have known Mr. Hope and worked with him on some of his television specials for our military. He was also a guest on my TV series, *Barbara Mandrell and the Mandrell Sisters*. He was so kind, and because of his enormous talent the world loved him!"
—BARBARA MANDRELL

"Martha Bolton and I have been good friends for about twenty years. I have read many of her books and from personal experience find her to be one of the greatest writers alive. I also must say as a comedy writer, she is the funniest lady on the planet!"
—DARRELL BLEDSOE, recording producer/music arranger/songwriter/author/publisher, former head of the Commercial Music Industry program, West Texas A & M University

"As a child of the 1950s and '60s, I grew up being entertained by Bob Hope. I loved his TV specials and movies. I thought he was the funniest man alive. Hope's USO Christmas shows were especially enjoyable. I went on to spend over twenty-two years on active duty in the US Army as a paratrooper and Green Beret. My service included multiple overseas and combat tours. Unfortunately, I never saw Hope in person. However, I was able to watch films of his shows and knew several fellow soldiers whom Hope touched personally. Martha Bolton's book is a long-overdue homage to the great service Hope provided to the troops. Even though this book concentrates on the G.I.s of WWII, it reflects the appreciation of the troops to whom he meant so much. Hope never forgot the G.I.s after WWII. He continued to visit troops in Korea and Vietnam, and during the Cold War and the First Gulf War. I heartily recommend this book. The letters truly reflect how multiple generations of G.I.s loved Bob Hope."
—W. A. "TONY" FUNDERBURG, Lt. Colonel US Army (RET)

DEAR BOB . . .

DEAR BOB...

**Bob Hope's Wartime
Correspondence with
the G.I.s of World War II**

Written and compiled by

Martha Bolton with Linda Hope

University Press of Mississippi ★ Jackson

The University Press of Mississippi is the scholarly publishing agency of
the Mississippi Institutions of Higher Learning: Alcorn State University,
Delta State University, Jackson State University, Mississippi State University,
Mississippi University for Women, Mississippi Valley State University,
University of Mississippi, and University of Southern Mississippi.

www.upress.state.ms.us

Designed by Peter D. Halverson

The University Press of Mississippi is a member of the Association of University Presses.

First printing 2021
∞

Library of Congress Cataloging-in-Publication Data available
Hardback ISBN 978-1-4968-3265-8
Epub single ISBN 978-1-4968-3266-5
Epub institutional ISBN 978-1-4968-3267-2
PDF single ISBN 978-1-4968-3268-9
PDF institutional ISBN 978-1-4968-3269-6

British Library Cataloging-in-Publication Data available

DEDICATED TO THE MEMORY OF BOB HOPE,

WHO GAVE SO MUCH TO THE TROOPS,

TO THE TROOPS

WHO GAVE SO MUCH FOR PEACE,

AND TO THOSE BRAVE SOLDIERS

WHO GAVE THEIR ALL

CONTENTS

FOREWORD

Linda Hope

MARTHA AND I HAVE WANTED TO DO THIS BOOK FOR MANY YEARS. THROUGH-
out my life, these letters have meant a lot to me in different ways. My first
memory was seeing them in their special boxes in my dad's home office. Their
orange spines and black-and-white-speckled sides stood neatly in a row on
a high shelf, and I was intrigued as a child. Time passed and I watched that
orange row grow, one, then two, then three rows, and on and on. Years later, as
a freshman in high school I remember having an assignment in my English
class, "Write about something that intrigues you."

I thought awhile and remembered those "mystery boxes" in my dad's office. I set about getting to the bottom of it. My first stop was Miss Hughes; yes,
"Miss Hughes" (not politically correct, but that's what everyone called her and
remember this was the 1940s). She was my dad's longtime secretary who had
been with him since I was a baby. I told her I was doing a report for my English
class on the contents of the orange boxes. "What's in them?" I asked. "It's history
. . . your dad's and our country's," she replied. "May I take a look?" She went on
to explain, "All of those boxes are filled with letters from our fighting men and
women who served at home and overseas, their family members back home
along with as many of your father's responses as he had the time to write, and
there were more letters than you can imagine. I'm amazed how he was able to
do all that he did and travel to as many places." She told me to come back later
and she would get down a couple of boxes for me to go through.

I wasn't at all surprised that Miss Hughes had organized all this correspondence, as she always carefully managed and kept meticulous records of all his
travel, show dates, and locations. Clearly, she was devoted to my dad and his
quest and did all she could to support his mission to bring laughter and a bit of
home to those men and women protecting this adopted country of his. Years
later, I grew to appreciate all she did to preserve my dad's legacy.

Each box contained a hundred or more letters, many with carbon copy (it
was the '40s), responses from my dad, which Miss Hughes somehow thought-
fully attached, knowing they would be an important part of the story of WW2.

As I was going through them, I was struck then, as I am now, that these letters really told the human side of what these men were going through and what Bob Hope and the laughter he brought meant to their morale and, not surprisingly, what these trips and the contact with the individuals serving meant to my dad.

Reading through these letters, which now reside at the Library of Congress, I was struck by how different our world was without the electronics and transportation we have today. In the forties, we had no computers, no e-mail, no instant communications, and travel that was done in much smaller, slower planes was far from the jet service of today. Even having lived through those challenging times I often forget what those days were like without our "modern conveniences." But it was also a time when everyone felt a commitment to work together and do their part. My dad was a great example of that. He had a gift for being able to make people laugh, and he shared it, willingly and without concern for his own well-being, and he enlisted others to do the same with their own gifts.

He always took a small troupe of fellow entertainers, who endured the endless hours of travel with many scary incidents, but who felt as he did about bringing a brief respite to those in great need (e.g., Frances Langford, a very popular movie star and singer; Patti Thomas, a young attractive tap dancer; Jerry Colonna, comedian; Tony Romano, a one-man band/guitarist; and Barney Dean, writer). They all traveled across the world together and faced all kinds of hell in order to do what they felt they had an obligation to do . . . entertain.

I remember as a child seeing them off as they boarded their plane for a very long flight. No flight attendants, no reclining seats, only semi-stale box lunches, many stops for fuel, and seemingly endless hours of uncomfortable flying ahead of them. We children waved good-bye while the adults faced fear and uncertainty, just like those serving.

I questioned my mother about why our dad had to leave us. She said, "Your dad is doing his part, and you and your brother must do yours. After all, he is only going to be gone for a few weeks, think of all the boys and girls who won't see their fathers for months or years, or ever." Throughout the war we were reminded of this each time my brother Tony and I grumbled that we missed our dad and wondered why he had to be away so much. He was so much fun when he was around, almost like having another playmate, and his absence left a hole in our lives.

We kept busy at home during those war years with all kinds of drives, collecting newspapers, tinfoil, Green Stamps, victory gardens, war bond drives, all in the effort to do what we could to help. Though I was quite young, I remember my mother signing up to serve in the AWVS (American Women's Voluntary Service). She wore a military-style uniform and took food to men stationed along the California coast, not too far from where we lived. She also helped establish other women's groups aimed at supporting those men far from home and the families they left behind. Another thing that was a part of life then were the blackouts and the fear they triggered, especially to those cities and towns situated along the coast who were constantly anxious about an invasion. There were curfews and we had to lower all the shades and pull the curtains so that our house wouldn't present a target.

One of the great joys back then were Dad's homecomings. It was a great relief to welcome him and his fellow performers. There was always a crowd of well-wishers and press wanting to get news from the various war zones, and a loved one hoping for a note or letter that my dad was given to deliver back in the states. G.I. mail often took weeks and even months to reach those waiting anxiously at home. On most of his trips, Dad would bring back trophies that had been given to him by the troops, different weapons and souvenirs of the war. One time he was up in his bedroom showing off his collection to us and giving my mother, my brother, and me small remembrances of where he had been. He picked up a gun that had been given to him, and my mother cautioned him to point it away from us, which he did as he pulled the trigger and said, "Don't worry, it's not loaded." With that there was a loud bang. My mother later had a picture of the gun painted on the cabinet pointing toward the bullet hole, with the words "And he said it wasn't loaded." He kept that reminder in his rooms as long as he lived.

Another reminder of those challenging days was the disease he called jungle rot that he picked up in the South Pacific. It was a nasty-looking infection that reoccurred on his feet and as a result he wore white socks as well as some kind of antifungal medicine. When I asked him about it one time he said he didn't mind, it made him think of all the diseases that our guys went through on those jungle-filled islands in the Pacific. That war and the horrors of it and mostly the sacrifice and determination of everyone during those times, especially our fighting men far away, were always with him.

Many years later, when he was in his eighties and in conjunction with the fiftieth anniversary of WW2, I produced a video, *Bob Hope: Memories of World War 2*. I was anxious to preserve those memories for posterity. We covered a lot of them, and I turned once again to those orange-spined, speckled boxes for inspiration, for a feeling of the times.

Dad had slowed down a bit by then and I was a little concerned how much he would remember, but as we were shooting, I was constantly surprised how vividly WW2 came back to him, especially when he told the story of he and my mother on board the *Queen Mary*, a very crowded ship bringing them back from England where the war had just escalated and Americans were urged to return home. He recalled word for word the special lyrics, a parody, he wrote to his theme song "Thanks for the Memory."

> *Thanks for the memory*
> *Of this great ocean trip*
> *On England's finest ship.*
> *Tho' they packed them to the rafters*
> *They never made a slip.*
> *Ah! Thank you so much.*
> *Thanks for the memory*
> *Some folks slept on the floor,*
> *Some in the corridor;*
> *But I was more exclusive,*
> *My room had "Gentlemen" above the door,*
> *Ah! Thank you so much.*

The ship's captain requested him to do a show that night to quiet the fears of the passengers who were anxious because of news that there were German subs lurking nearby waiting for orders to sink them . . . and he sang his song.

These and other memories, of sights he saw, of men and women he met and shared experiences with, the wounded he comforted, all remained a constant reminder to him throughout the hundred years of his life, of that special time when our country witnessed its "finest hour." These letters bear witness.

PREFACE

Martha Bolton

BOB HOPE. WHO WAS THIS MAN WHO EARNED SUCH LOVE AND RESPECT FROM the United States military that in 1997 he was named America's first Honorary Veteran by an act of Congress? A man who brought laughter to millions of soldiers, sailors, marines, pilots, guardsmen, officers, nurses, chaplains, and more for over fifty years in faraway lands and at home, bringing them a sense of hope when they needed it most. A man who dared to walk from bed to bed in military hospital wards, greeting the patients in body casts and traction with, "Don't get up." And the patients, some who for months hadn't cracked a smile or even talked, would laugh.

This "soldier in grease paint" traveled to some of the most out-of-the-way locations to perform for military audiences that would have easily filled football stadiums, while also being willing to show up for a handful of troops to perform from the back of a jeep or truck.

At the height of World War II, Bob Hope was receiving some 38,000 fan letters a week. He was the postman's nightmare and G.I. Joe's hero.

Over his remarkable one-hundred-year life span, he entertained eleven presidents (was friends and golfed with most of them), was named Entertainer of the Century, and has been called America's secret weapon and our nation's Ambassador of Laughter.

There wasn't a branch of show business that he didn't attempt and rise to the top of—radio, stage, film, television. He holds the record for hosting the Academy Awards (nineteen times) and had the longest-running contract with a television network in history (NBC, sixty years).

He was awarded five honorary Oscars for his contributions to entertainment and humanitarian efforts, he holds a Guinness Book World Record for being "the most honored and publicly praised entertainer" in history, and he was awarded the Presidential Medal of Freedom.

That was the man known as Bob Hope. And that's barely scratching the surface.

Anyone who knows Bob Hope, or read books about him or by him, or watched his movies and television specials, knows that the United States military held a special place in his heart. He hated war, just like most people, but he was always there for the troops. And they were there for him.

We hope by the time you finish reading *Dear Bob* . . . you'll understand why.

There were others who performed a good service by entertaining the military during World War II, and other wars, but no one did it quite like Bob Hope. Or as long. His was the show the soldiers requested most.

> "You are everybody's favorite because you can take it and you can give it."

> "Should you ever go into politics, you needn't worry about the votes. You already have all the servicemen's . . ."

These were the words of the soldiers themselves. They loved him like a brother, a father, an uncle.

Bob answered as many of the letters as he could, like this one response:

> **"Surely am pleased to know the boys out there really enjoyed our show. You know, my favorite audiences are those made up of G.I. Joes; and, as long as I'm assured they like our style of entertainment, they're going to get it."**
> **. . . Bob Hope**

What was it that set Bob apart from other entertainers, especially for these wartime shows? For one thing, Bob came across to the troops as one of them. He wasn't just another celebrity, looking to get some publicity. He was the champion of their complaints, the spokesman for their chagrins, and the bringer of home to their lonely hearts. Nobody did it better. And, more than anything, he respected them as men, even though many were mere boys.

There wasn't an area of service that he forgot either. He paid ample tribute to them all because he knew winning this war was a team effort, including those back home who were pulling and praying for them.

Bob would be quick to say he couldn't have done it alone. He had his faithful troupe that would answer the call at a moment's notice and travel with him. This team consisted of Frances Langford, Jerry Colonna, Patty Thomas, Tony Romano, and Barney Dean. Others would come along as guest stars on his radio shows—celebrity friends of his, actors, singers, sports stars, and more, but he depended on his core group most often.

Inviting one or two of the troops or brass to join him on stage was another aspect of Bob's live shows that he enjoyed doing. The troops loved this, especially when he had mail to share with them. Like the soldiers who got surprised by the first photos of their new baby back home they hadn't seen yet.

Just because he was on the entertainment side of the war didn't mean he didn't see any action either. There were times when he would arrive at his destination only to discover the enemy had bombed it just before he got there in hopes of taking out "America's secret weapon." Incoming would often happen during shows, exploding close enough to the stage that Bob could feel the heat and get his sideburns trimmed the hard way.

World War II news correspondent Ernie Pyle described the troupe's military travels this way: "It isn't often that a bomb falls close enough that you can hear it whistle. But when you can hear a whole stick of them whistling at once, then it's time to get weak all over and start sweating. The Hope troupe can describe that ghastly sound . . ."

The voices of the men and women included within these pages—and this is just a small sampling of the hundreds of thousands of letters that Bob received—tell a story. It's the ultimate "buddy" story from a man who knew buddy stories. It's a tale of adventuring into the unknown for the noblest of causes.

These letters moved Bob. He could hardly speak of them without being taken back to those years, those shows, and the memories they held. The men and women in uniform represented here, and in all the other letters he received, were his own sons and daughters.

As you read their words—funny, homesick, fearful, many penned under the most difficult of circumstances—we hope you see what we saw—how much the G.I.s loved and respected this man called Bob Hope and how much he loved and respected them right back.

Bob Hope could have done anything with his celebrity. He chose to dedicate it to our troops. We've shared some of Bob's life and career. These letters will share his heart.

DEAR BOB . . .

(Top) Bob Hope and Dolores Reade Hope stand on deck of the SS *Normandie* sailing to England from New York, August 2, 1939.

(Bottom) Bob and Dolores Hope's Toluca Lake home.

INTRODUCTION

— — — — — — — — — — — — — —

**"Contrary to what you've heard, I did not entertain the troops at
Valley Forge."**
. . . Bob Hope

The year was 1939. World War I had come and gone, leaving behind its scars
and old grudges. America was a decade beyond the stock-market crash and still
finding her way out of the Great Depression. By all accounts it was high time for
some laughter. One man, England born and American raised, was destined to
provide those laughs through the next world war that was brewing, and every
war that followed for the rest of the century. That man's name was Bob Hope.

Bob Hope came to America as a youngster, but even then, he knew there
was something about this new country that he loved.

**"I left England at the age of four . . . when I found out I couldn't
be king."**
. . . Bob Hope

Raised in Cleveland, Ohio, young Bob entered and won his first talent contest—impersonating Charlie Chaplin. That later led to stage shows with a variety of dance partners, vaudeville, stand-up comedy (before it was even called
that), and Broadway, where he met and married singer Dolores Reade.

Life was going well for this seemingly unstoppable talent. On the east coast,
at least. But what about Hollywood? Its warm weather and movies were en-
ticing, but he had tried that once. His less-than-promising screen test hadn't
opened any new doors for him. Maybe his timing would be better now.

Leaving behind the rave reviews of Broadway, Bob Hope and Dolores decided to move west and give Tinseltown another chance.

The newlyweds found their dream home on Moorpark Street in Toluca Lake,
California, a house that would undergo many renovations and additions over
the next six decades as Bob's family and career continued to grow.

This time Hollywood was more welcoming, and the offers started coming.

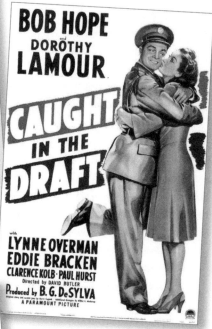

Bob Hope's 1941 film releases, Paramount Studios.

The Big Broadcast of 1938, which introduced the tune that would become his signature song, "Thanks for the Memory," was a huge hit, and the 1938–1939 Hooper Radio Ratings listed his new radio show at number 15 and climbing.

By 1940 his show had shot up to third place with a 28.2 share, nipping at the heels of both Jack Benny's and Bergen and McCarthy's radio shows (#1 and #2, respectively).

"I've always been in the right place and time. Of course, I steered myself there."
. . . Bob Hope

In April 1941, Bob Hope's film *Road to Zanzibar* released, followed by three other Bob Hope pictures later that same year: *Caught in the Draft* (July 4), *Nothing but the Truth* (October 10), and *Louisiana Purchase* (December 31). *Four* films releasing in *one* year. Bob Hope had become a major box office draw, no doubt about it.

Nineteen forty-one would also be the year that two completely different worlds would intersect. It happened at March Field in Riverside, California, on May 6. It was at this crossroad of celebrity and purpose that Bob Hope walked onto the stage and performed for his very first military audience.

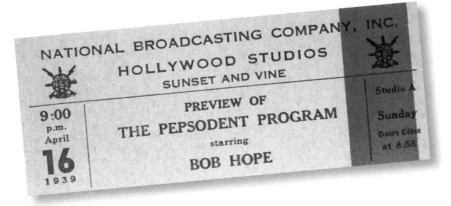

Ticket to a preview of Bob Hope's Pepsodent Radio Show, 1939.

DEAR BOB . . .

WE GOT DRAFTED. HOW'D YOU GET HERE?

— — — — — — — — — — — — — — — — —

IT WAS BOB'S RADIO PRODUCER AL CAPSTAFF WHO SPUN DESTINY INTO MO-tion. He thought it might be a novel idea to take Bob's radio show on location to a military base. Bob wasn't so sure. After all, his radio show was attracting some of the hottest stars of the day—Judy Garland, Doris Day, Frances Lang-ford, and many more, including renowned bandleaders Desi Arnaz and Les Brown. Bob was in his sweet spot and clearly having the time of his life. Why tinker with success?

Bob Hope and Judy Garland, Bob's radio show. Courtesy of Library of Congress and Bob Hope's personal files.

Bob Hope and Rosemary Clooney.

Bob Hope and Dorothy Lamour.

"What's March Field?" Bob asked Capstaff, still resisting the idea.

Capstaff explained it was a military base in Riverside.

"What do we do there?"

Bob couldn't see where Capstaff was going, but Capstaff wouldn't be deterred. He had an ulterior motive—his brother was stationed there. The pressure paid off. He convinced Bob to do the show, advising him to simply treat it like any other radio broadcast.

But March Field turned out to be no ordinary radio broadcast. That military audience was like no other audience Bob had ever experienced. And he loved every minute of it!

Bob Hope's radio show, March Field. Bob Hope Collection, Motion Picture, Broadcasting and Recorded Sound Division, Library of Congress.

By some estimates, nearly two thousand soldiers crammed into the March Field gymnasium that hot day in May—the high hitting a sweltering 94 degrees (and this was before central air conditioning). But the heat and overflow crowd didn't stop the laughs from coming. Once Bob heard the thunderous sound of grateful troops starved for laughter, he knew he had found his dream audience.

> **"These guys were glad to see me . . . One rookie came running up to me and said, 'Are you really Bob Hope?' I said, 'Yes!' . . . they grabbed his rifle just in time."**
> **. . . Bob Hope, March Field, 1941**

Joining Bob on the stage that day were Frances Langford, Bing Crosby, Jerry Colonna, Skinnay Ennis and the band, and Bob's regular announcer Bill Goodwin. The show couldn't have gone any better. Bob was thrilled and Al Capstaff was a hero.

America hadn't entered the war yet. What was going on over in Europe was something she had been observing from afar; keeping her eye on it, but also keeping a distance.

Then came December 7, 1941, and everything changed.

Color poster of Doris (Dorie) Miller by David Stone Martin. Library of Congress, Prints & Photographs Division, LC-DIG-ppmsca-40819.

Sunday News-Democrat headline, December 7, 1941.

After the battleship *West Virginia* had been torpedoed at Pearl Harbor, Dorie Miller found himself manning an antiaircraft machine gun (one that he wasn't even trained on) and is reported to have shot down several enemy planes. He was later awarded the Navy Cross for his courageous and speedy action.

The day after the Pearl Harbor bombing, President Franklin D. Roosevelt took to the airwaves and addressed the nation with these words: "Yesterday, December 7, 1941—a date which shall live in infamy—the United States of America was suddenly and deliberately attacked by naval and air forces of the Empire of Japan."

The surprise attack had caused heavy destruction and many lives were lost. America could no longer stand on the sidelines and watch. She was thrust into the middle of the conflict now and more than determined to help end it. Japan may have dealt a significant blow to America's battleships, but not to her spirit.

After the attack, Admiral Isoroku Yamamoto of the Japanese military was reported to have said, "I fear all we have done is awaken a sleeping giant and fill him with a terrible resolve."

He was right.

> **"I was in my car on the way to Lakeside Golf Course, listening to a football game from the Polo Grounds in New York. Suddenly, I heard words I couldn't believe. 'The Japanese have bombed Pearl Harbor.'"**
> **. . . Bob Hope,** *I Was There*

Across the country, men and women were enlisting. Young men, many still in their teens, were leaving families and friends behind and signing up to fight. Women joined as military nurses and filled other positions to help in the war effort. The draft was enacted. Everyone was needed.

Bob Hope was eager to do his part as well, but the powers that be felt his talents would be best utilized in another capacity—boosting the morale of the troops. An assignment he knew he could do and didn't take lightly.

"'Bing and I had an offer to become lieutenant commanders in the
Navy,' Hope said of the late Bing Crosby. 'But Roosevelt said no. He
said we'd be more valuable entertaining all the troops.'"
DEBORAH HASTINGS, Associated Press, May 18, 1990

Wherever our troops were stationed, Bob Hope was determined to show
up. No encampment was too small, no base too remote, no hospital ward too
hopeless to keep this "soldier in greasepaint" away.

Bob's original March Field experience now became the template for his radio
shows, which he figured could be broadcast from a variety of military bases
around the nation and the world. His material would focus on all aspects of
military life—the food, the accommodations, dealing with superiors, weekend
passes, missing family and sweethearts, and all those ever-changing topics in
the news. He set his writers to work, packed up his duffle bag, and waited for
his first orders to come through.

With five decades of future military shows waiting for him in the wings,
and with the blessing of his bride, Bob stepped into his new mission. For Bob
Hope, it was a perfect fit. As for the soldiers? They may not have realized it at
the time, but this new brand of comedian they called Rapid Robert, who only
needed a microphone and an audience, and on occasion a golf club, was about
to become their symbol of hope in every war to the end of the century.

The first stop following America's entrance into the war—Alaska.

The following excerpt from an interview with retired US Air Force colonel
Robert Gates, the man who flew Bob to Alaska and the Aleutians for his first
USO show, provides a glimpse into just how this Bob Hope/G.I. Joe relation-
ship was going to go:

One of many goodbyes.
Bob and Dolores Hope, 1943.

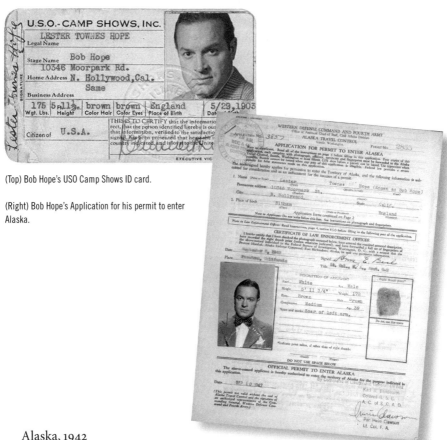

(Top) Bob Hope's USO Camp Shows ID card.

(Right) Bob Hope's Application for his permit to enter Alaska.

Alaska, 1942

. . . We arrived at Fairbanks and we walked into the Officers' Club, and lo and behold, there was Bob Hope with Frances Langford, and Jerry Colonna, and Tony Romano the guitar player, and an Army captain. And I introduced myself, and Bob says, "You're gonna fly us?"

I said, "Yes, sir."

And he said, "How old are you?"

I said, "I'm 22."

And he said, "You still got growing pains!"

And that was my nickname until about two months before he died [in 2003]. That was my nickname through 60-some years.

Nobody flew at night [in Alaska] because there were no radio letdowns [and navigational beacons] to speak of, except at Fairbanks and Anchorage, and at Elmendorf [Air Force Base].

So we went over to Valdez, the main port for Alaska. Bob did a show at about three in the afternoon for about half of the 600 or so servicemen who were there unloading the ships. And we were just ready to leave when the commander said, "Mr. Hope, only half of my troops got to see your show. Couldn't you do another one now?"

And Bob says, "Of course we can!"

And I said, "Bob, no we can't. We can't fly at night up here. We can't go back tonight."

"Oh, sure we can," he says. "It's only an hour and a half over there. We can do that."

So we did the show, and got back to the airport at about 9 p.m., and it's raining. And the mountains are 12,000 feet high there. So we did a tight turn at 12,000 feet through the rain and started on course, and we got into the ice and one engine quit. And then the radio went out. So there we were, the mountains higher than we were, losing altitude about 200 feet a minute, and how we got through is beyond me to tell you, other than God was looking out for us.

I remember Bob coming up and tapping me on the shoulder and saying, "Everybody back there is praying."

I said, "You tell 'em don't stop!"

The commander of the 11th Air Force had sense enough when they couldn't contact us to turn on all the search lights and point them to this same point in the sky over Elmendorf. And on our arrival, as we were letting down at about 6,000 feet, we saw the glow in the murk in the sky and let down on that and landed.

We couldn't taxi, we were all iced up, and had only one engine. So all the generals come rushing out of there, and the base commander and so on, and they were thanking Bob for a safe trip and everything, and I was the last one to come out of the airplane. And Bob put his arm around me and said, "Okay, now let's go to the barracks and change our drawers." And that's how we became the best of friends.

When I met him, at age 22, it changed my whole life.*

As challenging as that first Alaska trip turned out to be, Bob continued returning both during and after the war. Not only would he visit the troops stationed there, but Alaska became one of his favorite vacation spots for its unspoiled scenery and salmon fishing. Once, when asked why he didn't just retire and fish there full time, Bob explained: "Fish don't applaud."

---

* Used by permission from the author, Rebecca Maksel, *Air & Space Smithsonian Magazine*, January 2010 issue. Colonel Gates also flew Hope to shows in Europe after World War II, and to Vietnam in the 1960s. He spent over thirty years in the US Army Air Forces and Air Force, serving in Europe during World War II as a troop transport pilot for the 101st and 82nd Airborne.

(Top) Bob Hope, 1942, Umnak Island, Aleutian Islands.

(Middle) Bob Hope with troupe and others in front of the faithful-to-the-end *Growin' Pains* plane.

(Bottom) Bob Hope sits in the audience with Frances Langford, Jerry Colonna, and Tony Romano, Alaska USO show, 1942.

"You heard about the airman who was making his first parachute drop? Well, his first lieutenant told him which cord to pull, and told him when he hit the ground, there would be a station wagon waiting to drive him back to the base. So the airman jumped out of the plane and when he pulled the cord, nothing happened, and he said . . . 'And I bet the station wagon won't be there either.'"
. . . Bob Hope, Alaska

Those cold Alaskan temperatures and fluctuating flight conditions didn't slow Bob down for a second.

FAIRBANKS DAILY NEWS-MINER, Sept. 22, 1942—SEATTLE

Bob Hope, famous star of stage, screen and radio, is back in Seattle after having entertained soldiers in Fairbanks and other places in Alaska at the unprecedented pace of 58 benefit shows in eight days.

"It was a wonderful experience," he said. "One I wouldn't trade for the three years I've been giving shows."

"They're a wonderful lot of men in Alaska. They are doing a grand job."

Hope and his troupe immediately went to work on a new show that will be given first at McChord Field.*

Fifty-eight shows in eight days. No matter how you break it down, that's a remarkable pace by anyone's standards. Bob would probably say he did it to keep warm, but the troops knew better. They knew, even that early in their relationship, that this Hollywood star being sent to entertain them was different. He was one of them.

Whether it was, "This is going on at home so be glad you're away," or "This is what you're missing, so hurry up and get home and enjoy it, too," the troops couldn't get enough of "this Hope guy":

"We were on the coast of France on D-Day and I think when we heard your program that night that was when we most appreciated you . . ."

"I am writing you this letter for myself and my gang. My Gang is the Whole U.S. Army. We really think you are a great guy and you sure have done more for the boys than all the rest of them put together."

* Reprinted with permission, *Fairbanks Daily News-Miner*.

Bob Hope speaking to crowd gathered in Victory Square, Seattle, 1942. Photo courtesy of MOHAI, Seattle Post-Intelligencer Collection, pi28264.

"Many thanks for the thousands of laughs during the time when we needed them most."

"All hands say—Thanks for the finest memory we've had in ages, and thanks to every member of your entourage who gave us such a grand glimpse of an America we hope to return to soon, and then soon to go out again to defend—by definite and downright victory."

"We had no idea we were going to discover an audience so ready for laughter, it would make what we did for a living seem like stealing money."
. . . Bob Hope

Bob Hope and G.I. Joe were well on their way to a fifty-year unbreakable friendship. Whenever and wherever he was needed, he would go. He also kept up with his other career demands. And his growing stacks of fan mail. But every Tuesday night he was delivering his radio show from base after base across America and beyond.

(Top) A sampling of Bob's 1942 radio shows.

(Middle) Bob Hope and Lana Turner.

(Left) Bob Hope and Gloria DeHaven.

(Right) Bob Hope and Bette Davis.

(Bottom) Bob Hope and Lauren Bacall.

Babe Ruth, Betty Hutton, and the others listed on the 1942 itinerary were just some of the top-rated stars who appeared with Bob.

True to his commitment, Bob was bringing the troops high-quality entertainment and talking about the things they wanted to talk about. For Bob, a promise was a promise. He was determined to keep his side of the bargain and keep showing up no matter what and no matter where.

Bob Hope may have been the name most associated with these military shows, but the sacrifice made by Dolores and their four children over the years cannot be understated. Dolores selflessly partnered with her husband on this journey of celebrity for a remarkable sixty-nine years. Hollywood can be tough on a marriage, but theirs survived. As for the kids, perhaps son Tony summed up life in the Hope household best when as a youngster he welcomed his father home with this greeting: "Hiya, Bob Hope."

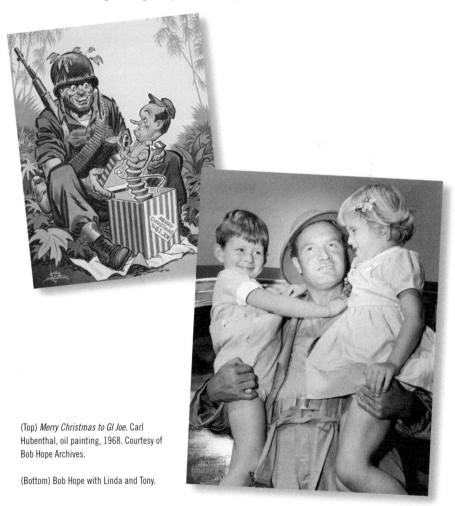

(Top) *Merry Christmas to GI Joe.* Carl Hubenthal, oil painting, 1968. Courtesy of Bob Hope Archives.

(Bottom) Bob Hope with Linda and Tony.

Bob and Dolores Hope with daughter Linda and son Tony Hope, Jerry and Flo Colonna and their son Robert at the Burbank Airport, home from the South Pacific . . . for a brief visit.

"I wanna tell ya . . ." That's how he'd begin. And you knew what was coming next: the jokes. Rapid fire, one after another and another, usually six to a minute, according to James Hardy, Bob Hope historian. Bob had incredible recall of the material, too.

> "During WWII his live performances were from memory. He used
> no notes. Cue cards were not invented until the early 50s."
> —JAMES HARDY

Bob Hope was a master at comedic timing, and he had a knack for self-deprecation humor. He was the everyday man who couldn't get a break, the guy who was more bravado than brave, more hapless than hero. This endeared him to the troops. He wasn't a celebrity just dropping in for a photo op. He wanted to be one of them.

> **"I had a wonderful trip out here from Los Angeles. You know
> those big streamlined trains that make it across the country in
> three days? Five of 'em passed the freight car I was in.**
> **"But I'm thrilled to be here. And what a wonderful welcome
> they gave me! As soon as I got into camp, I received a 10-gun
> salute. . . . They told me on the operating table."**
> **. . . . Bob Hope**

He delivered the jokes as only he could—perfectly timed, moving seamlessly from topics in the news to military life to sweethearts back home—all topped off with that famous Bob Hope sneer. And he did it from memory, the live shows. He would walk out on stage and deliver jokes that had just been written. He could use scripts for the radio shows, but not the live appearances.

Those six jokes per minute for an hour show calculates to three hundred and sixty jokes. From memory. Jokes that were constantly changing, according to location and whatever was happening in the news. And the troops couldn't get enough.

Many of these kids were barely out of high school, and some had never been away from home before. They were scared, uncertain about the future, and plenty lonely. It had to feel good to laugh.

Keep in mind, too, that in the 1940s, a letter to a loved one in the service could take weeks, months, and in some cases years to reach the intended soldier, following them around the globe from one base to the next. Many, too many, ended up never being delivered at all, leaving their love, tears, and all those "what might have beens" revealed solely to a government censor or postal clerk in the dead letter office.

> *Dear Bob . . . I just received your Christmas card yesterday and really appreciated it. It took exactly four months to the day to catch up to me . . .*

Imagine the loneliness of the World War II soldier, waiting for news from home. And imagine the anxiety of the families left behind, not receiving any word from their enlisted son or daughter for months.

Bob Hope would bridge that gap. He was a soldier's connection to home, and a family's connection to the battle zones. That's why they wrote to him. He was a friend of the family. They could tell him anything. And they did.

Family of a Portuguese dory fisherman staying close to the radio. Massachusetts: US Office of War Information, 1942. Library of Congress, Prints & Photographs Division, FSA/OWI Collection, LC-USW3-002070-C.

Mail Call. Edward
Sallenbach, li-
thographer, 1945.
Library of Congress,
Prints & Photo-
graphs Division,
LC-DIG-pga-08183.

Many of these letters didn't even have Bob's full or correct address. They would simply be addressed to "Bob Hope, in care of Paramount Studios." Or Pepsodent. Or NBC. Sometimes it was just, "Bob Hope in Hollywood," hoping the postman would know. Apparently, writing to Bob Hope was a little like writing to Santa Claus. Somehow, you just knew the letters would find their way to him.

In 1944, Bob Hope's cache of approximately 38,000 letters arrived in his mailbox every week. In some cases, the soldiers didn't even use regular envelopes or writing paper. They used whatever they could find to serve their purpose. Some wrote their missives on paper bags, coconut shells, and yes, even bathroom tissue.

Mail call could be a bittersweet scene with the troops standing around waiting, hoping to hear their name called. That's why Bob did his best to answer as many of their letters as he could. Not just a standard reply either. He would make it personal, often including funny comments and even a bit of personal news to help get their minds off the battles they were fighting . . . if even for a brief moment.

When Bob Hope left us in 2003 at the tender young age of one hundred, many of his professional papers were given to the Library of Congress for safekeeping and to be shared with the American people. His collection of military letters was among that donation.

★★★

(Top) US Navy, WWII mail clerk patch.

(Middle) No matter where Bob was, the mail always seemed to find him . . . even when addressed to:
Bob "location doubtful but probably near Hollywood, California" Hope.

(Right) All mail had to go through the security, receiving the censor stamp as on the V-mail shown here.

(Bottom two) Some soldiers got creative with their envelopes, sending Bob their original artwork.

Just a portion of the cherished boxes filled with soldiers' letters and other artifacts given to the Library of Congress from Bob Hope's archives. Photo by Frances Allhouse, Library of Congress.

(Linda) They were like a part of the family. In war years, they were a steady stream going in and out of the house. In times of peace, they represented some of Dad's most cherished and heart-tugging memories.

When I (Martha) first heard about the letters, I talked to Bob about the possibility of putting them into a book someday. There is so much history in this one-of-a-kind collection, so much reality of war, and life-sustaining laughter in the midst of it all. But what intrigued me the most was the obvious bond between Bob and the troops that comes through in every letter.

The letters also reveal some of the close calls he and his troupe experienced.

> "Your dad is the bravest man I've ever seen. He is fearless and he will go anywhere for a laugh."
> —MORT LACHMAN, writer for Bob Hope, to Linda Hope

DEAR BOB . . .

DROP ME A FEW LINES, WILL YA?

— — — — — — — — — — — — —

IT WAS THE MOMENT EVERY SOLDIER DREAMED ABOUT—MAIL CALL. THE troops lined up and waited. One by one, the lucky soldiers whose names were called stepped up and took their mail. Others held their breath as the mailbag slowly emptied. Only a half bag of letters left. Then, a quarter bag. Would the next letter be for them? Would they hear their name called? For a war-weary soldier longing for a word from home, there is no silence like that silence.

According to the Smithsonian Postal Museum, mail volume doubled between the years of 1943 and 1945. For some soldiers, a letter from home bore sad news—a loved one had passed away in their absence. For families at home, the letters sometimes told of injuries suffered on the battlefield. Other letters spoke of romance, and some were what became known as "Dear John" letters, announcing the long-distance romance had grown cold. Most of the time, though, mail call brought happy news from home, deeply felt love, care packages of toiletries, home-baked cookies, and other items that had a knack for arriving just in the nick of time.

Mail call aboard a transport ship, 1942. Corporal James G. Kissanitakis, mail orderly. US Army, image courtesy of Golden Gate NRA, Park Archives PAM prints collection, GOGA-1766.

(Top left) US Army troops sorting Christmas mail.

(Top right) A G.I. laments a common heartbreak: "No mail came in today."

(Right) Letting those back home know.

(Middle left) The United States Post Office provided V-mail, a sheet of stationary that could be folded and used as an envelope, to the troops for free, two sheets per customer per day.

(Middle right) Mail call in the barracks. Library of Congress, Prints & Photographs Division, FSA/OWI Collection, LC-USW3- 014340-D.

(Bottom) Almost everything a new G.I. needed to know about his or her WWII military service.

YOUR MAIL
(From the United States Government, Your Guide to Military Service, dated 1945)

No need to tell you the importance of mail to you as well as to those you love. Separation is a hard thing to take . . . but it's just as hard on those you are leaving behind. Make a firm resolve to keep that promise you'll soon be making . . . to "write often." As a member of the Armed Forces, you enjoy the privilege of free mailing of your letters . . . make use of it. Your Government is handling a staggering mail problem with great efficiency and sacrifice. It sees that your mail gets to you promptly . . . at all costs . . . every human effort is made to keep in tact the tie between you and your home.

Men receive their mail in fox holes on the battle line . . . in ships on the seven seas . . . everywhere. An elaborate system is maintained to insure the constant knowledge of your whereabouts. Delivery of packages may sometimes be slow, depending on where you are. Point this out to your family and ask them to watch published dates for Christmas mailing, packaging instructions, etc. Recommend and make use of the wonders of V-mail when overseas. No safer, surer form of mail service has ever been devised. Write often . . . don't put it off.

3/28/44

Dear Mr. Hope
Just a line to thank you for the lift you and Frances gave to my husband while you were on the Caribbean.

He's been there ten months now, and you're the first good news that's happened to him. When he wrote, he was very pleased as they were expecting you—and a prospective visit from Mrs. Roosevelt. What he said was, "Sure can use that 'Hope' guy. After you'd been there he told me how much they all enjoyed you, and remarked that he "can't see how that guy can stand up under it all."

Thanks again—you do wonders.
Sincerely,
Mrs. J. F. Sneed

Jan. 30, 1944

Dear Mr. Hope
I want to thank you from the bottom of my heart for your thoughtful-
ness in remembering my son "Bert McDowell" and sending me that
wonderful letter about him . . . He lost his own life by saving three
others, and yet he could not have a flag draped on his coffin after I
brought his body home from New Orleans, because the Merchant
Marines were not recognized by the Navy at that time. I had one boy
to visit me after he came out of the hospital to tell me how my boy
kept their courage up when they all were in the water. My husband
who is in the "Sea Bees" just came home . . . after being in N. Africa
for nine months. He was telling me what a wonderful show you gave
them over there.
*   . . . You will never know just what that letter means to me, so*
thanking you again.

I remain
Sincerely yours,
Mrs. Hattie Singer
Lima, Pa.

Dec. 1. 1944

Dear Bob,
*   . . . I haven't heard much about you lately in the papers, and I very*
seldom get a chance to listen to the radio. We were out at Normandy
on D-Day and lost our ship over there. I also lost all of my gear. And
your picture was in my sea bag.
*   If it wouldn't be too much trouble, would you send me another*
picture?
*   . . . I'm on a short leave now. And I am also married to a girl from*
around Boston here.
*   I've been with my wife for three days now, and we've been married*
a year.
*   . . . I hope you're well, and don't think me kidding or fooling when I*
tell you this, but the guys are praying for you . . .

Joe Cleary

Dec. 26, 1942

Dear Bob:
… This year's Christmas was the first one that I have spent away from home. The hymns and carols broadcasted throughout the day made me homesick and all "broken up" inside. I tried not to think of home, yet somehow I couldn't keep my thoughts from wandering back to those joyous moments spent on Christmas Eve and the following holiday week.

I tried to forget by reading, but it was to no avail. Then I happened to tune in on the variety program, in which you participated as M.C. After listening to the program, I felt greatly relieved. I know I'm just a home-sick rookie, but I'm sure those veterans of campaigns in staunch Australia, raging N. Africa, isolated Iceland, and those who went through hell in Bataan, Guadalcanal and Singapore would have forgotten some of the past, had they heard that wonderful program.

This line of thought compelled me to write and congratulate you. Keep up the good work, Bob, and may God bless you.

An Ardent Admirer

Italy
January 2, 1944

Dear Bob:
I want to thank you a million for the Christmas card. It was really swell of you. Honest.

Things are still about the same with me and the fellows over here, still hoping and praying that this old war will end soon.

… The boys and myself wish you all the luck in the world in the coming year.

Don't forget that fruitcake.

Sincerely yours,

Bob Wallace
P.S. Write soon

11/4/1944 (Italy)

Dear Bob Hope,
. . . What we would like to know is "are you married," and if so, who is the poor girl who's got to put up with you?
I hope you can find time to answer this letter as we would like to hear from you.

Sincerely,
Pte. R. Morrison

June 9, 1944
Pte. Morrison
Carrier Plt. "S" Coy
C.M.F.

Dear Private Morrison,
It's always good to hear from you boys. . . . Of course, I'm married! You don't think the girls would miss a chance like that, do you? Oh, yes . . . I'm a family man.
Speaking of Bing . . . he's just finished work on a new picture . . . and am I glad! It's hard work taking care of his kids . . . and I was tired of feeding his horses, too!
. . . There's my call . . . so will have to close now and get back on the set. So long now and the best of luck to you all.

Sincerely,
Bob Hope

"When we started to loop the loop, I said to the pilot, 'How come you're wearing a parachute, and I'm not?' He said, 'Well, they need me.'"
. . . Bob Hope on one of his military flights

Somewhere Over There
9 November 1943

Dear Bob:
Many things have happened since I had the pleasure of spending a
little time with you in Sicily. . . . I do want you to know that I appreci-
ate more than you can ever know the grand letter you wrote to my
wife. Frankly, I thought you might forget all about the poor Provost
Sergeant, but I should have known better as I had you rightly tabbed
as a "regular guy." I assure you that is not flattery, we old Army regu-
lars don't play that way. You either are or you aren't, and in your case,
you are. 'Nuff said.

Bill Cunningham

January 30, 1944

Dear Bob,
Received your lovely Christmas card and was very surprised to get it.
The reason it took so long to get to me . . . we have dropped our unit
number and are now called by our real names, "The Third Marines."
If there was a man ever more proud of a regiment than I, I would like
to see him. Maybe you have heard of us and maybe you haven't. We
[participated] in the Bougainville campaign. I know our outfit is a
crack outfit. I know that when they go out to do something, they do it.
. . . I have followed your travels a great deal. When you went to
Africa and cheered those boys over there, I knew then you were a swell
guy. I just wish you could have gotten to our place in the South Pacific,
but at least it makes me happy to read about you.
They say you're the eighth wonder of the world and I believe them.
Sometimes I wonder how you can carry on. You seem to keep on and
on, and there is no stopping you. You must have a swell wife to keep
you going, and I bet your kids are real proud of you. You're everything
a kid could want. I know your wife must love you dearly, and I bet it's
hard to give you up to the public. I just wish I could see you in person
and tell you how much I think you have done for the men overseas.
I've seen times when it was raining so hard that you could take a

shower, rinse yourself, row back to your tent, get in your bunk, dry yourself and float away in pleasant dreams.

. . . As for myself, I am just one of the rugged Marines. I know my duty when I see it and I'll carry it out to my best possibility. As the old saying goes, "It's the Marines who get the situation well in hand." We are fighting for men like you, Bob. Men who show us the happy side of life.

. . . I have a nice girl back home and just waiting to get home to marry her, but still, it's guys like you that keeps us going. I have been overseas now for about nineteen months . . .

Please do answer this.

Yours sincerely,
Carl—"Greeny" to my friends
Cpl. C. L. Greenfield
H & S Co., 3rd Marines—90 Fleet Post Office
San Francisco, Calif.

(Left) US Marines make their way through muddy terrain in Bougainville Island in Papua New Guinea on November 4, 1943. Library of Congress, Prints & Photographs Division, LC-USZ62-105509.

(Right) Bob Hope and Barney Dean on plane, Bougainville.

December 23, 1942

Dear Bob:

Of course it <u>might</u> be only a coincidence, but after your broadcast from Lowry Field #2 on December 15th, the entire camp was quarantined.

But there [are] no hard feelings among the boys as the quarantine has just been lifted and we are all once again as free as birds (yard-birds).

I just thought you would like to know.

Admiringly yours,
Private Sheldon F. Cooper
366 T.S.S. (Sp)
Lowry Field #2
Denver, Colorado

(Top) Bob Hope dances on stage at Bougainville.

(Bottom) Pilots cheer after Marshall Islands attack that downed seventeen out of twenty Japanese aircraft headed for Tarawa. November 1943. 80-G-470985. National Archives Identifier: 520896.

Somewhere in Holland

Feb. 26, 1945

Dear Bob,
Just a note to say hello, and to let you know how all the guys look
forward to your broadcast. Keep it up. I never knew before how much
the guys like you. I need my morale lifted, too, ya know. Well, this is,
as I said, just a short note. So give my love to all around the "club." . . .
Best to all.

Your pal,
Mickey (Pfc. Mickey Rooney)

May 15, 1946
Denver, Colo.

Dear Bob,
Most likely you won't remember me, but I worked for you and your
show while you were in New Guinea, and when you left you said drop
you a line some time, so here is one or two.

Pfc. Mickey Rooney imitates some Hollywood actors for an audience of infantrymen of the 44th Division. Rooney is a member of a three-man unit making a jeep tour to entertain the troops. T5c. Louis Weintraub, Kist, Germany, April 13, 1945. 111-SC-203412. National Archives Identifier: 531257.

I just heard your show on the air and it was said that the new Pepsodent tasted better than ever, well as far as myself and the boys go, that's awfully good. For a while we were in the jungle . . . we found we had a baker with us, so we all go out to find the things to make a cake. We found all that was needed . . . with the exception of flavoring. And after a long search with no luck, one of the gang showed up with a can of Pepsodent powder, and after everyone tasted it, we decided to use it as flavoring, and was very much pleased with the result . . . we all enjoyed our first cake in many a month, with the wonderful Pepsodent taste.

Keep the shows coming. You're still tops with my gang.

Respectfully,
Cpl. Earl G. Absher

Cpl. Earl G. Absher
US Army
Denver, Colorado

Dear Earl:
. . . No kidding . . . did you fellows really use that stuff (good ol' Pepsodent) in a cake? I've used it for about everything else. I've got to. My attic is full of it. Wish my sponsor would start paying me off in something else for a change.

. . . Expect to be in your city in a couple of days. Good luck.

Sincerely,
Bob Hope

Bob and that "Pepsodent smile."
Herman Freedman photo.

U.S. Naval Hospital
Ward "E"
Puget Sound Navy Yard
Puget Sound, Wash.

April 6th, 1944

Dear Bob:
Sorry that I didn't get a chance to see you while I was on leave in Hollywood. You were out on a camp tour.

I have been back in the States just seven weeks and was assigned a bed here on April 3rd. They are just giving me the double check. Incidentally, I have had so many malaria smears that when the corpsman comes into my room with his tray, I grease myself with oil and slide under his microscope.

. . . When we meet again, I will tell you about some of the unbelievable work and fighting that I saw and is being done.

You, too, are doing a grand job for the boys down under. For instance—I was chumming with a buddy in another hospital. (He has one leg now). . . . The topic was about the initial invasion of an island that he was on. In the landing barge that he was in, some were praying, some were silent, and some were sobbing, the tension being terrific. "Well," one Marine said, "I wonder what Bob Hope's program will be about next week." The last words heard from the airwaves were yours before going over the side. This same fellow had a Rosary in one hand and his rifle in the other.

To know that your clever humor was one of his foremost and inspiring thoughts should help me to try and let you know what your humor means to the armed forces. (He never came back.)

Should you ever go into politics, you needn't worry about the votes. You already have all the servicemen's.

You are a Will Rogers in your profession and the serviceman of all servicemen.

. . . if there is ever a time that I can do you a favor, just say so and it shall be done.

As Ever,
George T. La Clair, C.C.S.

Bob's War Department
Identification Card.

"I didn't see very much. And God knows I didn't do any fighting.
But I had a worm's eye view of what war was."
   . . . Bob Hope, *I Never Left Home*

Camp Bradford, VA
March 5, 1945

Dear Bob,
I'm writing this letter from the Naval Dispensary here in Camp
Bradford. While here I've been thinking about what you did for me the
night I was wounded. You will probably not remember me by name. I
was wounded Aug. 17th in Bizerte. While in the dispensary awaiting
treatment, you lit my cigarette and gave me a drink. I want to thank
you for the drink as it must have did some good. Anyway, I'm still
around. My chest is coming along fine, but so far I have not been able
to return to duty.
*   I'm thanking you again for that drink. I remain—*

Yours Truly,
James Ruffner

James Ruffner S 1/c G.M.
Amphibious Training Base
Camp Bradford, N.O.B.
Norfolk 11, Virginia

Dear Jim:
. . . Don't think I'll ever forget that raid at Bizerte. And don't
thank me for that drink I gave you while you were waiting [for]
treatment in that dispensary . . . I'm still thanking you . . . and
those other fellows . . . that I was in a position to give you a drink
. . . or anything else . . . that night! Best of luck!

Sincerely,
Bob Hope

"I've talked to lots of you guys in the field, and I've gathered that
the Armed Forces Radio Shows mean a lot to you. Believe me,
they mean a lot to us performers, too. So just keep your requests
coming by letter, postcard, V-mail, or put a note in a bottle and
drop it overboard. We'll get it somehow and shoot your request
right back. If you haven't got time to write, stick your thumbprint
on a friend's letter so we'll know you're all thinking of us, will ya?"
. . . Bob Hope over Armed Forces Radio

If Bob suggested it, the soldiers were all in. One
group of G.I.s sent their thumbprints to him on a
paper bag. They all cleared National Security.

11 Jun 45
Command Performance
Army and Navy Special Service Division
Hollywood, California

Dear Sirs:
... There are better than 1000 men in our unit, most of them have 2 ½ to 3 ½ years overseas.

After seeing a late film of Command Performance in which Bob Hope was MC, we took his advice as to putting our thumb print on an envelope ...

Sgt. Albert C. Easker
Base Surgeon's Office

June 18, 1945
Sgt. Albert C. Easker
Base Surgeon's Office

Dear Al,
Command Performances forwarded me your letter, along with the fingerprints. I've always been interested in fingerprints ... at least, since my brother went up to stay on that island in the middle of the bay off San Francisco.

Just returned from a tour of the East and it surely was good to be home again. Of course, it's a bit crowded ... my relatives are spending the summer with us. I really don't mind my relatives around the house though ... ***it's their relatives that are beginning to annoy me.***

Guess I'd better sign off for now. Good luck to you fellows out there ...

Sincerely,
Bob Hope

Making the most of their government-issued supplies, some letters were even written on bathroom tissue:

PVT. C. H. JONES
SAN FRANCISCO, CA
FEB. 5, 1944

AS YOU CAN PLAINLY SEE,

THIS NON-SKID, PRODUCED BY THE AUSTRALIAN

GOVERNMENT FOR THE IRRITATION OF AMERICAN

FRONT LINE TROOPS, SERVES A DUAL PURPOSE.

IT HAS SERVED ONE PURPOSE FOR US. YOU MAY

USE IT FOR THE OTHER. BUT WE BEG OF YOU—REMEMBER

THE IRRITATION. IF YOU DON'T, YOU WILL GET THE GIST

OF THE ABOVE PARAGRAPH IN THE END.

BEFORE WE GO ANY FURTHER WITH THIS, WE WILL

EXPLAIN WHY YOU WERE PICKED TO BE THE RECIPIENT OF

SUCH AN UNORTHODOX LETTER. YOU ALONE HAVE THE

SENSE OF HUMOR REQUIRED IN OUR CASE. WE GET A LOT OF

LAUGHS . . . AND WE FEEL YOU CAN LAUGH RIGHT ALONG
WITH US.

. . . HOW ABOUT IT, BOB? KEEP OUR SPIRITS HIGH. ANSWER

THIS MASTERPIECE.

SO LONG.
Private C. H. Jones and Company

Private C. H. Jones
San Francisco, Calif.

Dear Fellows:

Received your letter and I don't know just what to say about your choice of stationery. It's original, to say the least.

So you're in Australia! Well, you've been doing a rugged job over there and I know it's tough. But I'm going to send you a picture of myself . . . then you'll realize it could be tougher. After one look at me, everything else looks bright.

Hollywood is about the same . . . there's nothing much you can do to change it. . . . By the way, we've just finished another picture . . . Lamour, Crosby, and I. You know Crosby . . . Sinatra's father. Sinatra is now 4F. He's got a punctured eardrum from listening to those records of Crosby's . . .

Give all the boys my best and tell them I'll take care of the girls until their return. That will relieve them of all their worries . . .

Sincerely yours,
Hollywood's Greatest Lover
Bob Hope

Like Bob, popular music of the times tried to keep up the morale of the troops by ac-cen-tchu-ating the positive . . . Sheet music cover art courtesy of Edwin H. Morris & Company. A division of MPL Music Publishing, Inc. Used by permission.

United States Coast Guard
Vic Mature
(no date given)

Dear Bob-
Just a line to say hello and let you know how the boys at sea feel about you—you are undoubtedly the number 1 favorite. Your trips abroad have done things for you, not you of today, but that "Bob Hope" that will live on and on in the hearts of millions of soldiers and sailors forever. . . . If you ever get a chance on your program to plug the Coast Guard do so. You see, many people still think the Coast Guard only guard the coast when in reality every major engagement in this war the Coast Guard have participated and will do so on the ones to come.

My best to you and yours.
Vic [Victor] Mature, Chief Bosun Mate
U.S.C.G. Storis

DEAR BOB...

WE CAN DREAM, CAN'T WE?

—— —— —— —— —— —— —— —— —— —— —— —— ——

ON AUGUST 12, 1944, BOB HOPE QUIPPED ON HIS RADIO SHOW THAT WAS BE-ing broadcast from a naval hospital in the South Pacific: "We have a nice show here with Frances Langford, Jerry Colonna, Tony Romano, Patty Thomas, and Barney Dean. I know you'll enjoy the girls. You remember girls . . . ?"

The soldiers laughed and cheered. Bob Hope had hit on yet one more worthy topic of a soldier's misery—the severe shortage of potential sweethearts. Knowing this, Bob always brought along a handful of pretty gals to entertain the troops and remind them what they were fighting for. Then, he'd joke about his unwavering commitment to his work, "It's a tough job, but someone's got to do it."

Bob Hope and Frances Langford,
Odeo Leichester Square, London,
England, August 1, 1943.

21st Reconnaissance Troop
American Division
APO 716 c/o Postmaster
San Francisco, Calif
US Army

Dear Bob,
We could call you Mr. Hope, but as we have a favor to ask of you, we want to be good Buddies.

If your fan mail is as bad as we have heard, we should be in the same "foxhole," cause the women do not write to us either. . . . We thought that you could raise our morale by getting us a few pictures of young and upcoming actresses . . . We were going to write to Chaplin or Flynn, but we thought they would be having enough on their hands.

I guess you know we think your pictures are great and would like to have more of them out this way . . . in between your pictures our morale drops—that is why we want you to do this little favor for us to keep our morale at a high level in between your pictures. We would appreciate this very much.

. . . We sincerely hope that you can accomplish this mission that we are sending you on.

Waiting patiently,
Bill Pacheco
Wally Enz
Ben Yanish

June 27, 1944
Bill Pacheco
21st Reconnaissance Troop

Dear Bill, Wally, and Ben:
The thought of you boys . . . way out there in some forgotten foxhole . . . without a "pin-up" girl between the three of you . . . haunted my dreams last night . . . So early this morning I crept up to my attic and, with tears in my eyes, unpinned some of my most prized "pin-ups" to send you fellows. Take good care of them!

I'm glad you like my pictures ... I like them, too ... which makes four of us. I've just finished two more ... "The Road to Utopia" for Paramount; and "The Princess and the Pirate" for Goldwyn. My friends say that the best thing about my pictures is the title.

... I expect to leave on a tour of the South Pacific very soon now. May even get a chance to drop in on you boys, so watch out for me. In the meantime, take good care of those "pin-ups" ... will you?

The "Pin-Up" Collector,
Bob Hope

"When word got out that we had 10 girls with us, a squadron of fellas flew out to meet us—and some of them even had planes."
... Bob Hope

I A A F
INVITES YOU TO THE
BOB HOPE SHOW
Friday, Dec. 1, 1944

(Top) A ticket to a Bob Hope show was a prized possession to a G.I. starved for entertainment.

(Bottom) Tony Romano, Melvin Frank, Frances Langford, Jerry Colonna, Vera Vague, Bob Hope, Panama, March 1944.

23 May 1944—England

Dear Bob,
You were swell enough to send another crew your picture, so now you
have another eager beaver after you for another one. Our crew is fly-
ing B-24—oh, oh! Was just about to give the number, but happened to
think that they would censor that. We are fed up with pin-up girls (ha!
who said that? That's the funniest thing I've said all day!), and now I'd
like to pin you up. We always get a bang out of hearing you, the only
trouble is that we don't get to hear you enough.
    Lots of good luck to you always,

Another fan—
Bill Jones

(Top) June 11, 1944, Utah Beach, Navy Hospital corpsman. Official US Navy Photograph, now in the collection of the National Archives.

(Bottom) Bob Hope and Frances Langford, Italy/Sicily, 1943.

June 22, 1944
Sgt. Wm. E. Jones, 39559624
838 Sq. 487 Bomb Gp.
APO 559, c/o Postmaster
New York, New York

Dear Bill:

Was very glad to hear from you and, since you asked for it, am forwarding a pin-up of myself. I've had many requests for my picture . . . the fellas say that when they start feeling low, they go take a look at my picture . . . and realize how lucky they are.

I've been quite busy lately . . . Bing and I have been playing a lot of golf benefits. . . . I've always wondered why they had those flags on the course . . . but after a couple of shots of mine I found out . . . that's to tell you what country you're in.

. . . Will have to sign off now and get back to work. Tell the rest of the crew "hello" for me, will you? And the best of good luck to all of you.

Sincerely,
Bob Hope

Bob Hope, Frances Langford, Tony Romano performing in Italy/Sicily, 1943.

United States Naval Hospital
San Diego, CA

Dear Bob (Have a Heart) Hope:
From the Union ooo of Organized Wolves, we protest to your visit-
ing the Nurses and Waves at the U.S.N.H., as they will not look at us
Corpsmen since you have been here.

The poor little dears have been in a flutter and a daze for the last
twenty-four hours . . .

The next time, please bring along Dot Lamour, Betty Grable, Paulette Goddard, Lana Turner, Gene Tierney, and as many more of the
gorgeous stars as you can. In that way, making them jealous, we can
protect our interest in these organizations.

Maybe it would help to leave Cary Grant at home. It's a flip of a
coin to tell which one of you stirred up the commotion. Excuse me,
let's flip for odd man, maybe Colonna could take some of the votes.

Anyway, we enjoyed your program and we did get some laughs out
of it, even if we can't please the young ladies. So come back again.

Your Fellow Wolves
The Corpsmen
United States Naval Hospital
San Diego, California

(Left) Bob Hope with WACs, 1943, England.

(Right) Letter stamped with a Join the WAC ad
and censor mark.

Bob Hope's closing tribute to the WACs on his weekly radio show: "You know, ladies and gentlemen, before we leave tonight I'd like to say how really fine this set-up is here at Fort Des Moines. You know, we may kid a little about the WACs, but believe me, these girls aren't kidding. They're doing a job to be proud of ..."

Somewhere in England
May 9, 1943

Dear Bob:
Received your picture today, after it traveled all over the British Empire. I guess that is why you had such a tired look on your face ...
... Bob, why don't you give up trying to get Dorothy Lamour and give these English girls a chance? (They like anyone that even resembles a man.) All you have to do is brush up on your English accent and learn to drink tea.
... Well, it's 11 o'clock (2300 hours) and I've just finished my day's work at the canteen, so I guess I had better get in my mattress-less, spring-less, sheet-less, sleep-less bed. (Very comfy, though).

A-soldier-in-the-rear-rank

"One soldier went to the Hollywood canteen and danced with Hedy Lamarr, Betty Grable, and Lana Turner ... I don't know if it affected him or not, but he was a little late getting back to camp ... It was Tuesday before an anti-aircraft unit in San Diego could shoot him down."
... Bob Hope

Marlene Dietrich and Rita Hayworth serve food to soldiers at the Hollywood Canteen, November 17, 1942. Library of Congress, Prints & Photographs Division, NYWT&S Collection, LC-USZ62-113250.

"Here we are, doing the first broadcast from the Hollywood Canteen. Boy, this is really a marvelous place . . . Can you imagine all those beautiful hostesses . . . and only servicemen are allowed? I know one guy who got dressed up in a uniform so that he could get into the Canteen. But they knew he was a fake because the uniform fit him. . . . So, they threw me out."
   . . . Bob Hope

"A lot of these Waves wear x-ray equipment. And it is sure convenient for 'em. . . . If a sailor asks 'em for a date, they can look through his pockets and tell if he can afford it or not."
   . . . Bob Hope

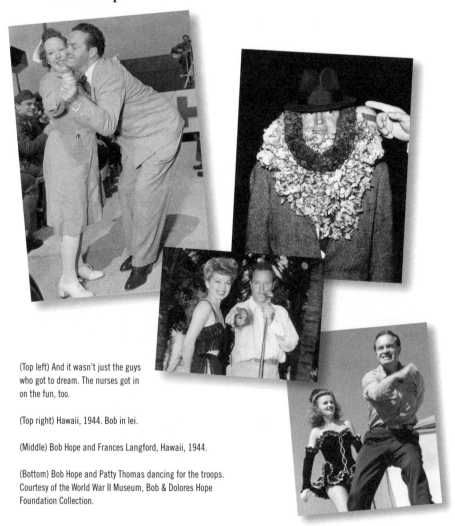

(Top left) And it wasn't just the guys who got to dream. The nurses got in on the fun, too.

(Top right) Hawaii, 1944. Bob in lei.

(Middle) Bob Hope and Frances Langford, Hawaii, 1944.

(Bottom) Bob Hope and Patty Thomas dancing for the troops. Courtesy of the World War II Museum, Bob & Dolores Hope Foundation Collection.

DEAR BOB . . .

THANKS FOR HAVING OUR BACKS!

— — — — — — — — — — — — — — —

ONE THING THE TROOPS KNEW BEYOND ANY DOUBT WAS THAT BOB HOPE HAD their backs. In training camps, on the battlefield, and most importantly, after they returned home, Bob Hope championed their cause.

If a soldier needed something, *anything*, Bob did his best to get it to them. If the request required the help of the American people to make it happen, he would make an appeal on his radio broadcasts. If he needed to go even higher, he wouldn't hesitate to bring the matter to the attention of generals, Congress, and even the president of the United States, if need be.

Both in print and over the airwaves, Bob paid meaningful tribute to each branch of the military, from the oft-celebrated to the oft-overlooked, he knew the important role that each of these brave men and women played.

After the war, Bob continued his commitment to making sure our GIs would never be forgotten in war . . . or in peace.

Bob with Tuskegee Airman, USO Tour, 1943, England.

England
May 8, 1944

Dear Mr. Hope,
This letter is in appreciation of last week's "Command Performance"
and the tribute you paid us, the Army nurses—God's forgotten chil-
dren. Really, sometimes we do feel that we're forgotten and our work
unappreciated, but your "Thanks for the Memories" at the close of last
week's program was a terrific boost for our morale.

I think that you've done more for our boys in the service than any
other star in Hollywood, and you're certainly tops with all the nurs-
es—It's between you and Jimmy Cagney—Mr. Cagney was here to see
us recently and we like him even better in person.

Thanks again for a swell tribute to our honest efforts. Good luck in
the splendid work you're doing.

Lt. Mary Rogers and "The Gals in Hut 109"

June 7, 1944

Dear "Gals in Hut 109":
That was a nice letter you sent me some weeks ago . . .

Perhaps you don't get much publicity, but I guess we all know
what a wonderful job you Army Nurses are doing. You're a vital
cog in this great war machine of ours . . . the war couldn't be won
without you. So just remember, we know you're in there pitching
. . . and we'll not forget you.

So it's between Jimmy and me, is it? Well, perhaps at that, I'm
better off than Crosby. You know, over here, it's between him and
Sinatra. It's made Bing quite moody . . .

I'd like to drop in on you girls in England, but this summer
I'm heading for the South Pacific, and Burma and China . . . if
possible. I'm going to try to bring a little entertainment to the
jungles . . . if the mosquitoes will let me in. Hear they have really
big ones down there.

My best wishes to you girls over there. And keep up the good
work . . . America really needs you.

Sincerely,
Bob Hope

Tuesday, 22 January 1945

Dear Mr. Hope:
My buddies and I wish to sincerely thank you for the wonderful work
you are doing on your "Command Performance" broadcasts. There is
nothing which makes a man happier than good music from his favor-
ites and a heap of laughs. My morale goes up forty points whenever
I hear one of your programs. And what is more, they are the only
programs which provoke laughs after laughs.
   We are very grateful.

Sincerely,
Ensign Ward Baxter

In a way that defied all celebrity boundaries before or since, Bob Hope, one of the box office sensations of his time, had become a literal pen pal to millions of military men and women. These are no ordinary fan letters. The link was on a personal level. You can tell that by the familiar tone in their correspondence. It was like they were writing to an old friend. They joked with him and he gave it right back. Even when he threw in a plug for his latest film, it was done in a newsy way with a healthy dose of self-deprecation:

> **"I'm pretty busy right now . . . making a new picture. It's one of**
> **those 'escapism' themes . . . the guy who's putting up the money**
> **keeps trying to escape."**
>   **. . . Bob Hope**

Nov. 19, 1943
Sgt. T. J. Martin
Nov. 19, 1943
Co. "C" 2nd Command Base

Hello Bob,
Well, here I am again writing to you and this time it's from a hospital
somewhere in Italy. It really isn't too bad, though, just a few pieces of
shrapnel in my left side and a gunshot wound in my left leg. Have been
in the hospital now about two weeks and am ready to go back to the
front lines again. This has been the first real rest I've had in a long time.

. . . I hate to bother you with my troubles because I know you are a very busy person, but gee, it sure does get plenty lonesome over here when you don't get any mail.

Wishing you and yours a Merry Christmas and a very Happy New Year, and please write soon.

Sincerely,
T. J. Martin

The Philippines
April 29, 1945
Keegan V. Day M.MM3/c
N. R. U. Navy 3149 Box E-5

Dear Bob,
Knowing your ability to delve into and solve problems, I thought you might do me a little favor by explaining the methods your cowboy friends use when fighting it out with their guns. They never have to re-load as the lead just pours from their six-shooters. We certainly would like the low down as we could put it to good use out here against the [enemy] . . . It would be very much appreciated, as we are connected with a P.T. outfit and would certainly benefit by it . . .

Keegan V. Day

"I think the He-men in the movies belong in the Army, Marines, Navy or Air Corps. All of these He-men in the movies realize that right now is the right time to get into the service. Every movie cowboy ought to devote time to the Army winning, or helping to win, until the war is over—the same as with any other American citizen. The Army needs all the young men it can get, and if I can set a good example for the young men, I'll be mighty proud."
—GENE AUTRY, joined US Army Air Corps 1942

DEAR BOB . . .

DID I REALLY SIGN UP FOR THIS?

WHENEVER A BOB HOPE MONOLOGUE TOUCHED ON FAMILIAR TOPICS SUCH as military food, physical demands, or dealing with superiors, the laughter was deafening. The soldiers couldn't figure out how Bob knew them so well. Had he been trailing them around the base, eavesdropping on their bunk-side complaints, listening to them in the chow lines? And how did he know which officers were the most demanding, or that the camp had just had an air raid the night before?

> **"My writers had a ball. There was hardly a subject we wouldn't approach. Laughs came from simple harebrained foolishness, reluctant heroism, and blatant cowardice set against a climate of high seriousness."**
> **. . . Bob Hope, *I Was There***

Bob shares a laugh with his writers. Nothing thrilled him more than working on his shows.

Bob knew early on that if he was going to have the kind of career that lasts, he needed a stable of the best writers around. Some of the writers for his radio show were Melville Shavelson (who went on to become president of the Writers Guild of America and wrote *The Princess and the Pirate*, *The Seven Little Foys*, and *Sorrowful Jones*), Sherwood Schwartz (future creator/producer of *Gilligan's Island* and writer for *The Red Skelton Hour*), Sherwood's brother Albert Schwartz (*The Jackie Gleason Show*, *The Milton Berle Show*, and *The Brady Bunch*), Norman Panama and Melvin Frank (*Road to Utopia* and *My Favorite Blonde*), and Milt Josefsburg (*The Jack Benny Show* and *All in the Family*). Mort Lachman (*All in the Family* and *The Stiller and Meara Show*) came on in 1947 and Larry Gelbart (*M.A.S.H.* and *A Funny Thing Happened to Me on My Way to the Forum*) joined the staff in 1948.

Bob Hope writers earned their money. Because of his many public appearances, Bob consumed material like no other comic.

Sherwood Schwartz often shared a story about how he, as the junior scribe on Bob Hope's writing team, was the one Bob would send out to get fudge sundaes. So established was this routine that after Sherwood completed his service in World War II, he surprised Bob by picking up a fudge sundae on his way over to his house. When Bob opened the door and saw the newly discharged Sherwood standing there holding the sundae, he simply took it from his hands and deadpanned that the errand had certainly taken him longer than usual.

From base to base, the G.I.s' complaints were relatively the same, and Bob gave voice to it all—C-rations, sleeping conditions, mosquitoes, snakes, weather, the terrain, and of course, the brass themselves. Bob was simply saying out loud what the troops were already thinking about and it helped take some of the edge off of the situation.

There were no canned guffaws or applause. These boys (and gals) were so ready for laughter, they didn't need them.

> **"The mosquitoes around Tunis are so big they have to use landing strips. But I got kind of used to their biting me. What I never could get used to was seeing them pull out a bottle of Worcestershire sauce."**
> **. . . Bob Hope, *I Never Left Home***

August 7th (no year given)
Major Neal Lang
Forward Ephelon
APO 350, NY

My dear Bob:
    ... We're in France now ... The mosquitoes are terrific ... they grow 'em like the P-38 over here ... two tails and you get the double jab with a single thrust. Last night I awakened to find two big ones reading my dog tags ... checking my blood type.
    The gang still talks about the shows you put on and they'd like to have you back. The entertainment end of the picture has dropped off badly during the past six months ...
    ... Good luck, Bob, and hope to see you soon again.

Neal

Dear Bob,

How are you today? Sorry I was called away so suddenly, as you understand Uncle Sam and I made a deal some time ago. You were out of town at the time Uncle picked up my option. Would of liked to had a little more time to make my decision, but it seems Uncle just couldn't wait.
    Well, Bob ... all my life, I wanted to be able to sit down and clip coupons. At last I have my wish. Now, all I do is go to the canteen with my canteen book, buy what I want, and clip coupons out of the book. ... But just the same, give me Hollywood.
    ... We drill every day. ... They have a great routine. Our first call in the morning for Revile is 5:30 am. We have to <u>line up</u> for roll call. Next we <u>line up</u> for breakfast. After breakfast we <u>line up</u> to wash our mess kits. Now, the next move is to <u>line up</u> and march back to the barracks, rest for ½ hour. Whistle blows, we again <u>line up</u> for general drill. Now, it is 12 noon, we now march back to the barracks to wash, so we <u>line up</u> to wash. Whistle blows again. <u>Line up</u> in front of barracks, march to Mess Hall, eat. We finish eating, now we <u>line up</u> to wash mess kits. Again, we <u>line up</u>, back to barracks we march, rest ½ hour.

Whistle blows, <u>line up</u> for general drill. We quit—4 pm. Now, they decide to let us have a little fun. We are going to play baseball until 5 pm. So we <u>line up</u>—to the baseball field we march. Now we have to choose sides, so we <u>line up</u> for that routine. It's time for dinner—break up the game. <u>Line up</u>—march to Mess Hall, eat. Finish eating—<u>line up</u> to wash mess kits. Then, <u>line up</u>—front of mess hall—march back to barracks to wash hands and face, then whistle blows. Again, we <u>line up</u> for Mess Hall. After dinner, they decide to take us to the show here in camp, so again, we <u>line up,</u> march to the show. This is a great life. "Line Marches On." Believe it or not, when we have to go . . . some places we <u>line up.</u>

Well, Bob, sure would appreciate a letter from you. . . . Will close, old Boy,

Mickey Cohen

"I looked down at the guy marching next to me and said you're pretty short to be in the Army. He said, I'm not so short. When we started this hike, I had legs.

"This camp is so big, you need a six-hour pass to get a six-hour pass.

" . . . It's so big, you have to go AWOL twice before you're out the front gate."
. . . Bob Hope

Food was a favorite topic for these military shows, and Bob was more than happy to provide plenty of laughs about the rations. He ate what the troops ate much of the time. They called it lunch, Bob called it research.

"I have wonderful memories . . . like box lunches and yellow fever shots . . . and I've learned to say Kaopectate in nine languages."
. . . Bob Hope

There were plenty of references to a certain meat product that had been appearing on their meal trays a little more often than they would have liked. You guessed it—SPAM.

"Spam is a ham that didn't pass its physical."
... Bob Hope

General Dwight Eisenhower was even moved to write a letter to a Hormel executive, both praising and questioning this new and unconventional dining selection. The former president's letter read in part: "During World War II, of course, I ate my share of Spam along with millions of other soldiers. I'll even confess to a few unkind remarks about it—uttered during the strain of battle, you understand. But as former Commander-in-Chief, I believe I can still officially forgive you your only sin: sending us so much of it."

"Now I lay me down to sleep,
I pray the Lord the Spam don't keep."
... Bob Hope, March 11, 1946, *Life* magazine article

In World War II, news commentator Mike Wallace served in America's navy as a communications officer, and actor Richard Burton served in the Royal Navy. Audrey Hepburn, a child at the time, was a courageous courier for WWII resistance fighters in Holland. And actor George Kennedy served with Patton, and following the war he played the general in a film. The entertainment industry was well represented in uniform.

"I joined the navy in 1942. ... After four months of training at Notre Dame Midshipmen's school, I was assigned to C1139, an antisubmarine patrol craft, as a communications officer. I looked great in my dress uniform, but nothing else about my service was distinguished. With a green crew and a captain who had never been to sea, we were one of the most incompetent ships in the navy. Our first time out of port in New Orleans, we backed into another ship and almost sank it. Then, on our first sighting of a Japanese submarine in the Pacific, a nervous sailor released a depth charge instead of a depth charge marker and blew us up. I was bruised and had internal injuries. Then I became deathly ill with severe cramps and a high fever which turned out to be amoebic dysentery. At the San Diego Naval Hospital, I was an inpatient and then an outpatient for several months prior to my honorable discharge in June 1944."
—KIRK DOUGLAS, recalling his World War II memories*

* From *Kirk and Anne: Letters of Love, Laughter and a Lifetime in Hollywood* (Running Press), by Kirk and Anne Douglas, Copyright 2017, The Bryna Company. Used by permission of the authors.

DEAR BOB . . .

HERE'S WHAT'S SHAKIN'

— — — — — — — — — — — — —

THROUGH THESE LETTERS, AND THOUSANDS MORE, THE SOLDIERS KEPT BOB abreast of whatever was going on in their lives. That is, as much as they could share under the censor's watchful eye. They wrote about the latest happenings around the base, how much they looked forward to their next weekend pass, and whatever else they deemed newsworthy.

Not only did Bob enjoy reading these chummy communications, but they also provided plenty of "behind the scenes" information so Bob and his writers could tailor the jokes accordingly.

If a soldier wrote and complained about the rainy conditions in his area, then you can bet that rainy conditions was a topic in Bob's monologue whenever he performed there. Like this letter:

> *"South Pacific"*
> *May 20, 1944*
>
> *Dear Bob:*
> *. . . Thanks for the memory*
> *Of dehydrated spuds*
> *Assorted dusts and muds*
> *For sagging tents*
> *With gapping vents*
> *That let in frequent floods,*
> *We thank you so much . . .*
> *[written by a Marine who served on Guadalcanal]*
>
> *Sincerely,*
> *W. H. Mayes*

Bob also liked to throw in the names of familiar hangouts, commanding officers, and so on. The troops always appreciated this extra effort that personalized the material to them.

Something else Bob enjoyed doing during the military shows was calling a soldier up to the stage and bantering with him. It was especially fun if the soldier was a new father who had not seen his baby yet and the Hope troupe could surprise him with photographs. This had to be worked out ahead of time, of course, but the results were well worth it. Today the scene would go viral on YouTube. Back then it was just between Bob and some 30,000 G.I.s spread out over the landscape.

There were other bits of news that the soldiers had to share with their pal Bob. And they did it—one letter at a time.

> *Battey General Hospital*
> *Rome, Georgia*
> *May 11, 1945*
>
> *Dear Mr. Hope:*
> *Naming a combat plane and selecting a proper and fitting picture has been a major problem in the Air Force, or so it seemed in my outfit, the 484th Squadron, 505th Bomb Group (VH).*
> *. . . As you can see by the enclosed pictures, my crew and I fell along the wayside in making this selection for our B-29. However, we do not consider it a complete flop because when we started making those low level attacks on Tokyo, we could look down and see the [enemy] running like mad—terrified—not because of the bombs, but because of the horrible effigy streaking through the sky. (Even Crosby's horses would have run.) Without a doubt, that caused more havoc in Japan than all the incendiary bombs to date. No doubt it was felt that the tremendous protrusion, resembling a nose, could ferret (one way or another) anyone from any place of hiding.*
> *. . . Believe me, the HOPE-FULL DEVIL died a gallant death, battling an extremely rough sea—20 foot swells—remaining intact until all crew members were safely out and in life rafts. Not being able to brace myself, unfortunately, I suffered a fractured back—but at a time like that, a broken back is a minor detail in getting out. Each man came thru with flying colors. THEY'RE A GREAT CREW!*
>
> *The crew consisted of the following men:*

Col. C. L. Macomber, Co-pilot	*S/Sgt. G. Westmoreland, Radio Operator*
(along for the ride)	*Sgt. L. L. Melesky, Radar Operator*
Lt. J. A. Ptaszkowski, Navigator	*Sgt. M. L. Binger, Left Blister Gunner*
Lt. C. R. Gustavson, Bombardier	*Sgt. J. R. Rivas, Right Blister Gunner*
M/Sgt. R. J. Aspinall, Engineer	

As we were not "toting" guns at the time, Sgt. J. C. Edwards, CFC Gunner, and Sgt. D. L. Riddlemoser, Tail Gunner, were not along on the mission.

. . . In case you are interested, Sgt. Melesky (who also suffered a fractured back) was studying for the ministry prior to entry into the Army, so it was always a practice to have a short prayer before the take-off of each mission. You will note that one of the pictures was made during the prayer, just before our last mission. (This prayer was evidently too short.)

. . . The HOPE-FULL DEVIL was a proud ship, always leading the Squadron and had several missions over Tokyo, one mission to Ota and one mission to Iwo Jima.

But lest we forget, fifty percent of the credit goes to the exceptionally fine ground crew, under the capable Crew Chief, S/Sgt. Horace Brown, who kept her ticking in topnotch condition . . .

Bernard L. McCaskell, Jr.
Captain, Air Corps
Aeroplane Commander

Crew prays by the Hope-Full Devil plane.

June 11, 1945
Captain Bernard L. McCaskill, Jr.
Battey General Hospital
Rome, Georgia

Dear Captain:
Received your letter with the pictures of the HOPE-FULL DEVIL and I don't have to tell you I got a great big kick out of them. So glad the ship served its purpose. It must have been pretty hard steel to withstand that puss of mine.

I have another plane somewhere in the Pacific, a B-17, BOB'S HOPE. It was named after me because of the trouble the fellows had in keeping its nose down. That plane, also, went through about fifty missions and finally was so bullet-riddled that they sent it to the junk pile.

I do hope that you are mending down there in Georgia; and, also, hope to have the pleasure of meeting you sometime. Please don't be bashful about making yourself known if you ever hit Hollywood or are ever in the vicinity of one of our shows when we are on tour. I'm leaving this Saturday to play eight weeks in the European field of rubble for hospitals and camps there. But I'm returning about the middle of August, so time yourself accordingly.

Give my best to the whole crew and tell them I hope they're enjoying good old America . . . because they surely deserve it.

Sincerely,
Bob Hope

Captain Chesley Sullenberger may have impressed us all by landing a US Airways airplane in the Hudson River in 2009, but he isn't the only one who's made a heroic water landing.

On August 14, 1944, pilot James Frank Ferguson had the responsibility of bringing down a crippled Catalina PBY carrying Bob Hope, Frances Langford, Patty Thomas, Tony Romano, Jerry Colonna, and Barney Dean. Bob had been trying his hand at flying the plane when, through no fault of his own, an engine went out. The pilot rushed back to his seat, took back the controls, and with great skill brought the plane down in the Camden River, near Laurieton, which is about four hours south of Sidney, Australia. The emergency, which nearly somersaulted the aircraft, ended with the plane finally coming to rest on a sandbar. Thanks to a local fisherman, Alan Wallace, the lucky survivors all made it safely back to land.

At first, Alan didn't realize who it was who was dropping out of the sky on their small community until he started helping to take the survivors ashore.

The local postmaster, Mr. Plunkett, didn't believe Bob when he showed up at the town post office a short time later wanting to send a telegram to let folks back home know they were all okay. Bob introduced himself to the postmaster, but Mr. Plunkett wasn't buying it.

"Young man, it's Monday, I'm much too busy for your jokes," Mr. Plunkett is reported to have said to Bob.

(Top) Bob's plane arriving in Laurieton the hard way. Photo by Scott Sheppard, used by permission.

(Middle) Bob Hope's plane makes crash landing in Laurieton. Photo by Scott Sheppard, used by permission.

(Bottom) Rescued, Bob Hope and troupe live to laugh another day. Photo by Scott Sheppard. Courtesy of Scott Sheppard and the Camden Haven Historical Museum.

Eventually, Bob convinced Plunkett of his identity, and the postmaster ended up loaning the cashless celebrity eleven pounds for a hotel room and food.

Word quickly spread of the emergency landing throughout the entire Laurieton community, and Bob and his troupe were coaxed (quite willingly) into giving a show for all the townspeople. This spur of the moment event took place at the Laurieton School of Arts. Bob and the gang put on the same show they had been giving the G.I.s, only this one, according to reports, closed with the audience doing the Hokey Pokey along with Bob and his guest stars. Whether it was the locals who taught Bob the dance or he did the teaching, a good time was had by all. The celebration of Bob and the troupe's recovery from the incident is said to have lasted until 4 o'clock in the morning!

For many years, Bob continued sending Christmas cards to people he'd met in Laurieton. Apparently, bonds made during the Hokey Pokey are stronger than one might think. And, according to Mitch McKay, the Laurieton postmaster was repaid every bit of that eleven-pound loan to Bob Hope.

(Top) Bob Hope getting into the fishing boat. Photo by Scott Sheppard. Courtesy of Scott Sheppard and the Camden Haven Historical Museum.

(Middle) Bob Hope and troupe after Camden Haven River plane crash. Thanks to the skills of pilot James Frank Ferguson, all survived. Photo by Scott Sheppard, with special thanks to Peter Dunn, Mitch McKay, Gregory Ferguson, and the Camden Haven Historical Museum.

(Bottom) Once on solid ground, Bob lets those back home know he's safe. Photo by Scott Sheppard. Courtesy of Scott Sheppard and the Camden Haven Historical Museum.

"Our landing in the Camden Haven River reminds me of how much people pulled together during the war years. Our South Pacific tour had been demanding. We often entertained in the rain and the mud because we had promised to be with our boys wherever they were. We wanted them to feel a touch of home. I represented each boy's sister or girlfriends and was proud to do so."

—PATTY THOMAS, as told to Mitch McKay, It's Not Hollywood, but . . . *

"For three days, Dolores heard reports that our plane was missing. I later learned that had our plane hit the sandbar first, it would have exploded."

. . . Bob Hope, *I Was There*

---

* Used with permission of Mitch McKay.

(Top) Photo shoot, 1944, on Green Island, about twenty miles off the coast of Cairns, Australia.

(Bottom) Bob Hope in Australia, 1944.

The annual Laurieton celebration of Bob's unexpected plane crash and visit to the area. Photos courtesy of Mitch McKay.

To this day, the people of Laurieton celebrate the anniversary of when Hollywood suddenly dropped in on them. Food (including Bob Hope's favorite pie—lemon meringue), fun, and memories are shared, as well as several rounds of the Hokey Pokey.

Lt. Cdr. Holman Faust, USNR
Staff, ComSerOnSoPac
c/o Fleet Post Office
San Francisco, Calif.
16 August, 1944

Dear Bob:
It was a shock to get the first flash yesterday that you folks had been in a forced landing, and a tremendous relief to hear you'd all come out entirely all right. We're waiting rather anxiously to get the full details, which we hope will come today. What a set of experiences you've piled up in the South Pacific! It was certainly a source of great gratification to have worked with you folks. You did a wonderful job for our boys, one that they'll long remember and that they've been writing home about. . . . You gave them wonderful entertainment, and a touch of home that did much for their morale. I guess you know now what the distance from home and the loneliness of the forsaken Pacific Islands means.

Who (at home) can understand the rigors of your trip, the constant traveling, playing, traveling, playing? How're you ever going to get anyone to believe that show in the tropical downpour, with no one in

the audience making any move to leave, even though they were soak-
ing—and all you folks were soaked, too?

    I don't know how to express completely our admiration for the job
you're doing, and how impressed we all are at your stamina and de-
termination to entertain all possible men. As a matter of fact, we don't
know how you stand it. But you do and continue to deliver heart-
warming entertainment with unfailing good humor.

    Maybe someday we can all sit down together and rehash your tour
of the South Pacific. I hope so. There'll be some interesting memories.

    Please give our very best regards and warmest thanks to all the
gang. We grew to like and admire all of them very much. . . .

    "Well done, Bob," and "Thanks for the memories."

Holman Faust
O. in C.
Welfare & Recreation

"We continued on to Wakde, Owl, Aitape, (can you believe these
names) and took PT boats to do shows on the islands of Woendi
(referred to as 'Wendy' by the Navy), Endila, Lumbrum, Los
Negros, Manus, Ponam, and Pitylu. . . . Eighteen years later, in the
Rose Garden at the White House, President Kennedy presented
me with the Congressional Gold Medal. Later he told me he
was one of those guys who sat in the rain on Wendy Island and
watched our show."
. . . Bob Hope, *I Was There*

An interesting tradition carried on during World War II was called "short snorters." These were dollar bills or bank notes that were signed by a group of people who had all been together at some point and time. Each person would sign their own dollar, and then get everyone else in attendance to sign their dollar, too. The arrangement was that whenever they ran into each other again, they would each have to produce their "short snorter" as proof they had kept it with them at all times, otherwise they would have to pay the other person a dollar or buy him or her a drink (hence the term "short snorter").

    Some of the famous names who have signed short snorters include Eleanor Roosevelt, Harry Truman, Francis Cardinal Spelling, and many more, including Bob Hope. Even Joseph Stalin signed one.

(Top) Bob Hope and Jerry Colonna, signing
short snorters, 1945, France.

(Middle) Eleanor Roosevelt signs some short
snorters for the troops on March 27, 1944, during her visit to the
Panama Canal Zone. Photo by Signal Corps - US Army. (Photo
courtesy of The Franklin D. Roosevelt Presidential Library and
Museum.)

(Botttom two) Short snorter signed by Bob Hope and Troupe. The
Series of 1935-A $1 HAWAII note at right, from the Mark Hotz
collection, features signatures of Bob Hope and his entire USO
entertainment troupe. *From left to right*: Barney Dean, Patty
Thomas, Bob Hope, Jerry Colonna, Frances Langford, and Tony
Romano. Courtesy of Mark Hotz.

DEAR BOB . . .

GREETINGS FROM THE FOXHOLE

— — — — — — — — — — — — — — —

"... And you should see this base. They live in Quonset huts here.
Quonset hut—that's a foxhole upside down."
    ... Bob Hope

One would think that in a foxhole writing a letter to a celebrity would be the last thing on your mind. Yet some soldiers did exactly that. If there was a lull in the action, and someone else was keeping watch, some soldiers took advantage of that moment to write a quick V-mail right then and there under the light of the moon ... or exploding bombs in the distance. They would write to their mother, father, brother, sister, sweetheart, or Bob Hope. When they were finished—either with the whole letter or a portion of it for the day—they'd tuck the paper back into their pocket and carry on with the battle.

Bob enjoyed hearing from these soldiers who were right in the middle of the fighting. Some of the letters even listed "foxhole" as their return address.

"They let me fire one of the anti-aircraft guns today.... I won't
say those guns have a lot of kickback, but it's the first time I ever
fired a gun and had my backbone dig a foxhole at the same time."
    ... Bob Hope

Major Stanley Bach
Hq. 1st Division
APO—1
New York
11 June 44
"Somewhere in France"

Dear Bob,
A lot of things have happened since you and I visited 10 Downs Street
with Senator "Happy" Chandler. I well remember you trying on Mr.
Churchill's hat and gloves ...

I was in the Invasion—landed at H + 3 hours on D-day, plenty scared, too—noise, mortar shells . . . keep a fellow from sleeping on the beach. A little rough for a few days . . .

I did get a promotion, too—helps the check, you know.

. . . "Come over—the foxholes are fine."

"BERLIN BY SEPTEMBER."

Stanley Bach

March 28

In the Philippines

My dear Bob:

. . . You're a popular guy out here, Bob—just as popular as you are everywhere else—and deservedly so.

Getting along swell, tho' a bit rugged in spots. Our landing was exciting, and there were a few times that I thought St. Peter and I were going to be on speaking terms in double quick times. But someone's prayers overcame the devil's agent and I'm still around and happy to be around. I suppose as usual you're bouncing around the country, doing more than your share of service work. How about autographing the enclosed and sending it back for my foxhole decoration?

. . . My best to you, Dolores, Tony and Linda, the Jack Hopes, the Colonnas, and my good friend, Barney Dean.

Sincerely,

Abe

MT Sgt. A. L. Marontz

A popular WW2 song, "Praise the Lord and Pass the Ammunition," written by Frank Loesser and published in 1942 by Famous Music Corporation.

May 19, 1944
Pvt. Augie Pecorelli
Pvt. Johnny Ficorelli
Anzio Beachhead, Italy
Bob Hope
Universal Studios
Hollywood, California

Hello Bob,
What's jiving, pal? My buddy Fick and I are in a foxhole somewhere
in sunny Italy where the sun isn't shining for right now it's pouring. . . .
Man, as we're writing to you, there are things a-popping around us,
and man, when they pop, they don't sound like any fire cracker or
Gabriel blowing his horn.
One day over here, pal—my buddy and I were in a foxhole when
everything started coming—from bullets to [the] kitchen sink. Man,
they were coming thick and fast! My buddy looks at me with a blank
expression and says, "Augie, you hear what I hear?" I look at him
and say, "What are you? A comedian?" I hear 'em. My eardrums ain't
punctured! Quickly, he goes for a pack of butts and I fumble around
for my matches . . .
More to come . . .

Pick and Fick

(Apparently, the situation called for Pick and Fick's undivided attention. Some
time later, they were able to continue with their letter . . .)

May 19, 1944
Anzio Beachhead, Italy
(Continuing)

Hello, pal.
[So] I go to strike a match, but the cover is wet. We looked at each
other and said, "How are we gonna get a light?" Still, them shells
are dropping around. Suddenly, my buddy grabs a match and says,
"Watch." At that moment, we hear the whistle of another shell, my
buddy raises his arm, match in his hand, and strikes it on the bottom
of the oncoming shell. No kidding, Bob. We know you and Bing have

World War II matchbooks.

had many exciting adventures on your Roads to Morocco and Singapore, but Fick and me are having the same on "The Road to Rome."

Say, pal, we hope you're still knocking 'em in the aisle with your gags as "The Voice" is with his yodeling. Give our regards to Bing. How's his horses doing? Drop us a line, buddy. Good luck to you.

Pick and Fick

---

3 Dec 44

Dear Bob,
I hope I am not offending in calling you Bob. I've admired you so long though, you seem like an old friend, at least you do to a serviceman.

I read in a paper tonight of your little squabble with your studio. (Incidentally, it was rather an old paper.) The way I get the story is that you insulted a few officers and their wives for taking the choice seats at one of your shows.

Not knowing the whole story, I would like you to know the majority of this army's officer personnel feel like you do. There is not enough that can be done for that G.I. Joe in the foxhole and other branches of the service. An officer is there to lead his men in dangerous times, and when the time comes for the glory or rest, he should step back.

I too have seen it too often where some officer thinks because he wears the bars, he can step all over G.I. Joe. But, Bob, you didn't find it difficult the closer to the front you got? I don't know why I'm writing this letter tonight except to tell you we all think you're a great guy and *to thank you for the happy moments you have given us. Keep plugging for all the Joes, we'll sure back you. If you're ever in France again, look us up. We're a Combat Engr. outfit made up of the grandest bunch of men in the U.S. I'll guarantee you that the officers in this outfit won't have the best seats for any show. We give those to the guys that carry out our orders no matter how dirty or dangerous—G.I. Joe.*

Yours truly,
Charles H. Cole

Santa Monica
January 25, 1947

My dear Bob:
. . . It was at G-25 (Ashchurch) in England that you objected to the brass (officers) seated in the front row. During the second show we complied with your request, but in the meantime, my Special Service Officer was really sore.

. . . C. W. Richmond
Colonel, U.S. Army, retired

Bob Hope's closing tribute to the American G.I. on his radio show:

. . . We've covered plenty of land, sea, and air since Pearl Harbor and visited many a cog in our fighting machine. But tonight we're face to face with the number one boy of the Armed Forces—the man in infantry, Johnny Dough-boy himself. When you snap on the radio these days, you hear the roaring dramas of men who fly through steel and fire to sink a [Japanese] carrier or blast a Nazi submarine and then come limping home on a wing and a prayer. We don't hear much about a guy with a stripe on his sleeve and a gun in his arm, the biggest hero of them all. He's just plain Joe Infantry—an all-around soldier who stands with his two feet on the ground and slugs out the final round of fight. He's the man who stormed to the top of Hill 164, fighting through more hell per square foot than any man has ever known. The fella who swept down the other side of that hill throwing cold steel to the Ger-mans and pushed onto the streets of Tunis and Bizerte, a little closer to Berlin. And he is the guy who tonight is pushing through the red and white snow of

Attu Island, a little closer to Tokyo. Just plain Joe Infantry, no silver wings, no glamour, but mister, he's the guy who day and night, and I mean every day and night, is taking this country a little closer to victory. Thank you, fellas.

(Top) WWII trench art. Soldier Wade C. White, US Army. Engagements listed: "Leyte Manilia Philippines, Eniwitok Perry Marshalls. Pearl Harbor Hawaii, Okinawa Ryukyus, Ulithi Atoll Carolines, Los Nigros Manus Admiralty, Mariana Islands, Coral, Bismark & China Sea."

(Bottom) June 9, 1942, at Bob's 200th performance at camps. And to think he was just getting started. Everett Collection Inc / Alamy Stock Photo.

DEAR BOB . . .

TELL MY MOM I MISS HER

— — — — — — — — — — — — — — —

> "[My mother would] get out a big washtub and give us a bath
> in the kitchen, taking us in the order of our conduct during the
> week. If we'd been good, we got fresh water. That's why I was
> tan—at least beige—until I was 13."
> . . . Bob Hope, on growing up the fifth of seven sons

Many of the troops in World War II were still "wet behind the ears." Seventeen-
and eighteen-year-old kids, and even younger if they fudged on their enlistment
papers, which a few did. Like Seaman First Class Calvin Leon Graham, who
joined the navy when he was only twelve years old.

This youngest enlistee of World War II (that we know of) was wounded
in the Battle of Guadalcanal and earned both a Purple Heart and a Bronze
Star Medal. When his true age was discovered, he was given a dishonorable
discharge and his awards were revoked.

Years later, he managed to get the matter worked out and the dishonorable
discharge was changed to honorable. Two years after his death, his dutifully
earned Purple Heart was presented to his widow by then Secretary of the Navy
John Dalton.

Twelve may have been unusual, but eighteen certainly wasn't. Leaving their
homes behind, these young kids were signing up to fight a war they hadn't
asked for, nor did they want. But America had been attacked, war had been
declared, and without hesitation they went, determined to make a difference
in the outcome.

Once the rush of the induction process and training wore out and these soldiers were shipped off to faraway places, thousands of miles from the familiar,
in jungles or deserts, that's when the loneliness would set in. For the soldiers,
and for their loved ones back home.

A tradition, which began in World War I and continued through World War
II, was the hanging of a service or Blue Star flag in the window of the homes
that had a family member serving in the military. There would be one star for
each son or daughter in the war.

Two Blue Star flag.

Mrs. Esther McCabe of Lilly, Pennsylvania, had the most children serving in World War II. This brave mother watched eleven offspring go off to war. Eight of those served in the United States Army, one was a merchant marine, and two were in the navy. What's even more remarkable is that they all returned home.

Other mothers weren't so fortunate. Their son or daughter made the ultimate sacrifice.

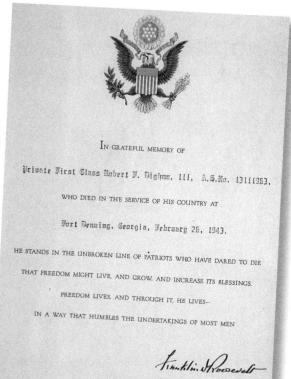

In GRATEFUL MEMORY OF

Private First Class Robert F. Bigham, III, A.S.No. 13111363,

WHO DIED IN THE SERVICE OF HIS COUNTRY AT

Fort Benning, Georgia, February 26, 1943.

HE STANDS IN THE UNBROKEN LINE OF PATRIOTS WHO HAVE DARED TO DIE THAT FREEDOM MIGHT LIVE, AND GROW, AND INCREASE ITS BLESSINGS. FREEDOM LIVES, AND THROUGH IT, HE LIVES— IN A WAY THAT HUMBLES THE UNDERTAKINGS OF MOST MEN

Franklin D. Roosevelt

PRESIDENT OF THE UNITED STATES OF AMERICA

(Left) WWII Gold Star pin.

(Right) President Franklin D. Roosevelt–signed letter honoring those who gave their all.

Many had their family trees forever changed due to the conflict.

One mother was especially impacted. The five Sullivan brothers of Iowa served together on the USS *Juneau* in the Solomon Islands. All five lost their lives on November 13, 1942, when their ship was torpedoed and sank. In a single day, this dear lady became a Five Gold Star Mom.

Due to the Sullivan Brothers tragedy, and the potential risk for similar situations to occur, regulations were changed to limit the number of siblings that could serve together on the same military assignment.

Since Bob Hope and his mother were always close, he knew how important it was for a mom to hear from her son or daughter serving so far away from home and in harm's way. He also knew what it meant for the soldiers to get word from their moms that all was well back home.

Whatever he could do to help bridge that gap, he would do. His favorite being this: before or after Bob's shows (and sometimes during), soldiers who managed to get close enough to Bob would sometimes ask if Bob would call their moms when he returned to the States and let her know that he had seen them and they were fine. Even if that soldier was laid up in a hospital bed, he'd ask Bob to make it a good word.

the five Sullivan brothers
"missing in action" off the Solomons

THEY DID THEIR PART

Office of War Information, 1943.
American Legion Collection.

Commander Motor Torpedo Boats
Pacific Fleet
Oct 14, 1944

Dear Bob:
It was really grand of you to call my mother and pass on your lasting cheer to my family. It eased their minds considerably. I could've asked of no man nothing more; the zeal of private friendship will always exist here.

. . . I feel I should tell you this, there are undoubtedly millions of people that realize the lively interest and fine work you accomplished in all theaters of this war. . . . Your many side trips to reach the few out of way places was one of the many considerations you showed the plain guy—few entertainers have been out here, but those few failed to exert that extra effort. Those thousands in the out of way places, as well as those on the main line, respect you and your company for what you achieved, which strengthened the very foundation. You left an indelible impression on the service, and I say this from consensus, you accomplished more than any one other man, admiral or private. . . . In closing, you have my gratitude and sincere regard for many acts of personal kindness and attention. Remember me to Barney, Frances, Tony and Pat. See you when it's over.

Sincerely,
Zub . . . Sgt.

V-mail for Mom.

Dear Mom, a favorite
request of the troops.

Dear Bob,
Just to let you know that I am well and hope you are the same. Bob, I
hope you will write to me and let me know if you sing this song for my
Mother on Mother's Day. I don't know when Mother's Day is, so will
you sing the song—the name is "Dear Mom," then she will know that I
am O.K., and by the song she will know that I love her very much.
    Well, so long and God bless you.

Earl J. Rowley, U.S.N. Seabees

V-mail for Mom from across the
miles on her special day.

Sent from American Red Cross
April 9, 1944

Dear Bob,
Even though it is a little difficult to write to you in an upside down
position, I felt it the least I could do to show my appreciation for
making me a little more comfortable while I lie here on my back in a
traction bed. My neck is in a halter with a weight attached, and it has
been this way for the past two weeks when I met with an accident. I
had to come back from 18 months foreign duty without anything hap-
pening, and now this.
    . . . You know, Bob, right now I have a wish to make, for my birth-
day is the 15th of this month. It would be the best birthday present if
you could arrange to give a show from this camp in the near future,
and I would be able to see you in person. . . . The only thing I will ask
is that you don't mention my name. My mother thinks I am O.K., and
that's the way it will have to be, as she has a weak heart . . .

One of your fans,
PFC Sidney Tenenbaum

October 26, 1942
Pvt. Victor Torre 36129164

Dear Bob:
Just a few lines to let you know we just heard your program, "Command Performance," starring Judy Garland and Lana Turner, and a few others. And if I'm not mistaken, you dedicated a few numbers to the boys overseas. And we sure would appreciate "Dear Mom" for Vic Torre, George Cocca, Steve Jarski, Marvine Veach. And Bob, we really miss our Mom. We really mean it.

We are doing our part in Australia. Whereabouts is a military secret.

Here is hoping we hear from you soon . . . And, Bob, if you answer this letter, the boys sure would get a bang out of it.

Thank you, Bob. So long.
Your soldier friends overseas

Bob didn't leave the dads out either:

14th December 1943
Capt. Herbert Ernest
Somewhere in Italy

Dear Bob—
Here's hoping this gets through your pyramid of fan letters. My mail was held up for a couple of weeks because of my change in location—but when I finally got it—I received an enthusiastic letter from Dad telling of your phone call to him. I can't quite tell you how deeply I appreciated your taking time out to go to that trouble. Thanks are hardly sufficient, but from where I'm sitting they'll have to do. We're in Italy now baking more than we ever thought we could—for the fighting Fifty Army—makes our African adventure a mere piddling! We're happy to be where it counts and are all optimistic about the way things are going.

Best regards,
Herbert Ernest

DEAR BOB . . .

JUST HAD TO SEND IT

— — — — — — — — — — — — —

THE SOLDIERS MAY HAVE HAD A LITTLE TOO MUCH FUN WITH SOME OF THESE letters and gifts that they sent Bob, especially some of the rare and interesting photos that they happened to "stumble" upon in their travels.

It has been rumored that we all have a "twin" somewhere in the world. Not an authentic twin, but someone who looks remarkably like us. We might catch a glimpse of this person as he or she walks by us at an airport or in a crowded mall. Or perhaps a friend will send a selfie with the lookalike.

Bob received more than his share of old-fashioned snapshots and artwork from soldiers who were convinced they had found his "lookalike." One soldier didn't have to look very far at all to find the Bob Hope lookalike—he was staring right back at him in the mirror.

> *Torpedo Squadron 46*
> *United States Pacific Fleet*
> *March 14, 1945*
>
> *Dear "Ski Nose" Hope,*
> *After seeing the enclosed picture of myself, I have decided to commit Hari-Kari—but then maybe I ought to change my mind and sue you for scaring my mother.*
>
> *All is forgiven,*
> *Ed A. Zurlinden*

"On the Road to Tokyo."

June 6, 1945
Lt. E. A. Zurlinden
Torpedo Squadron 46
c/o Fleet Post Office
San Francisco, Calif.

Dear Ed:

Dropped by my home last night and was greeted by my wife . . . who asked if I would stay the night . . . by my children . . . who wondered who that man was . . . and by a stack of G.I. Mail.

Just back from a tour of the East. It was really wonderful . . . they went for me in New York . . . they went for me in Chicago . . . but in Kansas City . . . they caught up with me! But it's good to be home. . . . While I was in Cleveland I went back to my old neighborhood to meet my old friends. I met the Mayor . . . and I asked him if there had been many reforms there since I had left. He said, "No . . . that was the last one!"

Thanks for that picture of yourself. It is rather rugged; but I'm mailing you one of myself . . . which you will find is even harder to take. So . . . good luck!

Sincerely,
Bob Hope

The mysterious photographs and drawings weren't only of Bob. Other resemblances were brought up, too.

2 May 1945
Somewhere in Germany

Dear Bob,
Our purpose in writing you and enclosing the photo is due to the fact that we believe you might recognize the individual to whom we refer. Your aid and assistance will put our minds at ease in establishing absolute identity.

We don't recall the personal appearance of the "Kraft Blue Ribbon Boy" in this area at any time, but with the heavy undergrowth and foliage, it seems apparent that he did sneak through an alley or two with a thumb pointed toward friendly positions, groaning "Going My Way."

The facial camouflage would have come in handy after the noted owner had handed out six straight tips (losing) at Santa Anita.

We are undecided as to whom the photo should be sent, but we think it a mean trick of the person to mislead his public in such a way.

. . . In the event that you have the same difficulties that we did in identifying the individual whose likeness appears on the enclosed photo, it appears to be a man with a face, two eyes (complete with eyebrows), a high (high) forehead and a chin well upholstered. Physical capabilities are unknown, but a good set of pipes must be present for anyone to protect them from elements the way this person has.

Thanking you in advance for your loyal cooperation in this matter, we remain . . .

Very truly yours,
Captain Charles E. Paggi

Even Bing Crosby had his lookalikes.

P.S. Any similarity between the above character and any other person living or dead is purely coincidental.

June 18, 1945
Capt. Chas. E. Paggi
Hq. Btry. 379th AAA AW BN

Dear Chuck:
Thanks for your letter. It surely was thoughtful of you to send me the photograph . . . I'm going to show it to the "Croaner" one of these days . . . when he's feeling strong.

. . . **Guess I'd better sign off for now. I may be dropping in on you fellows in a few days for I'm headed your way. In the meantime, best of luck to you.**

Sincerely,
Bob Hope

Another Bob Hope lookalike, in a Dürer painting.

Salzburg, Austria
October 10, 1945

Dear Mr. Hope:
Hate to disturb you, but the other day I was looking through a Nazi library and found this page with the famous Durer painting of the Adoration of the Holy Trinity.

My eye fell on a certain figure in the ensemble . . . a knight in armor . . . How did you ever get in that painting in 1511? I'm a Catholic priest and don't believe in this migration of souls business, however, not only I, but a lot of the officers and men here thought the resemblance striking.

Incidentally, I wish to apologize for any disturbance of your program awhile back. I flew low over your audience with one of our goofy artillery pilots . . . I think it was Furth or Schweinfurt or Nuremberg. Remember? You looked up and waved.

Greetings and all that kind of thing.
Charles G. Erb
Chaplain

Others were compelled to send Bob the same image . . .

American Red Cross
14 April 1945

Dear Mr. Hope,
I have come across this reproduction of a painting by Albrecht Durer
in my travels thru the Reich, and from the looks of this heavily plated
gentleman, it seems possible that our generation has not been the only
one to be fortunate enough to number you among its constituents.

Harvey C. McClintock
Captain F. A.

Germany
Jan 29, 1945

Hello Bob,
Bob, you carry your age pretty good. . . . I picked the enclosed picture
up in a fox hole somewhere in Germany. No fooling, Bob. It looks a lot
like you, I think. Keep up the good work, Bob. We think you are tops.
But we never have time to see the show, and there isn't a radio for
miles of where I am. But this can't last forever.

A fan forever,
James F. Moore

June 6, 1945
Pfc James F. Moore
Btry C 927th F. A. Bn.

Dear James:
. . . I'm always glad to hear from you fellows. Of course, if I
continue to receive those pictures you've been sending me, I'll be
able to paper the walls of my den! Will have to get back to work
now, so here's wishing you the best of luck.

Sincerely,
Bob Hope

697 Sgt. W. H. Pegg
R.A.F.T. Transport Command
Gander Airport
Newfoundland

Dear Bob:
. . . I don't have the gen on this Christian knight, but as far as looks go, there is a definite similarity.

Very sincerely,
Bill Pegg

Germany
6 April 1945

If the enclosed picture from a magazine found in one of the German homes used by us for shelter gives you a belly laugh like it did us, this letter will not be in vain. No offense meant, Bob, and I won't tell Bing.
But all kidding aside, I and the boys enjoy your broadcasts over here and want to thank you.

Sincerely,
Capt. Mloock

Bob was turning up everywhere. And sometimes, it wasn't even "him."

To: Capt. L. S. Mloock
June 6, 1945

Dear Captain:

... Thanks for the picture. Doesn't she have a terrific nose though! Glad I have a classic profile. You boys must have seen a lot of strange sights since you've been over. What's this I hear about green, pink, blue, etc. hair in Paris? I'll be over soon, so watch out for me.

Sincerely,
Bob Hope

Somewhere in New Guinea
June 5, 1944

Dear Bob:

After reading an article in our New Guinea rag concerning the sale of Frank "Swoonatra's" silk panties, for such unheard of prices, we are enclosing the following items—one pair of G.I. drawers (we regret that they can't be silk, but we are not swooners. Just plain fighting men of the U.S. Army). We are also enclosing four other items in the hope that you, a man [who] in our estimation is doing more for the soldier than anyone we know, will auction said articles for whatever Bonds they will bring. We are really anxious to see if a fighting man's drawers rate.

We have been over here 29 long hard months and we are still able to stand up and wear these things.

Please [accept] our apologies for the slightly worn socks as the rats have terrific appetites over here.

In closing, we wish to remind you that our slogan is "More of Lamour, Hope, and Crosby and less Sinatra."

Signed—
Pfc. Bill Israel—Drawers (not panties)
Pfc. Ed Kelly—Undershirt
Pfc. E. G. Gulledge—Shoe strings
Pvt. N. J. Lee—Socks (slightly worn)
Sgt. M. D. Lawrence—Handkerchief

The soldiers got creative with their gifts to Bob. Most were handmade items, and a few were, well . . . a little more imaginative than that. Like the letter from a soldier who shaved off his goatee and mailed it to Bob for a souvenir! Imagine Bob opening up that envelope! After the initial "gift" was sent, the soldier wrote a follow-up note to Bob's secretary at the time, Marjorie Hughes:

Overseas
Sept. 16, 1944

Dear Miss Hughes,
I'm the fellow <u>without</u> the goatee. Remember, I sent it to Mr. Hope some time ago.
*   . . . No doubt my letter (and goatee) has been cast aside and forgotten. But you might remember that I vowed to meet him if it took to my dying day.*

Goatee-less,
Clayton R. Kern

P.S. If Mr. Hope is back from the S. P. [South Pacific], at least tell him about the goatee. He might get a bang out of it.

Miss Hughes certainly remembered the original "gift" and responded accordingly:

October 5, 1944
Clayton R. Kern S 1/c
Armed Guard, Pacific
S. S. ROBERT D. CAREY

Dear Mr. Kern:
Your letter came as a bit of a shock. I remember that goatee, right enough, but haven't the vaguest idea as to where I "filed" it! My private opinion is that once a person decides to part with such a bit of personal property . . . he should definitely decide to part with it . . . no qualms, no passing regrets, etc. In other words, "Be Brave!"
*   Mr. Hope finished work on "The Princess and the Pirate" before he left on his South Pacific tour the first of July. He just got back from a short tour of the Eastern states . . . including Canada. He is scheduled to make a couple of pictures in the near future, but I have no idea as*

*to just when he will start work on them. Frankly, I believe he'd rather
tour service camps and play for you boys.*

*... If you come to Los Angeles be sure to get in touch with Mr.
Hope through the studios ... Paramount. He's always glad to talk to
you fellows if he's on the set.*

Sincerely,
Secretary [Marjorie Hughes] *to Mr. Hope*

April 18, 1944

Dear Bob:
*I don't have any metal to mold my own "Oscar"—so let this be the
reasonable facsimile.*

*I know that the laughter of countless servicemen scattered over the
globe is more than ample payment for your tireless efforts—BUT—I
would like to add my own two cents. You've done a swell job and a lot
of gents in this man's army won't be forgetting you for a long time to
come—if ever ...*

Cpl. H. R. Biedinger

Soldier's artwork and portion of
original letter.

March 23, 1943

Dear Bob:
I suppose I should start this letter off "Dear Mr. Hope," but I have heard you on the air so often that I feel I know you and I am sure you will not take offense at the familiar use of your name. I assure you I mean no disrespect.
   While listening to your program this evening I heard you were broadcasting from Catalina Island. This "rock" is just 25 miles further out than Catalina and has none of the facilities for entertainment that they have in Avalon. . . . I was wondering and hoping, Hope, if it could be possible for you to make the journey to this island for one of your broadcasts. . . . We do not get ashore very often and what with the loneliness and the barrenness of this place, a little entertainment would certainly go a long way toward increasing the morale of the men.
   I am not sure if I am doing the correct thing in addressing this letter to you without going through official channels, but I ran into you one night last July near Burbank in a filling station, and you gave me a big grin and a "Hi, fellow," which made me pretty sure you're a regular guy and wouldn't mind my blowing off this way. . . . I can promise you some good fishing if you do come out. . . . Incidentally, if you are ever in Dallas, Texas after we have won the war, drop out and we'll barbeque a steer in your honor . . .

Yours very truly,
George Kent
Royal Australian Air Force
450 Squadron
Central Mediterranean Force

---

7 Jan 44

Dear Bob Hope,
We want you to adopt our Squadron! How about it?
   I suppose that the above flat statement does not convey much to you other than that a Squadron wants you to become their "Father."
   Well, you see, it's like this . . .

*All the best Squadrons these days are having themselves adopted
by some famous personage, preferably a film or radio star. Being one
of the better of the best Squadrons, we have decided that we would
like to have a "Father" and a "Mother" (the decent thing, you know), so
we've written to Greer Garson, asking her to be our "Mother" . . .*

*Now, to tell you something about the Squadron that we would have
you take up parental duties for—*

*Firstly, we are an Australian Squadron (don't hold that against
us) and, to help us out, we have New Zealanders, Canadians, [an]
Englishman, and a South African. We have had two Americans with
us, but both eventually escaped.*

*We fly P.40 Kittybombers and our motto is "We Harass" (you
should see us in a city). The Squadron's number and name is 450 "Desert Harassers" Squadron, Royal Australian Air Force.*

*. . . The Squadron has shot down forty-nine enemy aircraft con-
firmed, that have happened to try and interfere with this harassing
business.*

*. . . If you decide that you could stand being called "Dad" . . . then
let us know.*

Lt. R. H. Burden

Feb. 25, 1944
R. H. Burden, F/Lt.
Royal Australian Air Force
Central Mediterranean Force

Dear Lt. Burden:
Or should I say, "my son?" Of course, I accept this heavy respon-
sibility which has been thrust upon me. No <u>man</u> would leave a
woman to cope with . . . how many? . . . "harassers." I shall stand
beside your new "mother" in this grave emergency.

But as your new "father" I must assert myself to demand more
information . . . names, biographical notes, reports on behavior
. . . you know what I mean. Get busy!

I'm afraid that is about all I have to say at the moment. It's a
great shock, this business of becoming a father . . . and on such a
large scale!

In the meantime, be good boys and do your "harassing" where it will do the most damage.

Your "dad,"
Bob Hope

Throughout the war years, Bob's "military family" kept growing.

(Germany)
March 18/45

Dear Bob,
As you know, we G.I.s are in the habit of adopting beautiful women, dogs, and what not. We thought we would be different and let you adopt us. You see, we belong to the fifth section and make a sport of weight-lifting. . . . We read your pretty book, "I Never Left Home" . . . but we orphans never had a home and don't know the emotions of leaving one. And here we come to the point. Can we call you Daddy? That's swell! Now that you're our papa, how's mama?
. . . A little about ourselves now. We hope to visit the Adolph Hitler Hotel (to be renamed the Roosevelt Parkway), the "most bombiest" place on earth, boasting the world's largest cellar, incidentally.
. . . Your seven sons-a-guns,

"Johnny" Frost
"Jodie" Boddo
"Jimmy" Durentiss
"Don" Sudano
"Dunny" Dunstan
"Steve" Hornacek
"Ray" Zuramel

June 6, 1945
Pvt. Don Sudano 20248001
"B" Btry 258 F. A. Bn.
APO 339, c/o Postmaster
New York, New York

Hiya, fellows:
. . . Glad to hear from my seven boys! . . . I'm due over Germany
sometime soon, so may drop in on you boys. Until then, best of
luck to you.

Sincerely,
Bob Hope

(Letterhead: American Red Cross)
Pfc. Chas. Boghosier (Bogie)

Here is a little something you might like, and again you might not.

*There was a doggie, Swobby, and a Marine—went into a café to eat.
The waitress asked the Doggie what he wanted, and he in a tough
voice said "A steak and make it raw." She took the order and went on
to the Swobby. The Swobby also said in a tough voice, "Bring me a
steak and make it bloody." Pretty tough boys, she thought. Then, she
came to the Marine and asked for his order. He said, "Just bring me in
a couple slices of bread and run a bull through here."*

A Marine in the Pacific

Another letter written on bathroom tissue:

Dec. 9th, 1945

*Dear Bob,
Please [accept] this letter, not as a mere joke, because this letter is
written in all sincerity. . . . We are a couple of young returning sailors
who need a good start for a business, monkey or otherwise. We don't
want to start at the bottom of the ladder to attain our goal . . . that*

happens every day. We, depending upon your generosity, could skip a few rungs.

We remain, "your dependents"
Rudy and Peter

P.S. Send all donations, and in equal shares, to:

R. A. Caputo   *P. H. Rubbicco*
Revere, Mass   *Medford, Mass*

P.P.S. If you fail us, we still have faith in "Crosby."

P.P.P.S. We thought of Rockefeller, but he only gives out dimes.

P.P.P.P.S. Please excuse the stationary, but that's all that's available here aboard ship.

February 20, 1946

Dear Mr. Caputo:
(I feel, since we are discussing a financial matter, this should be kept on a very formal plane!) I received the letter sent to me by yourself and Mr. Rubbicco and have studied it carefully.

You boys have made a great mistake! Don't you know Crosby's the one who owns the mint? And, besides, my last contract with the Secretary of the Treasury left me with a saddened outlook on life.

But seriously, I'm glad to know you're back in the good old U.S.A. Here's hoping it will be a long, long time before you do anymore "traveling."

Sincerely,
Bob Hope

Italy
April 24, 1944

Dear Bob,
Just a few lines to say hello to our Old Morale Builder . . . We wrote
Bing a letter a few weeks ago, and he hasn't answered as yet.
    . . . To get to the bottom of this letter, we will quit beating around
the bush, all we want is a small stinky little fruit cake, not less than 5
lbs. and not more than 10 lbs. If you can send it, it will be greatly ap-
preciated by us all.

PFC Bob Wallace
Joe La Rocca
Mike Navarra
Bill Williams

To: PFC Bob Wallace
New York, NY

Hi, ya, Fellows:
. . . You mustn't be too hard on Bing. He's probably so worried
about his new competition that he doesn't have time to write. . . .
I finally won a couple of bucks from Bing the other day, but it was
hardly worth while . . . at least he might have ripped it out of the
mattress first . . . What would I do with a mattress?
    I'm working on a pirate picture now. This time it's a picture for
Sam Goldwyn. Paramount, of course, was very reluctant to lend
me out, but Goldwyn was anxious to get me . . . he says he has to
do something to cut down on his income tax.
    I'll see what I can do about that fruitcake. You know, here
in California it isn't exactly the time of year for such. But I'll
look around. There've been a lot of great cooks in my family. My
uncle, in fact, once cooked for the governor . . . his reprieve came
through in time. Well, I'll say "so long" for now. Give my best to
the rest of the boys.

Sincerely yours,
Bob Hope

Contrary to what one might think, during World War II fruitcake wasn't sent to Allied soldiers for bridge-building purposes. The troops actually requested the dessert, filled with its variety of dried fruits and nuts and capable of holding its flavor and same texture for years, perhaps even decades. As a matter of fact, there is a report of an elaborate wedding fruitcake, prepared during Queen Victoria's reign and stored at a London bakery since 1898, that miraculously survived the World War II bombing of London.

> *Received March 26, 1945*
> *Armed Forces Radio Service*
>
> *Hello Bob:*
> *. . . Would you mind sending us a pin-up picture of you in a bathing suit? If the Japanese get a look at your super frame, we know they will throw in the sponge and quit.*
>
> *We have the greatest confidence in you, Bob. Speaking for the gang of the instrument section here, I hope you will oblige us with three photos.*
>
> *Can't rely upon the dames these days, but we know you won't let us down.*
>
> *Thanking you.*
> *Your sincere admirers,*
> *Cpl. Hilland D.*
> *Royal Canadian Air Force*
> *OVERSEAS*

June 6, 1945
Cpl. Hilland D.
Royal Canadian Air Force
OVERSEAS

Dear Corporal Hilland:
Dropped by my home the other day to see if there [was] anything that had to be taken care of before I left for overseas, and I found a stack of mail from you boys . . . some of it rather ancient.

Just got back from a tour of the East . . . Chicago, New York, Washington. The California Chamber of Commerce said my trip

was another Victory tour . . . they claim it was a victory to get me out of the state. But it surely was a thrill to get back to Hollywood . . . My regular waiter at the Brown Derby had tears in his eyes when he saw me. I was so impressed I said, "From now on I'll always leave a tip on the table." He said, "Never mind that, Hope, just leave the tips that are on my other tables!"

I'm sending you the three photos. However, I was advised not to send ones of me in a bathing suit . . . my friend said you boys still have a fight ahead of you . . . why make it any more difficult! Best of luck to you.

Sincerely,
Bob Hope

War Show poster, Bob's head in poster, LA.

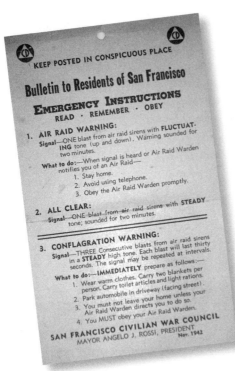

1942 Air raid bulletin to
San Francisco residents.

Many items were sent to Bob as a souvenir of the war. And vice versa.

Jan. 27, 1945
A.P.O. 403
Luxembourg

Dear Mr. Hope,
We've heard so much about your new book, "I Never Left Home," and ever so anxious to read it.

Being with the 3rd Army and 80th Div. Inf. at the front, it's pretty hard for us to get this book. We would appreciate it very much if you would send us an autographed book.

. . . Well, I guess that's all for now, and hope you won't disappoint us. Best of luck to you and your gang . . .

Two G. I.s
Pfc. Joe Billonitz
Pfc. Tony Izzo

P.S. If you can't send the book, send Frances Langford.

Excerpt from Bob Hope's closing tribute on his radio show from Fort Jackson:

You know, battles are fought on land and water and in the sky, and wars are finally won on the ground. And tonight I'm looking at the man who'll win this war on the ground. Men like the engineers who whack out little jobs like the Panama Canal and the Alaskan-Canadian Highway. Men who go in first and come out last when the going gets tough. The men who build desert roads so fast, the infantry can march full speed behind them. Sure, you can soften up the enemy from the air, but before he's licked, the infantry must take his factories and cities and farms, and the artillery must run interference with the infantry, blasting holes in the enemy's lines, fighting off his planes and protecting our men and equipment. . . . No, sir, there isn't a tougher fighting team in the world, and if you didn't know it before, you know it now for you watched them carry the ball in North Africa, and mister, when Uncle Sam gets down close to that Berlin-Tokyo goal line, just watch these Fort Jackson guys go over that final touchdown.

> " . . . I wanna thank the soldiers here at Fort Jackson for the swell reception they gave me when I arrived here. Gee, I didn't expect to be carried on their shoulders for miles. . . . I didn't expect to be put down in Lake Murray either."
> . . . Bob Hope

A piece of Japanese propaganda that was found by a soldier.

DEAR BOB . . .

I'M MISSING MY SWEETHEART

LONELINESS WAS A TOPIC THAT ALWAYS HIT HOME WITH THE CAMP AND radio audiences. The enlisted men and women, as well as their sweethearts back home, knew that feeling all too well. Laughter and romantic ballads were worthy antidotes for such a condition. Bob knew this and packed plenty of both into his shows. Jokes about dating, marriage, and romance were soldier favorites, as well as popular love ballads of the day. Songs like "I'll Be Seeing You," "We'll Meet Again," "You'd Be So Nice to Come Home To," and so many others could take a soldier on "A Sentimental Journey" right back into his sweetheart's arms again . . . if only in his mind.

And just like he did for their mothers and fathers, whenever he was asked Bob would happily pass along any messages the troops had for their sweethearts, too.

> October 6, 1944
> Mrs. Gordon A. Johnson
> Montevideo, Minn.
>
> Dear Mrs. Johnson:
> I just wanted you to know our troupe played for your husband down there in the South Pacific and he told me to say "hello" to you for him, and also to tell you to be sure to write.
> He looked fine when I saw him, and I trust he still is. I hope this mess will be over soon so all the boys can return to a normal life. Will you please include my best wishes when you write to your husband?
>
> My best regards,
> Bob Hope

US Army Signal Corps, Homefront Sweetheart locket, WWII.

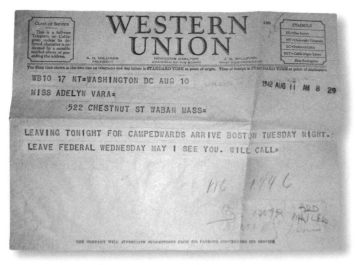

Soldier's telegram: "Leaving tonight for Camp Edwards.... May I see you?" Sent August 10, 1942.

Sept. 17
A.P.O. 920
S.W.P.A.

Mr. Bob Hope
I want to take the opportunity and write you these few lines and thank you from the bottom of my heart for doing what I asked you to do for me—by calling my wife up in L.A. and giving her the message I sent thru you. . . . that one call made her very happy I know. . . . I have a son in the service also—he is on a Liberty ship—somewhere in the Pacific, and my wife wrote and told me she has not heard from him in five months. So that is why I am so grateful for you for calling her at the time you did. . . . she was pretty worried about us over here. But speaking to someone who had seen me and knew I was okay—helped her a lot I know.

So once again, Bob, I want to thank you for all your trouble and appreciate it very much.

And I would like to tell you just how much us boys over here really enjoyed your show—it was really sweet and helped a lot. A show like yours and a letter over here is worth a million dollars or more to us fellows.

Thanking you once more, I remain—

Sincerely yours,
S/Sgt. A. C. Baker

Guitarist Tony Romano accompanies Frances Langford in an impromptu performance, 1944. Bob Hope Collection, Library of Congress.

October 5, 1944
Mrs. Richard Rogers
Auburndale, Mass.

Dear Mrs. Rogers:
I just wanted to let you know that we saw Captain Rogers down there in New Guinea and he looked very well.

Captain Rogers was our Special Service Officer in his area and he did a great job for us, really treated us fine. He told me to say "hello" to his daughter, Lynne, and to say her Daddy was thinking of her.

There's no need to tell you that we had a very exciting trip visiting all the boys. I surely hope they will soon be able to return to a normal life. When you write to the Captain, please say "hello" to him for me.

My best regards,
Bob Hope

October 25, 1944
Charleston, S.C.
Stark Hospital

Dear Bob:
Your reply to my letter came as a most pleasant surprise.

It is quite encouraging to hear that you may have the opportunity to visit Stark Hospital while on your "Southern tour of the 'you'all' states. I, for one, certainly hope that you can make it, since my morale has hit a new low recently.

You asked about Petey McDade. She has an adorable baby girl, by name, Kathleen Sue White. At the present time she is living in Chicago, Illinois. Her husband was injured in Germany, and is now in a hospital "Somewhere over there." He has never seen the baby, and it will be quite interesting when he sees what a really charming daughter he has.

My husband is overseas now, serving under General Patton in France. I haven't heard from him in over a month, and naturally, it has me quite worried.

Well, Bob, thanks again for the letter, and we'll be looking for you when you come down south.

Wishing you much continued success,
T/5 Elaine Mulligan W.A.C.
Stark Hospital
Charleston, S. C.

My wishes, Husband Dear, are for
A Christmas so complete,
Good luck will smile on all your plans
And keep a lifetime sweet;
My wishes, like my love, reach on
Into a future far....
Because my Hearth of Happiness
Is only where you are!

Yours Forever and
Ever,
Audrey:

WWII 1943 Christmas card sent to newlywed husband, Army Pfc. Leon Vaughn, who was later killed in action, October 18, 1944. Leon's son was born eight days after his death.

Hawaiian Isl.
Wednesday 2110
23 May 1945

Dear Bob "Stateside" Hope:
Say, Bob, is there a chance that you'd play a song for a buddy and me?
Neither one of us has a special girl. Both of us had some other fellow step in on our heartthrobs, so we'd like to dedicate "Close to You" to all the girls in the good old U.S.A., and we'd like to have Ginny Simms sing it. We would appreciate it very much.

Thanks.
Sincerely yours,
Robert P. Connell S 1/c (Los Angeles)
Johnny Preston S ¼ (Houston, Texas)
A.T.B. Navy 900

Robert P. Connell S 1/c
A. T. B. Navy 900

Dear Bob and Johnny:
Received your letter and sent your request on to the proper department of AFRS. Hope your song is played for you very soon.
. . . Wish I could visit you boys out in the Pacific again this summer, but USO thinks you have enough in the way of hardships without having me along, too. I'll have to get back to my packing for I am hopping off for Europe any minute now. Here's wishing you both the very best of luck.

Sincerely,
Bob Hope

" . . . I'm back at Paramount, you know. There really wasn't any serious trouble between me and the studio . . . just a slight technical dispute about salary . . . they didn't want to pay me any."
. . . Bob Hope

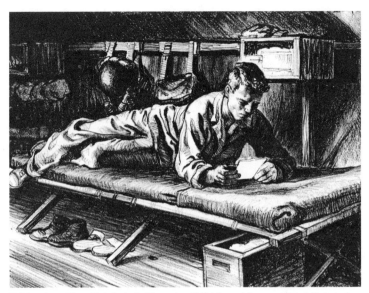

Mail from home, Edward A. Sallenbach, lithographer, 1945. Library of Congress, Prints & Photographs Division, LC-DIG-pga-08182.

(To Bob Hope)
I'd like to know if you could help me out—you are the GI's best friend.
Bob, do you know some girl that will write me a letter and send me
her picture?

Joe, somewhere in Germany

Matchmaking requests, such as the above, were made by the soldiers, although these were usually for dates with celebrities. In these situations Bob would at least send fan photos of their requested favorites. And at least once Bob was brought in for relationship intervention.

According to an NBC news item dated April 13, 1942, and titled *Bob Hope Finds Shangri-La in Army Camps*, Bob helped out a young draftee at Camp Roberts who had just received his engagement ring back from his sweetheart. Broken-hearted, the soldier needed someone to help him patch things up and he was convinced that Bob Hope should be the one to intervene. Bob couldn't speak directly to the girlfriend live on air during his broadcast, but he agreed that after the show, he would place a call to the ex-fiancée. Using his best humor and persuasive skills, Bob managed to talk the young lady out of the break-up. The engagement was reinstated and, thanks to Bob, at least one more "Dear John" letter of WW2 was happily reversed.

DEAR BOB . . .

HOW 'BOUT IT?

— — — — — — — — — — — — — — —

IF A SOLDIER ASKED FOR IT, BOB HOPE WOULD DO EVERYTHING IN HIS POWER to make it happen. From paying a visit to their particular base or hospital, to sending jokes or photos of his celebrity friends, and yes, even fruitcakes and harmonicas, Bob always did his best to accommodate each and every request of the soldiers. He may not have worn the uniform of an enlisted man, but his heart stretched across every branch of the military. It's no wonder there was such confidence among the soldiers that they could write and ask Bob Hope for just about anything and receive it.

> *Italy*
> *13 Nov 44*
>
> *Dear Mr. Hope:*
> *Missed you in Tunis because I was sent there to draw a beer ration for the men. Missed you in Bizerte because we were in the staging area just out of town. Missed you at Taborka because you didn't show up.*
> *Think I deserve a raincheck, so if and when I get back to the States, would like to attend one of your performances.*
> *. . . Save a ticket for me to one of your shows, if I don't laugh loud enough I will gladly return the ticket.*
>
> *Merry Christmas to you and yours.*
> *Sincerely yours,*
> *Jonathan Edwards*
>
> ---
>
> **June 6, 1945**
> **Lt. Jonathan Edwards 0–1112671**
> **Co. "C" 16th Arm'd Engr Bn**
> **APO 251, c/o Postmaster**
> **New York, New York**

Dear Jon:

... So you've missed me all over the globe ... Some fellows have all the luck! If you ever get to Hollywood, contact me through the Studio and I'll arrange for you to see a broadcast or visit the lot. In the meantime, good luck to you.

Sincerely,
Bob Hope

"Rembrandt Hope. That's me. Always on the canvas."
 ... Bob Hope, on his short-lived boxing career

Bob Hope signs autograph in England, 1943, as Mickey Vance, deputy boxing commissioner, looks on.

L.A.C.
1584936 L Dixon D.
32.E.F.T.S.
Bowden, Alberta
Canada
29.4.44

My Dear Mr. Hope—
I do hope this letter won't cause you too much annoyance, because it contains a request which I should imagine is made very often to you.

I have been in America and Canada for some time now training as a pilot, and before returning to England, want to get something my fiancée there would really be thrilled with. As she is a keen autograph

*"fiend" and her favorite films have been the "Road to Morocco" series,
I wonder if you could let me have your autograph, please?*

Dennis Dixon

June 7, 1944

Dear Dennis:
Received your letter and hope it isn't too late to send you that
autograph for your fiancée. You'll find it enclosed.

As long as she enjoyed the "Road" series, you might tell her
that we've just completed another one of them, "The Road to Utopia," this time. Dorothy, Bing and I have a lot of fun making these
pictures . . . probably that is one reason so many people seem to
like them. Of course, Bing has been a bit sulky about this one . . . I
get the girl! He surely must be losing his grip.

The whole troupe had a wonderful time on the tour last summer and I was pleased to be able to stop in England and see the
fellows there. Wish I could do it again soon, but this summer I'm
headed for the South Pacific. Will probably travel by mosquito . . .
for I hear they have them large down that way.

. . . Anyway, the best of luck to you.

Sincerely yours,
Bob Hope

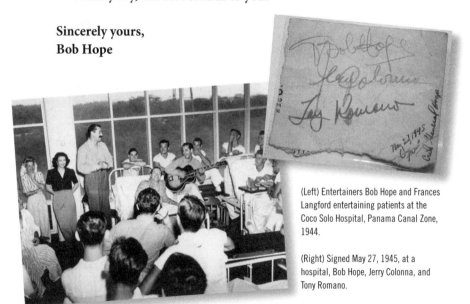

(Left) Entertainers Bob Hope and Frances
Langford entertaining patients at the
Coco Solo Hospital, Panama Canal Zone,
1944.

(Right) Signed May 27, 1945, at a
hospital, Bob Hope, Jerry Colonna, and
Tony Romano.

Dorothy "Dottie" Lamour autographed photo for soldiers.

Lieutenant A. J. Davis
April 18, 1944

Dear Bob,
Here we are in the middle of the jungle, no Dorothy Lamour and without hope. We have two fellows who can play the mouth organ, but we've no mouth organ (harmonica)—can you do anything for us? (Please.) . . . We've written to thousands, and you're our last Hope.

All the best from the boys of No. 1 Commando. India Command

---

17 Feb. 1945

Dear Mr. Hope,
I've enjoyed your radio program for a long time, your two books gave me a big bang, and I wouldn't miss one of your pictures.
Now, I'll stop licking your hand and tell you what I want. My request is this—if you ever put on your show here at Fitzsimons Gen. Hosp., Denver, Colo., will you please visit on our ward? Several movie stars have put on shows at this hospital, but none have come on Ward

C-2. They visit the enlisted men's wards and smile . . . when their pictures are taken . . . and we get to see the results in the Post paper.

Mr. Hope, it's a funny thing, but we officers would like to meet you folks also. Believe me, I'm not trying to run down enlisted men. I'm lamenting the fact that we are left out in the cold. I have T.B. and so will be operating at the same old stand for at least another year. So if you come out, please don't forget us!

Sincerely,
Ens. E. L. (last name illegible), U.S.N.R
Ward C-2 Room 14
Fitzsimons Gen. Hosp.
Denver, Colo.

United States Marine Corps
Office of the Commanding General
Camp Joseph H. Pendleton
Oceanside, California
14 January, 1943

Dear Bob:
. . . You and your gang were simply swell to come down and put on such a great show. . . . We hope to see you again sometime in the near future . . . we are 100 per cent for you down here at Camp Pendleton and you can tell the crazy world I said so.

Very cordially yours,
J. C. Fegan

Major General, U. S. Marine Corps, Commanding
February 3, 1943
Major General J. C. Fegan
United States Marine Corps
Camp Joseph H. Pendleton
Oceanside, California

Dear General:

Received your letter, and I just want to send a little missive to apologize for a belated departure from your Officers' Club the other night. But everybody was having such fun, and Colonna had so many stories to finish that it looked like we never would get away from Camp Pendleton.

Anyway, the memories of you and your hospitality will always be refreshing. The whole gang still talks about the great time we had there. Let's hope we can do it again some time.

My best wishes to Mrs. Fegan.

. . . Pepsodentally yours,
Bob Hope

USS Cascade
May 8, 1944

Dear Hope-
. . . All the guys in this compartment think you are one of the most promising young stars in Hollywood. . . . By the way, I just happened to think; we would like to have a "pin-up" picture. We are saving a place for you between Dorothy Lamour and Betty Grable.

Best Regards,
Elton M. Garner

Elton M. Garner MM2/c
USS Cascade

Dear Elton:

Glad to hear from the Navy. Took your letter right over to Paramount, with that part about my being one of the "most promising young stars in Hollywood" underlined. I was always of that opinion, but it's just as well to let the Studio see that others do believe it, too.

. . . Give my regards to the boys . . . and do put my picture in a safe place.

Bob Hope

Dear Mr. Hope,
While we were stationed at Camp Legune, North Carolina, some of our buddies wrote to Bing Crosby and told him that they would like to pitch one more liberty before shipping out, but they were broke and so they asked Crosby to send them ten dollars or they would tell you what a cheapskate he was.

In reply to their letter, Mr. Crosby said "due to the Federal taxes he has to earn one hundred thousand dollars in order to get a net profit of ten dollars," and as it would take too long to earn such an amount, he sent them 6 expensive pipes instead with his name engraved on them.

So Mr. Hope, due to the fact that Mr. Crosby has a larger family than yourself and naturally has a larger financial burden than yourself, we have come to the conclusion that you can afford to top Crosby's gifts.

If we do not receive an answer in reply to this letter in a reasonable amount of time, we are going to write to Crosby and tell him what a cheapskate you are.

Hoping to hear from you soon, we remain . . .

Yours truly,
4 Marines
Pvt. John Winkler
PFC John Kerwood
Pvt. John (unreadable)
PFC Teddy Stark

June 6, 1945
Pvt. John Winkler 972880
32nd Replacement Draft Co. B
First Marine Division
c/o Fleet Post Office
San Francisco, California

Hiya fellows:

... Sorry old Slab Flab couldn't see his way clear to loan you boys that ten dollars! He's getting so he won't trust his best friend for a buck! In fact, I had quite a time "hitching" my way home from New York.

So long, and good luck.

Sincerely,
Bob Hope

Ward M-11

Dear Bob:
A tail gunner, Sgt. Tommy Gilmour, is a member of the crew of the B-24 Bomber christened last week, "Bob's Hope." The gunner is a typhus patient in Ward M-11. Can you spare three minutes to say hello to him and for me to stand by and do a story for YANK? He (and I, too) would appreciate it greatly. Thanks.

Donn Hale Munson
YANK Field Correspondent
(Ex-Columbia Script Dept.)

Bing Crosby, stage, screen, and radio star, sings to Allied troops at the opening of the London stage door canteen in Piccadilly, London, England. Pearson. August 31, 1944. 111-SC-193249, National Archives Identifier: 531210.

"Aerial gunnery . . . that's the science of shooting at something that ain't there and hitting it when it's where it wasn't."
. . . Bob Hope

(Top) Bob autographing for the soldiers.

(Bottom) Bob signs mirror for troops.

DEAR BOB . . .

WORDS AREN'T ENOUGH

— — — — — — — — — — — — — — —

MANY SOLDIERS FOUND THAT WORDS WEREN'T ENOUGH FOR THEM TO EX-
press their gratitude to their World War II pen pal. But in the loneliness of
their barracks, in the homesickness of the holidays, on the eve of battles and
unknown outcomes, words were all they had.

Some letters were short, a few lines and a signoff. Others went on for pages.
When gifts were sent they were often sacrificial. One of a kind items that they
had made or found. Souvenirs they could have kept for themselves, but they
wanted Bob to have them. Personal items, the goatee the most unique among
them, were mailed to their "brother" in Hollywood for safekeeping, and perhaps because they knew, of all people, Bob would appreciate their significance.

Letters, V-mail, packages, and postcards by the tens of thousands showed
up in Bob's mailbox for the duration of the war and beyond, all trying their
best to convey the gratitude they felt for Bob Hope for all he had done and was
continuing to do for the troops.

> **"I've been asked to run for President of the United States, but my
> wife doesn't want to move to a smaller house."**
> **. . . Bob Hope**

Mail call postcard, Camp
Croft, South Carolina. US
Army. Stationed at Camp
Croft during WWII were
artist Henry Martin Gasser
and Secretary of State
Henry Kissinger.

Naval Air Station
Astoria, Oregon
Nov 14, 1944

Dear Bob:
. . . I am taking this means to thank you very much for the little bit of sunshine that you have brought into my heart and millions of other servicemen in the last few years. I have never been lucky enough to be where a big time star came, but I sure do hope to see you someday. You may not be in the service because of age, but <u>you are doing your part.</u> I thank you for the little spark of happiness you put into our lives each week, and if you ever have a chance to come where . . . shipyards send their ships before they go to sea, please do, as I hope to be waiting for you with the rest of the boys here. We only have one radio and it is small, but the entire house is full to try to hear one good joke, and when you make one, it is relayed back to the boys who can't get close enough to hear. Thanks for taking time to read this. I know you have all you can do.

Yours truly,
William H. Taylor, S 1/C

---

1 July 1944
Mr. Bob Hope,
New York, NY

My Dear Mr. Hope,
Just finished reading your book "I Never Left Home." But O boy, you sure were "Home" to those who did leave home. [You] brought joy and happiness to them and they who were left at home.
  The words you used in the Preface, "I could ask for no more" comes from the bottom of your heart I know, and adding to that thought, you donated the royalties from your book to the National War Fund, which is just another one of the "Hope Ways" of bringing cheer and happiness to us who serve. As one soldier friend, who served in the thickest of the fight, and was wounded, wrote me, "I sure was down, but to see and hear Bob Hope, I never for a minute lost hope. With a guy like that giving his all to us, it makes it really worthwhile to fight for his life and what he represents in our land of freedom."

May I end this note of appreciation with the thought that must be in the mind of every man, woman or child who has someone who left home for here or over there . . . "With Bob Hope and his show, we could ask for no more."

Sincerely,
A soldier of 29 years' service
Frederick E. Wade

Chief Warrant Officer U.S.A.
Headquarters E.D.C.
Governors Island, New York

Motor Torpedo Boat Squadrons
Pacific Fleet, Navy
August 9, 1944

Mr. Bob Hope
Paramount Studios
Hollywood, California

Bob, the surest way to tell what the boys out here are thinking about is to censor their mail. We have to do that anyway, by regulations. May I say that you and your troupe who visited us are the main topics of correspondence? The jolt in the arm which we so sorely needed was supplied with your humorous hypodermic. I cannot express in adequate English how much your visit meant to all of us.

All hands say—Thanks for the finest memory we've had in ages, and thanks to every member of your entourage who gave us such a grand glimpse of an America we hope to return to soon, and then soon to go out again to defend—by definite and downright victory.

Good luck and best wishes from all the crowd.

Sincerely,
R. H. Smith
Lt. Comdr, USN
Brks B-1 USNTC

American Expeditionary Station
Dept. C; Navy 3237
Fleet Post Office
San Francisco
Sept. 10, 1944

You'll never know how much good you did coming through here. Re-
ally the guys are still talking about you and your gang. . . . As much
as they all enjoyed and appreciated you, though, everyone hopes that
next summer it won't be necessary for you to visit a battlefront area
. . .

Regards,
T/Sgt. Hal Kanter

---

26 May, 1945

Dear Bob,
I'd like to tell you just how pleased we were to have you pay us a visit
last week.
    To begin with, this is one place celebrities just never seem to visit
. . .
    Anyway, the scuttlebutt about your coming started lots of other
scuttlebutt—that someone in Welfare and Recreation had fouled
things up and you couldn't make it, and other various and sundry
rumors. Not until the morning of Tuesday 22 May were we sure you'd
come.
    Then came the biggest question of the day—who would get to see
you? We knew that you'd raise a row—maybe even refuse to perform
if the audience consisted mostly of officers. Close on the heels of the
discussion came the announcement that there'd be 3 tickets for the
show—3 tickets for 20 of us in the Recruit Personnel Office! Of course,
we were pretty disappointed. The inner-office distribution was very
fair. Three slips marked "B.H." were placed in a gob hat, along with 17
blanks, and we all drew. Those of us who weren't lucky enough to have
a ticket tried to figure out just how we could get around to attending
the performance. Finally, someone hit upon the idea of forging tickets.
One of the fellows placed a mimeograph stencil over a ticket and

traced the lettering, and printed up some good-looking substitutions.
We all agreed Charles had missed his calling . . .

We even gave the tickets a good working on, so that they'd look like
the real McCoy—just in case the seaman guard scrutinized them. Well,
sir, we were all pretty proud of ourselves for devising a way to evade the
ticket shortage.

At five minutes before five (I'm really not salty enough to say 1655!),
we learned that the show would be at Ingram Field, instead of at
Sullivan Auditorium. I'm very happy to tell you that no one who had
wanted to see and hear you missed out. We all appreciated the fact,
too, that it was plenty chilly out there on the platform—Seneca Lake's
breezes are something to be sneezed after—not at.

Those who saw you at various places around the base were impressed by your informality and friendliness. Boy—you were given
verbal orchids all over the base, and that's no boloney! Saw you outside
the stadium myself, but didn't dare to speak to you.*

So I'll say, "Hello, Bob" now. Silly, huh?

Again, our sincere gratitude. You really gave our morale a man-sized
boost. And that last word is spelled with a double "oh" too—double oh
also means, "plenty of okay" here.

Gratefully yours,
Ronnie McFarland Y 3/6 (WAVES)

*Too much gold braid hoovering about!

June-28-1944
France
United States Navy

Dear Mr. Hope,
We are on an LST somewhere. There are very few people who know
what an LST is, in fact, we don't even know. We are the Amphibious Force of the U.S.N. We have just finished listening to one of your
programs. Of course we only hear the rebroadcast from London, but
it is about the same thing as the original. We and the rest of the crew
enjoy them immensely. After a hard day's work, we immensely enjoy
you and your gang. You will notice that we used immensely twice very

close together. We just picked that word up so we thought we would use it on you. Hope you like it.

We of the Amphibious Force are not very well known and this might not be flattering, but all of the other branches of the Army and Navy have a pin-up favorite. We of the Amphibious Corps have selected Mr. Colonna for our favorite. The reason for our choosing Mr. Colonna was due to a vote between Mr. Sinatra and Mr. Colonna. Mr. Colonna won by a large majority. We have picked you as our favorite comedian. We realize of course that you receive a lot of fan mail, and that you yourself might not see this letter, but we hope our little message gets passed on to you and Mr. Colonna.

We were on the coast of France on D-Day and I think when we heard your program that night that was when we most appreciated you and the rest of your gang.

(No name given)

U.S. Naval Hospital
Ward 5–2
San Diego, Calif.

Dear Sir:
I have just finished listening to your program from Chicago and to say it was tremendous would be belittling it. The speech you made about Bonds after the program was enough to stir the tightest skinflint into action.

I was wounded in the Battle of Guam; however, that was (I speak of my service) trivial, considering what you are doing. Keep it up, the fellows overseas don't get enough of you.

I was fortunate enough to see and have my picture taken with Miss Langford when she was here. I hope someday to see you in person and possibly thank you myself for what you have done and are doing.

You may not hold a rank in the Naval Service of the United States, but I'm sure you hold a top one with the men in service.

Sincerely,
P.F.C. William Adams (U.S.M.C.)

June 6, 1945
PFC William T. Adams USMC
U.S. Naval Hospital Ward 5–2
San Diego, California

Dear Bill:

Sorry to be so late in answering you fellows, but I have been rather busy these past few months and haven't had much time for my G.I. Mail. I'll have more time now . . . since I gave up that paper route.

Just returned from a short tour. Traveling is really rough, and there's always a slight delay in securing tickets nowadays. A "slight delay" . . . that's an ODT expression meaning, "Bring your own field rations and don't forget to leave a forwarding address in case your Social Security comes due!"

. . . I'm getting set for another trip overseas. Of course, my sponsor was sorry to have me go off the air for the summer . . . and there's absolutely no truth in the rumor that Pepsodent will start manufacturing aspirins when I start broadcasting again in the fall.

It's always good to hear from you fellows. Hope by now you're up and about again. Here's wishing you the best of luck in the future.

Sincerely,
Bob Hope

"You hear people go on about unpopular wars, but show me a popular one. Nobody in their right mind wants to go to war, but when it happens you have to get behind your troops."
—DAME VERA LYNN, British wartime entertainer

Vera Lynn sings to workers during a lunchtime concert at a munitions factory, somewhere in Britain.

Bayside, Long Island, New York
February 6, 1944

Dear Bob:
I am a schoolgirl in 8A. You may wonder why I start a sentence
like this. In school, my class was assigned a composition on morale
builders. Morale builders were people like you and many others who
entertain the service men and women. When time came for all of us
to read our compositions, everyone wrote about you going overseas
and having your own radio program. So Bob, I wrote to tell you, you
and Pepsodent are doing a swell job. Keep it up, Bob.

Sincerely,
Miss Helen Becktel

**"Boy, these pilots really handle their planes rough. One boy went
up in a Douglas dive bomber and after the third loop, Douglas
bailed out."**
 . . . Bob Hope

Bob and some of the "gang." Library of Congress, Recorded Sound Section, Bob Hope Collection.

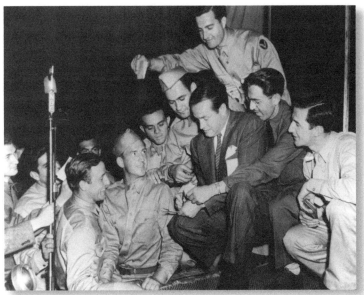

Bob's either signing autographs or getting their take-out orders.

Somewhere in the Pacific
October 15, 1944

Dear Bob,
I am writing you this letter for myself and my gang. My Gang is the
Whole U.S. Army. We really think you are a great guy and you sure
have done more for the boys than all the rest of them put together. You
are everybody's favorite because you can take it and you can give it.

We just read an article about the time you were giving a show and
some boys marched 10 miles to see it, and when they got there, there
were already so many G.I.s that they couldn't see, so they started to
walk back. And when you heard about it, you hopped in a jeep and
overtook them, and performed for 40 minutes in the rain. That is just
what a real soldier would do, and we Aviation Engineers are proud of
you, Bob. I hope your secretary doesn't throw this away without show-
ing it to you. Won't you drop me a line so I can show the boys what an
obliging fellow you are. Of course, if you are too busy, we can under-
stand. If I knew you'd get this, I'll really write a nice long letter . . .

Sincerely yours,
Pvt. Dick Grainey, U.S.A.A.F.E.

"He and his troupe would do 300 miles in a jeep, and give four shows . . . One of the generals said Hope was a first-rate military target since he was worth a division; that's about 15,000 men. Presumably the Nazis appreciated Hope's value, since they thrice bombed towns while the comic was there."
—QUENTIN REYNOLDS, war correspondent 1943

October 5, 1944
Commander E. H. Kincaid
Commanding
U.S. Naval Advanced Base No. 158

Dear Commander:
. . . The whole gang sends its regards and best wishes, and the next time we have a show, let's not have an explosion in the background. I don't know if any other actors could stand it. If there's anything further you need for your show, or anything at all I can do for you, just let me know.

Best regards,
Bob Hope

12-6-44
Lt. J. W. Moore
Pensacola, FL

Dear Bob-
I am writing this while listening to your war bond program tonight and want to mail it before it seems like a silly thing to have written. It's not of much importance, but I do want you to know that I'm exceedingly proud to be holding up my small part in this outfit, knowing that men like yourself, Bing and all the rest who have done so much, are backing us.

I will be on my way overseas very soon and will be doing so feeling happy to have known you if only over the air. If and when I return,

I'd like to stand at the nearest bar and buy you a drink, not because you're Bob Hope, but because you're the same kind of guy I've been flying with, the same man that would protect your tail in a fighter attack, and the same buddy I'll buy drinks for when we get back. I hope this hasn't sounded trite, but lying here in my bunk I got this feeling of wanting to express my small thanks in some way. Will let the little part I may be able to play in the near future stand as my appreciation. . . . proud to be fighting for you.

Sincerely,
A Marine Pilot

Oct 15, 1944—Netherlands East Indies

Personal—NOT FAN MAIL

Dear ["Bob" is written, then crossed out and replaced with] Mr. Hope:

I'm not a stage struck fan that's batty over movie stars. This is the first time I've ever wrote one. But I have a darn good reason besides helping me (I'll tell you later).
    You have done wonders for the morale of men overseas. If they drafted you, it would be too bad for us. You're doing more than any civilian I know of to aid the war effort. I read how much trouble you go through to put on shows for us. Taking the shots is enough trouble itself. You really have guts. I saw you in Guinea before I landed here on D-Day. I really thought I am fighting for something and somebody after you gave us the talk. And if every civilian, yes even servicemen, was like you, it would shorten the war.
    Now, I'll tell you how you helped me. I'm in a hospital and was almost dead. But I started to get well, and last night I saw a short about you and Lana Turner frying steaks, and Betty Hutton and Judy Garland. I laughed myself almost sick again, but you really lifted up my spirits. Thanks a million, Mr. Hope, and God bless you.

Sincerely,
Roland (last name illegible)

United States Army
Corps of Engineers
May 1st, 1944

My dear Bob,
You will probably recall the writer as being at your home last Oct.
with my wife, visiting our friend Elma Aarons. Since then I have gone
overseas and am now in this far off reaches known as the China/
Burma/India section of the war front.

Bob, the reason why I am writing to you is to give you an honest
report on how much the American soldier really thinks of Bob Hope. I
spent thirty days on a ship getting here and every day we had record-
ings of different radio programs. Well, yours were played and asked for
about 72% of the time. In a crowded ship going through sub-infested
water, it was a big thrill to me to hear the boys laughing their heads
off at your jokes, Colonna's comedy, and then, get a wistful look as
they heard Frances Langford's songs. . . . What I'm trying to say, Bob,
is that to us . . . you really typify our way of living and you bring us
thousands of miles back to our beloved country. Thanks, Bob, keep it
up, and may God spare you for many years to come. We need you as
much as everything else that we are fighting for.

John Mattiello

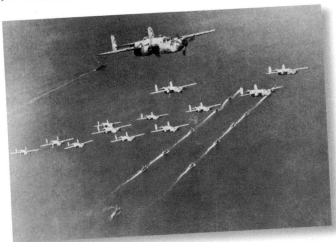

Southwest Pacific—It's D-Day in the South Pacific and this photo depicts a momentary junction of American air and sea forces on the move. The B-25s (North American) en route for Rabaul to blast Japanese airdromes while the invasion convoy, several thousand feet below, spreads toward the Green Islands. US Army A.A.F. photo. Library of Congress, Prints & Photographs Division, LC-USZ62-105185.

Bob Hope signing off his radio show from Pensacola Naval Air Station (May 4, 1943):

... In the months to come when we invite our memories in, this night will be a permanent guest. We're moving on now, but here's a parting word to these Navy fliers. They're a modest bunch of fellows who I must say that they're training and flying their hearts out, and they love it. You know, we've seen our scientific laboratories work to protect the life of the individual. Well, this big naval air station here is a laboratory protecting the life of the whole nation. The scientists here are scarcely more than boys, but they're boys who are becoming super pilots. For when the Navy trains a pilot, he's a gunner, a bomber, a radio man, and pilot. And because of the men in Pensacola, America will lead the aviation world of tomorrow. For that's the Trail of Peace. But first, there's another trail that leads to Tokyo, Rome, Berlin, and flying his Douglas Dive Bomber, his Wildcat, his CorseAir, his Coronado, and Avenger, the Navy fliers are out there tonight blazing their trail. And brother, when I say blazing, I mean he's really making it hot for the enemy. Thanks, fellas.

Nov. 18, 1944

Dear Bob:
It has been quite a little while since I saw you at Tulagi. Am wondering if you and Colonna got that Tulagi mud off your shoes? You gave a wonderful show for the boys there. We all thank you and your troupe.
... We have a title all cooked up for a new picture—you and Crosby—"The Road to Manila."
Brother, it is advisable to lay off for a little while because that's a "hot" road. Tom and I were at Leyte on the initial landing. It was hot there, believe us, and it wasn't the weather.
... Here are two bucks. Will you please send us a copy [of your new book on the South Pacific] as soon as it is available?
Too much can't be said about the effect of your wit and humor on the men on the fighting fronts all over the globe.
Would like to hear from you, if you get a chance to write. I know you are busy, we are all busy out here.
... Best regards to you from the crew and officers.

Sincerely,
W. W. Bralley
Lt. (jg) U.S.N.R.

P.S. I have plenty of Pepsodent on hand. It's everywhere.
P.P.S. The two bucks—did you find them? Send bill if book costs more.

June 6, 1945
Lt. (jg) W. W. Bralley USNR
U.S.S.P.C. 623
c/o Fleet Post Office
San Francisco, California

Dear Lieutenant:
Before taking off on this summer's tour, I felt I should dash off a
few notes to you fellows who have been kind enough to write . . .
thus keeping my fan mail up . . . and my sponsor happy.
**   It's surely good to get home and rest for a few days.**
**   . . . I'm returning your two bucks . . . I can't take money from**
you boys. Besides, that new book hasn't been started yet. When
you hear it's on the market, write to me again and I'll see to it
that you get a copy. In the meantime, my best to you all.

Sincerely,
Bob Hope

April 18, 1945

Dear Bob,
You have been told many times, I'm sure, how much pleasure the
servicemen get from your appearances—personal, radio, and film. I
thought, however, that you might be interested in the scene here this
evening. Our radio is on full volume, and as our "recreation room" is a
tent, it can be heard over quite a small portion of the hospital. As your
voice and the roars of your "real" audience have drifted out, the men
have drifted in. They are a conglomerate group: ambulance drivers
with red-crossed helmets waiting to go out with patients being evacu-
ated, ambulant patients in pajamas, with or without robes, sometimes
with field jackets and combat boots, and men of our own detachment

just released from twelve hours on the wards, in surgery, mess, supply or other departments of a busy hospital. I know of few programs which draw so many so quickly.

... With sincerest appreciation for all you have done for service people at home and overseas.

Barbara Hall

(John Mark Running)
USA AF
13 January 1947

Dear Mr. Hope:
... I am taking this opportunity to write you and personally thank you—THANK YOU FOR SAVING MY LIFE.

You wonder how? It was a joke—

Remember those programs of yours that used to be broadcast from records overseas? Well, it was because you were so funny and told such a good joke on one of those programs that I am able to write and tell you now just how much I appreciated and do appreciate your worthy efforts.

They say that we Navigators were worth about $100,000 apiece. They also say that the value of what was in the plane the day you told that joke was worth $4 million.

... We were going into Vienna that day in January, 1945—Sunday it was—and a clear day, too. All the fellows on our crew were sweating out the graduate Nazi gunners below some thirty thousand feet. Me, I'm just tucking my flak suit and tin hat over me to keep warm in the -40 atmosphere.

I remember the way the shells exploded and made black smoke like a Jersey fog, and now and then a light of burst would light the way (to Heaven we thought)—we're on a bomb run, see ... seven minutes of blazing, cold silent hell when your mind ain't on dames, drink, and dazzling light, but on [those] who killed the guy who was your buddy, brother, or you.

A few things happened and [we] were as full of holes as a shot-gunned tomato can, but we made it outta that inferno on two and a half engines and a lot of something else like guts 'cause guts is all you got at times like that—they ache so much.

I recall looking back at the parting clots of soot over the guys behind us—that's all . . .

The next thing I knew someone had me by the head and was hollering, "Running! For %@@&'$*%! Get this on and get some oxygen into you!"

That co-pilot had the radio on and had turned on the Bob Hope program and was listening to you when I went out, but it was only because one of your jokes was so funny that the pilot called me up to see if I got it, that they found I wasn't getting oxygen (and you know what that means at 30,000 feet)—so I lived.

Well, Bob, what I wonder is . . . what that joke was—I was unconscious when you told it—yet it saved me, and I don't know what it was to this day.

Very seriously, I remain your most sincere and LIVE-ly fan.

The above is true and can be verified, so I just want to thank you again.

John Mark Running
USA AF

Even if they had to come on stretchers, the G.I.s were determined to see Bob's show.

Bob Hope sharing a canteen with troops in North Africa, 1943.

A. C. Swann
Mount Hope
Hamilton, Ontario
CANADA

Dear Mr. Hope,
Many thanks for the thousands of laughs during the time when we
needed them most.
    ... Before coming to Canada, a friend and myself saw the "Road
to Morocco." At that time we were both due to go overseas. My friend,
a Sgt. Airgunner, made the remark [that] he would enjoy the sand. If
you could see the funny side of a camel, so could he.
    He went to N. Africa, where he was awarded the D.F.M. before be-
ing killed in action.
    The memory of him I will always associate with you, as we saw all
of your films together, and had many laughs at your jokes. I know he
would have liked me to have said thanks as well. . . . I would much
appreciate it if I could have a photograph of you to place beside his. I
shall enjoy your films in [the] future more no doubt as I shall feel he is
watching them too.
    Thank you again . . .

Yours very sincerely,
A. C. Swann

April 24, 1944

My dear Mr. Hope,
This letter may bring back to you the memory of my son, Bernard
Klein, though I realize that you have met many servicemen during
your tours of the battle zones.
   Bernard wrote to us after meeting you and told us about taking
pictures of your show. He was a photographer with the Army Signal
Corps, and at that time was a Corporal.
   It is with regret that I inform you of his death in action.
   Bernard gave his life in the Anzio Beachhead invasion in Febru-
ary. . . . That your presence among the boys gave Bernard a bit of hap-
piness and relaxation, is greatly appreciated by me.
   . . . Those of us on the home front owe our future peace and secu-
rity not only to those actively engaged in fighting our battles, but also
to those who maintain the spirit, morale, and the will to win of our
fighting men . . .

Sincerely yours,
Harry C. Klein
Trenton, New Jersey

"Believe me when I say that laughter up at the front lines is a very
precious thing—precious to those grand guys who are giving and
taking the awful business that goes on there . . . There's a lump the
size of Grant's Tomb in your throat when they come up to you
and shake your hand and mumble 'Thanks.' Imagine those guys
thanking me! Look what they're doing for me. And for you."
   . . . Bob Hope, 1944

South Pacific
May 29, 1944

Dear Bob,
   . . . I suppose you wonder why I am writing to you, well, you see, I just
got done reading an article in the "Reader's Digest" on the tours that

you made for us guys, and in this article I happen to read that you are from Cleveland. Well, I happen to be from Ohio myself, maybe you know where I live . . . it's a small town 55 miles north of Cleveland, named Orville . . . it's pretty little, so I suppose you never heard of it.

Well, it sure is a wonderful thing you are doing for us guys in the service, and you don't know what it means to us. I use to listen to you all the time on the radio when I was home, and I hope to see you personally one of these days, if you ever get down about the South Pacific. Don't forget to drop around and see us, as we would sure be glad to see you. This island is sure a swell place . . . it is quite small, but there's plenty doing here.

. . . Well, so long for now.

Your sailor pal,
Jack Frey

June 7, 1944
Jack L. Frey
Navy 203
c/o Fleet Post Office
San Francisco, Calif.

Dear Jack:
Received your letter and was surely glad to hear from a fellow-Clevelander . . . or, at least, from one who has lived practically in my own home town. Seemed like old times.

So you're in Bora Bora . . . Maybe I can make that spot while I'm down that way this summer.

. . . Well, I'll have to close now and get back on the set. Give all the boys down there my best and tell them I hope to be seeing them soon.

Sincerely yours,
Bob Hope

"A lot of these sailors sleep in hammocks. You know what a hammock is, don't you? That's 'government issued curvature of the spine.'"

 . . . Bob Hope

Bob Hope and Ernie Pyle sit in a pile of rubble and deep thought, Palermo, Sicily, 1943.

DEAR BOB . . .

THE BEACHES LOOKED BETTER IN THE BROCHURE

Letters from the South Pacific

According to Jim Hardy, Bob Hope historian and archivist, during Bob's South Pacific tour the summer of 1944, the indefatigable entertainer traveled some 30,000 miles and gave roughly 150 performances. These were not easy audiences either. Some of the bloodiest and toughest battles of World War II were fought in the South Pacific—the Battle of Midway, the Battle of Guadalcanal, Leyte Gulf, Iwo Jima, and Okinawa, just to name a few. Each battle that happened there would ultimately bring us closer to the end of the war. But the cost was great. Conditions in the South Pacific took their toll on the soldiers. Diseases, such as malaria, were widespread, and the terrain and weather conditions added to the challenge.

1944, Admiralty Islands, Bob waits backstage before a show. A rare pensive moment, away from the troops.

Many of the letters that Bob received from this part of the world told of boys who had sat in his audience and laughed at his jokes only to lose their life in the very next battle. Show after show, Bob had to look out at those faces in the audience, fully realizing that, no matter how much he reminded them of home, many of them were never going to see it again. That reality sat heavy on Bob Hope's heart more often than he ever let on.

Bob never wanted the soldiers to see any of the troupe cry, especially while they were visiting the hospitals and surgical centers. He believed their job was to bring a much-needed reinforcement of laughter and smiles to these brave men and women, no matter how grim the scene. That was the miracle drug they needed more than anything, and he made sure he delivered plenty of it whenever he went.

The soldiers, some too weak to even lift their heads off their pillows, recognized this man as soon as they heard him enter the room. Even if they couldn't lift their heads, or see out from behind their bandaged eyes, they knew his voice from radio and movies, and some had already corresponded with him.

To the surprise of the medical teams, Bob would connect with soldiers who had previously refused any visitors at all. Those who had withdrawn from others since their initial injury, somehow managed to smile for Bob, or even laugh. And a few uttered the first words they had spoken in weeks or months.

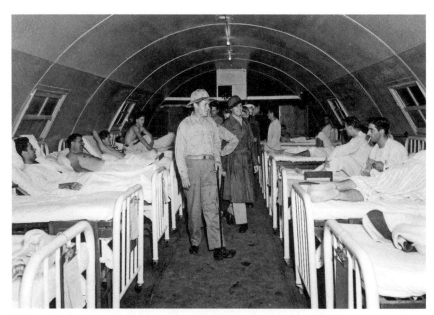

Bob Hope always made time to visit the wounded, and this war had more than its share of them.

After the surprise attack on Pearl Harbor in December of 1941, Japanese forces soon captured Manila, and on April 9, 1942, the United States surrendered the Bataan Peninsula. Some seventy-five thousand Filipino and American troops were captured and forced to participate in what became known as the Bataan Death March. These prisoners of war hiked over sixty miles to prison camps with no food or water, while being subjected to severe beatings and worse. Those who fell by the wayside were either left behind to die, killed, or their fellow soldiers carried them.

After the surrender of the Bataan Peninsula on the Island of Luzon, General McArthur told General Wainwright, "I'll come back as soon as I can with as much as I can. In the meantime, you've got to hold."

Pictured here at the far left is T/Sgt. Ed De Pompa with fellow POWs who were also in the Bataan Death March. Like Bob Hope, Ed was a boxer. But when America entered World War II, Ed operated a B-17 tail gunner in the Pacific, ending up in Bataan, where he became a prisoner of war in 1942 for forty-two months.

April 10, 1944
BURMA

Dear Bob "I Hope":
We're two soldiers who have been in the jungles of Burma quite some time. We read recently in the Reader's Digest that you have appeared in almost every theater of war. We are wondering if it would be possible for you to appear in the C.B.I. theater?

There isn't much enjoyment in this part of the world. We had a few actors and actresses here, but really would enjoy your appearance here. If possible, bring along Betty Hutton.

Think this over, Bob. I'm sure the boys in this theatre would really enjoy your appearance. God bless you.

Yours truly,
Pvt. Sherman G. Abel
Please answer
Excuse the spelling, we lost our dictionary.

General Douglas MacArthur wades ashore during initial landings at Leyte, P.I., October 20, 1944. Later that day, he made a long-awaited announcement on a radio show: "People of the Philippines, I have returned!" Cropped from Select List number 150, National Archives Identifier: 531424.

"I was in World War II; I cried when they took me in the Navy. That was the last time I cried."

—DON RICKLES, who spent two and a half years in the Philippines

---

June 9, 1944
Pvt. Joseph S. Saccaia 32745160
5303 Hq. Co. (Prov.)
Area Command, APO 689, c/o PM
New York, New York

Dear Joe:
 . . . Just as soon as I finish this picture I'm now making for Sam Goldwyn, I'm heading down for the Southwest Pacific Theater. Am going to try to make Burma and China, if it's at all possible. Surely would like to drop in on some of you fellows in that section. So watch out for me, maybe I'll be seeing you before long.

 Since I intend to be traveling again this summer, I had to go down to take a physical the other day. I went to see my own doctor first. I don't know if my heart's good or not . . . but he listened to it a few minutes, then he said, "I was going to give you a little time to pay your bill, Hope . . . but under the circumstances, you'll have to pay cash!"

. . . Well, I'd better close now and get back on the set. Better try to get a few laughs in this picture I'm stealing money for. Give the boys down there my best and tell them I hope to see them soon.

Sincerely,
Bob Hope

May 11, 1945, USS *Bunker Hill* hit by two kamikazes. Official US Navy photograph.

43rd Bomb Group
64th Bomb Squadron
March 25 / 45
The Philippine Isles
API 74

Dear Bob,
During your tour of South Pacific outposts, you visited a tiny island in the area of the Netherlands E. Indies, and there with you present, a Liberator was christened in your honor, "Bob's Hope."

It may be that in your tours many planes have been named for you, but so far as we here know, this is the only one, and I thought that perhaps a brief report on the activities and fate of "Bob's Hope" might prove interesting to you.

Lt. Dick Hill flew the ship across (I flew one of her sister ships), but soon after you christened her, Dick was sent on O.S. to another outfit and she was virtually my "baby."

If you hoped she would . . . destroy enemy installations from . . . China and Formosa, not to mention the Philippines, and always bring her crew back safely, you have cause to be proud of her, just as I have been proud to fly her.

You know, Bob, when you fly a plane through thick and thin, it becomes more than a highly specialized mass of steel destruction. It takes on a personality, and you treat it with as much patience and care as you would your best girl. So it has been with "Bob's Hope" and I grew to know all her qualities, treacherous characteristics, and peculiarities.

Although it is not unusual for a man and his plane to end their combat days together tragically, it is to me a pleasing coincidence that Bob's Hope and I ended ours together happily. She will never fly again. We were shot up by flak over Formosa quite badly on my last mission. None of the crew was seriously injured, but she had a motor gone and was holed like a sieve. She limped, but she came through her last long flight and brought us back to safety.

Bob, if you ever have occasion to, please mention a great old plane, "Bob's Hope" and her squadron, the best in the business, in your program, articles, or books. It would please everyone in the outfit. I would personally prefer not to be mentioned.

. . . I hope this has gotten thru the censors and your secretary. If not, well, I made a good try anyway.

Sincerely and admiringly yours,
(Name withheld at soldier's request)

P.S. Excuse the slant [of the writing on the paper]. The wind blows a lot here—so hard in fact, the words get twisted like this before they hit the paper.

June 6, 1945
43 Bomb Group, 64th Bomb Sqdn.
APO 74, c/o Postmaster
San Francisco, California

I want to thank you for giving me that report on the activities of "Bob's Hope" and her squadron. I'm almost as proud of her as you are . . . that's saying a lot, isn't it? I'm planning on writing up my experiences in the South Pacific and may be able to use that material. Wish I were coming back to see you fellows again this year, but I'm due to go the other way. So in the meantime, the very best of luck to you all.

Sincerely,
Bob Hope

" . . . the fellas here are so nice. Today they took me for a spin on the plane. But it's the first one I ever took while tied to the propeller."
 . . . Bob Hope

Left to right: Colonel Hawthorne, Bob Hope, Patty Thomas, Frances Langford, Barney Dean, Jerry Colonna, Tony Romano (with guitar), and "Bob's Hope."

"Like Bob Hope, the Texaco Star stood by our GIs throughout World War II and beyond. This shared respect and gratitude for the men and women of our Armed Forces forged a bond between Bob and Texaco that remained for much of his career. Bob Hope appeared in many Texaco commercials, and Texaco was a proud sponsor of many of Bob's entertainment shows."
—John C. Harper, historian, Policy, Government, and Public Affairs, Chevron Corporation. Courtesy of Chevron/Texaco

July 17, 1944
Mr. Bob Hope
c/o Special Service Officer
Headquarters, S.O.S., Southwest Pacific Area
Finschhafen, New Guinea

Dear Bob:
. . . I have been overseas with my outfit for two years, and we're presently located on New Britain. Am serving as Special Service Sergeant of our Regiment, and upon hearing the news of your arrival in this area, confided to my cohorts that I was "a friend" of yours. The response was overwhelming and the immediate request was that I make an attempt at getting you over here to entertain the boys.

It really was a source of great delight for me to learn that you and Frances Langford were in (or coming to) New Guinea on tour, so I'm herewith appealing to you fervently, wishing you might swing such a deal enabling your troupe to pay us a visit. Truly, Bob, the boys in this neck of the woods would go wild if I could tell them you had accepted my invitation.

On this island, and I believe much more so than any other of the Islands in this vicinity, we've been in desperate need of a morale booster. I know without a doubt that you and Frances could remedy the situation beautifully.

. . . If you can find it possible to fulfill this great desire, would you please insist on coming directly to Talasea, New Britain first to entertain our outfit? Your reception will be deafening I'm sure, and we can certainly accommodate your troupe and Miss Langford. The chow is naturally lousy, but your previous expeditions have undoubtedly adjusted your appetites accordingly. However, if I knew you were coming, and knew approximately when, a detail of men could be sent to our nearby island which abounds with wild cattle to get a couple of calves for a nifty meal. Please let me hear from you as quickly as possible, will you Bob?

Sgt. Jon Torrence—19098055
Service Company, 185th Infantry

(Top left) Guadalcanal patch.

(Top right) Bob Hope and troupe with soldiers in New Guinea, August 26, 1944.

(Middle) Bob Hope with 1st Marine Division, Russell Islands.

(Bottom) Bob Hope having a fungus on his foot checked out—one of his least favorite souvenirs from the war.

Excerpt from Bob Hope's closing tribute to the Seabees delivered on his radio show:

. . . If you wanna know what Seabee means, skip the dictionary and go to Guadalcanal in North Africa, to Attu Island in God-forsaken sand piles in the Pacific, for that's where you'll find the Seabees. Iron men of the Navy. Their motto is "We build, we fight." And they can do both at the same time.

> **"Well, ladies and gentlemen, tonight we're broadcasting for the Seabees. . . . These fellas here are doing a great job. They're always first on shore. They land with the Marines. In fact, by the time the Marines have a situation well in hand, the Seabees have a bridge across it."**
> **. . . Bob Hope**

August 1944

Dear Bob:

. . . If you recall your itinerary of your trip in the S.W.P.A., you can place this particular spot of Eden, as you gave us a show this afternoon about 1 o'clock. I enjoyed your show so much that I thought I would write to let you know how much. I, and I am sure all the men up here, appreciate your efforts.

. . . Personally, I think your services to the Government are comparable to any line soldier, or I should say at least a platoon. You're no kid and yet you probably take more punishment in one of your tours than we take under other than combat conditions.

So in closing, I wish again to express the appreciation of a G. I. who is far from the Bronx, New York where he comes from, for one hour's entertainment that was both heartily needed and appreciated.

Yours for a furlough for both of us,
Cpl. James McKeon, 32171840
Service Co., 503d Parachute Inf.

October 6, 1944

Dear James:

I wish to thank you for writing me. Surely am pleased to know the boys out there really enjoyed our show. You know, my favorite audiences are those made up of G.I. Joes; and, as long as I'm assured they like our style of entertainment, they're going to get it.

But it was great to get back home.... Everybody was glad to see me ... my first trip to Paramount was really a red-letter day ... when they heard I was coming, they all stayed home and read letters.

All kidding aside, the entire troupe enjoyed the trip down to see you boys. The folks at home are proud of you and know you'll finish up that little "job" you have on your hands. So long now, and good luck.

Sincerely,
Bob Hope

5135 Lieut W. G. Booth
1 En Fiji Infantry Reg.
Suva. Fiji Islands
13/4/44

Dear Bob:
I suppose you are wondering who ... this letter is from. To begin with it's from a bloke who was born in the same town as you were, and that is why I am taking the liberty of dropping you a line.

Whilst in the U.S. Naval Hospital at Tulagi in the Solomons, I was glancing through a Reader's Digest dated I think August 1943, and came across an article entitled, "WHILE THERE'S HOPE, THERE'S LIFE." Imagine my surprise when I came to the part where it said that you were born at Eltham, near London. Well, I was certainly tickled pink to think at least somebody from the old town has made good.

... When war broke out I was in Suva owning a hotel. Not long after, I gave it up and joined up with the above Regiment. A year ago today we embarked for the Solomons. Malaria got me pretty bad and towards the end of last year, I was shipped back home. Our boys are

(Left) Bob takes a peek inside his childhood home on Craigton Road in Eltham, England. During the war, Eltham and the surrounding area sustained sizable bomb damage.

(Right) Bob Hope in the South Pacific, 1944.

now getting their fair share of action alongside the Americans on Bougainville, and am glad to say they are doing a good job of work and are thought a lot of by the American soldiers.

According to the American Papers . . . after your European job is finished you are going to the Pacific, so I trust that you will see something of them. If you come across a Battalion of smiling happy go lucky Fijian Natives, it's them. They all know about you, so they will welcome you as the flowers in May . . . and if you stop over in Suva on your way down, I will not take much finding.

When all this business is over, I am taking the first plane back home. My people are still living at Eltham, although the old town has had a very bad hammering. Maybe you will let me call on you when passing through the States.

All for now, Bob. Carry on with the good work, you are doing a fine job. Haven't seen you on the movies, but have heard you over the radio. Cheerio and good luck.

Bill Booth

July 8, 1944
5135 Lieut. W. G. Booth
1 Bn Fiji Infantry Reg.
Suva FIJI ISLANDS

Dear Bill:

Just a short note to thank you for your letter of some time ago. It surely is good to hear from someone from your own home town!

I'm going to the Southwest Pacific area, right enough . . . in fact, I'm practically on my way. Have a few things to straighten out and a few clothes to pack, but that won't take long. Hope I'll see you and the boys.

If you're ever in Hollywood, contact me through Paramount Studios. If I'm out of town, my office will try to arrange a pass for you to see the studios from the inside. In the meantime, my best to you.

Sincerely,
Bob Hope

"He promised to keep a supply of my blood type on hand, even if he had to kill the chicken himself."

. . . Bob Hope, on an admiral's support of Bob taking his shows into combat areas

Bob Hope, World War II.

The following letter could have been the beginnings of *The Bachelor*:

Sunday, November 6

Dear Bob,
. . . We gathered from [a] few of your phrases in your book that you have gained the friendship of that beautiful and glamourous Paulette Goddard. Now we wish to ask a favor of you and hope that you will help us out. . . . how about arranging a date for each of us, when we get back to the good old U.S.A., with Paulette Goddard?
. . . Last but not least, how about a picture of yourself? For we have a hole in our tent and finally decided it needed patching and knew that a picture of you would scare anything away, even rain.

Two leathernecks on a lonely Pacific Island.
P.F.C. Ernest E. Semsky, USMC Unit #495-L
Pvt. R. Patrick Meehan, USMC Unit #495-L

"I said (to the pilot), 'It's a little rough out there. Don't you think we should have parachutes?' He said, 'Don't be silly. The ones with parachutes jumped out an hour ago.'"
. . . Bob Hope

July 24, 1944
Ruocco's Modern Service Station
% Tarawa

Subject: Bill for gas
Welcome to our island! May you take all the advantages of our gracious hospitality.
The gasoline that has been "dumped" into your plane, is the finest for we received it from Jack Benny . . . we believe that Jack Benny's gas is the best that could be had, for he used it many times, over and over again, with much success and we imagine that it can still be used.
Please sign here in acknowledgment of receiving the gasoline.

By order of Pvt. Guy Ruocco

★ ★ ★

When the USS *Indianapolis* was hit by Japanese torpedoes at 12:02 a.m. on July 30, 1945, it was returning from a highly secret mission to Tinian Island. The crew, unaware of the full details of their mission, had just delivered a special package containing needed parts and enriched uranium for "Little Boy," a secret weapon that would soon be assembled and loaded onto a plane christened the *Enola Gay*. This clandestine delivery by the Indianapolis would soon bring about Japan's surrender.

Since the precise location of the *Indianapolis* had been a closely guarded secret, their distress signal was not picked up. Now, with parts of the ship burning and other parts taking in water faster than the ship could handle, everyone began to abandon it. The USS *Indianapolis* sank in only twelve minutes, taking three hundred lives with her.

The rest went into the water, trying to stay afloat on whatever they could find. Of the original 1,196 on board, only 316 would eventually survive the ensuing four and a half days of dehydration, starvation, and shark attacks. Of further note, according to Wikipedia Commons, a lucky few found crackers and, you guessed it, SPAM, among the ship's debris to aid in their survival.

"Everybody was scared to death," said Harlan Twible in his personal account documented for the World War II Museum. "These were all 18- and 19-year-old kids."

(Top) USS *Indianapolis*, twenty days before her sinking on July 30, 1945. Official US Navy photograph.

(Bottom) Survivors of the USS *Indianapolis*. Official US Navy photograph, now in the collections of the National Archives.

(Top) Peleliu invasion, September 15, 1944. US National Archives, 80-G-283753.

(Middle) A navy corpsman offers a drink of water to a marine wounded in the Battle of Peleliu.

(Bottom) Soldiers in a hospital on Guadalcanal who were wounded in the Battle of Peleliu. Soldier in the lower right on the bed with a bandage on his head is Pfc. Marcel (Sal) M. Baldinger of the 1053rd Platoon, 3rd Battalion, 5th Marines, 1st Marine Division. United States Marine Corps.

Years after being court-martialed for "failure to zigzag," Captain Charles B. McVey III of the *Indianapolis* was eventually exonerated of any wrongdoing. On October 30, 2000, President Clinton signed the resolution that Congress had passed clearing the captain's name posthumously.

> "I think one of the most emotional shows I ever played is when I played for the 1st Marine Division at Pavuvu down in the South Pacific . . . We were playing on this island called Banika . . . and this fella flew over and said, 'Could you possibly do an extra show for the 1st Marine Division? They've never had a show, and they would really love to see you. And they're going to invade Peleliu.' And so, we flew over the next morning. And you knew when you

walked out there that you're playing for 15,000 kids, that a lot of these guys you'd never see again. And as it worked out, 60% of those kids were knocked off in this invasion of Peleliu."
... Bob Hope, recalling the Pavuvu show, prior to the invasion of Peleliu, 1944

"He wasn't a guy working for money anymore. He was like a guy on a mission. He found something that was bigger than money, bigger than anything—which was filling the need of those guys. The desperate need they had to laugh."
—MORT LACHMAN, writer/producer

"There were these guys, maybe some—a number of them—were going to go die. And they were all laughing together. That's a real service."
—ALAN ALDA on Bob Hope's military shows, from National Archives video

"Some months later I was going through a military hospital in Oakland, California, doing the usual 'Don't get up' routine for a ward full of wounded Marines when a guy, half-covered with bandages, suddenly stuck his hand out of the bed covers and hollered at me, 'Pavuvu.' He didn't have to say anything else. I just went over and shook his hand, turned and walked away. I just couldn't handle it."
... Bob Hope, *I Was There*

Back to a Coast Guard assault transport comes this marine after two days and nights of Hell on the beach of Eniwetok in the Marshall Islands. His face is grimy with coral dust but the light of battle stays in his eyes. February 1944. 26-G-3394. National Archives Identifier: 513202.

February 27, 1945

My dear Mr. Hope,
. . . I was fortunate to see you, Frances Langford, and Tony [Romano]
in person when you boarded a Pan American clipper at La Guardia
Field in New York. I was standing on the sea wing right near the hatch
and all of you had to pass me to get into the plane. I put in nineteen
months of service with P.A.A. as a member of the beaching crew. I am
now a buck private in Uncle Sam's army and I'm somewhere in the
Philippines. No one is more anxious than I am to get this mess over
with as I have a wife and four children waiting for me.

. . . Sincerely yours,
Pvt. Peter J. Ferdico, A.S.N. 42175792

"The cost of freedom is always high, but Americans have always
paid it. And one path we shall never choose, and that is the path of
surrender, or submission."
—JOHN F. KENNEDY, 35th US president

"Victory at all costs, victory in spite of all terror, victory however
long and hard the road may be; for without victory, there is no
survival."
—WINSTON CHURCHILL

USS *Pennsylvania* and battleship of *Colorado*
class followed by three cruisers move in line into
Lingayen Gulf preceding the landing on Luzon.
Philippines, January 1945. 80-G-59525. National
Archives Identifier: 520627.

DEAR BOB . . .

REMIND THE FOLKS BACK HOME TO
DO THEIR PART . . . AND WE'LL DO OURS

—— —— —— —— —— —— —— —— —— —— —— ——

THE TROOPS WERE DOING MORE THAN THEIR SHARE, BUT THERE WAS STILL plenty to do back home to support them. From rationing products such as gasoline, sugar, nylon, rubber/tires, and more, to growing extra food for the soldiers and collecting scrap metal, the country did without so our fighting forces wouldn't have to. Rationing became a way for everyone to help.

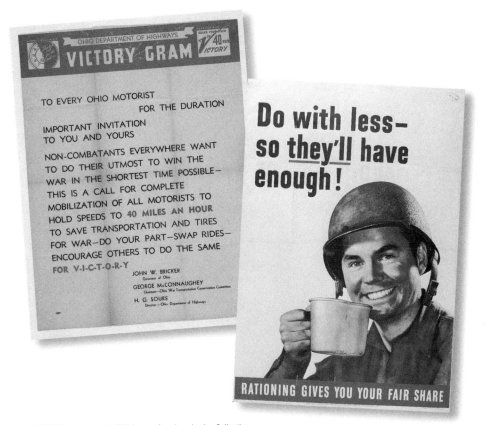

(Left) Ohio Department of Highways, American Legion Collection.

(Right) Knowing what was at stake, the home front didn't mind sacrificing so the GIs could have what they needed.

(Top) Sugar rationing. 208-AA-322I-2. National Archives Identifier: 535570.

(Middle left) Saving a necessary commodity for the troops. Poster by Roy Schatt, 1942. 44-PA-1688. National Archives Identifier: 515359.

(Middle right) Office of War Information, 1943. American Legion Collection.

(Lower left) Rationing stamps.

(Bottom) World War II ration book, ca. 1943.

(Top) Harvesting bumper crop for Uncle Sam. Movie star Rita Hayworth sacrificed her bumpers for the duration. Besides setting an example by turning in unessential metal car parts, Miss Hayworth was active in selling war bonds. 1942. 208-PU-91B-5. National Archives Identifier: 535932.

(Right) War Production Board, 1942.

(Bottom two) Office of War Information, 1943.

Conscientious objectors, pacifists, and non-resisters (such as Amish and Mennonites), helped out in other ways—growing crops and raising livestock for the soldiers, doing forestry work, and assisting in mental hospitals. According to American Psychiatric Association's *Psychiatric News*, " . . . over 1,000 Mennonites performed their civilian public service (CPS) work in mental hospitals." Their passion for humanity, as well as their personal observances, resulted in major changes and humane improvements in the way psychiatric hospital patients were being treated.

Another way folks back home were helping in the war effort was by buying war bonds, and Hollywood and Washington, DC, gave them every opportunity to do it.

> **"Good evening, Mr. President. I heard you just had a conference with Winston Churchill on a battleship about war strategy. War strategy, meaning, 'Where will we attack the enemy, and how are we going to keep Eleanor out of the crossfire?'"**
> **. . . Bob Hope, White House Correspondents' Dinner, 1943**

War Activities Committee, 1945.

1944 White House Correspondent's Dinner program, signed by President Franklin D. Roosevelt.

April 30, 1942—Eleanor Roosevelt on the White House lawn with entertainers setting out on the Hollywood Victory Caravan, a national war bond tour for the US Department of the Treasury. *Seated, from left*: Oliver Hardy, Joan Blondell, Charlotte Greenwood, Charles Boyer, Risë Stevens, Desi Arnaz, Frank McHugh, writer Matt Brooks, James Cagney, Pat O'Brien, Juanita Stark, Alma Carroll; *standing, from left*: Merle Oberon, Eleanor Powell, Arleen Whelan, Marie McDonald, Fay McKenzie, Katharine Booth, Eleanor Roosevelt, Frances Gifford, Frances Langford, Elyse Knox, Cary Grant, Claudette Colbert, Bob Hope, Ray Middleton, Joan Bennett, Bert Lahr, director Mark Sandrich, writer Jack Rose, Stan Laurel, Jerry Colonna, and Groucho Marx. Photograph by Gene Lester. Bob Hope Collection, Motion Picture, Broadcasting and Recorded Sound Division, Library of Congress.

Besides Bob Hope and his regular troupe, the actors, actresses, sports figures, big band leaders, and singers who helped provide entertainment for the soldiers during World War II, either in the traveling shows, at the canteens, selling war bonds, or in so many other ways, read like a Who's Who of Hollywood. The list includes such notable entertainers as:

Fred Astaire	Walt Disney
Louis Armstrong	Errol Flynn
Lucille Ball	Cary Grant
Frances Langford	Fred MacMurray
Patty Thomas	Rita Hayworth
Judy Garland	Betty Hutton
Milton Berle	Don Ameche
Carole Lombard	Stan Laurel and Oliver Hardy
Jack Benny	The Three Stooges
Katharine Hepburn	Angela Lansbury
Dorothy Lamour	Tony Romano
Irving Berlin	Louis B. Mayer
Martha Raye	The Nicholas Brothers
Humphrey Bogart	Roy Rogers and Dale Evans
Boris Karloff	Joe E. Brown
Mel Blanc	Jane Russell
Babe Ruth	Jimmy Dorsey
George Burns and Gracie Allen	Red Skelton
James Cagney	Ethel Waters
Cecil B. DeMille	Tommy Dorsey
Marlene Dietrich	Shirley Temple (stateside)
Bud Abbott and Lou Costello	John Wayne

Bette Davis pointing out pictures of movie servicemen to Marlene Dietrich and Bob Hope in the Hollywood Canteen, Hollywood, California. Acme Newspictures, Inc., photographer. Library of Congress, Prints & Photographs Division, LC-USZ62-112143.

And so many, many more. All the greats were showing up to do their part—working in the kitchen, serving the food, dancing with G.I.s. In World War II fame and competition were checked at the door of these canteens, replaced by a spirit of service and gratitude.

(Top left) "Kilroy was here" was a popular WW II symbol that made its way onto buttons, clothing, and as graffiti on walls, mystifying the enemy as to what it meant. Its exact meaning is debatable, but its familiarity, and the frequency with which it turned up, offered some solace to the troops.

(Top right) National Museum, US Army.

(Bottom left) War Activities Committee pin, Motion Picture Industry.

(Bottom right) Bing Crosby and the Andrew Sisters. *Billboard* magazine, October 30, 1943.

"I was never on a train that bounced around so much in my life. I couldn't sleep, so finally I called the conductor and said, 'Isn't there any way to smooth out these tracks?' He said, 'What tracks? We went on a salvage drive and I guess we overdid it.'"
. . . Bob Hope, on his travels to shows around the USA

"This is our great free country and everyone should feel some obligation to serve in some way at some time—to give something back. That doesn't mean only military service—it means more broadly, service to others. Everyone should find a time to do just that. My time was World War II. Serving was an honor and a privilege. I was a tiny part of something noble, and my military experience honed my respect for 'Duty, Honor, Country.'"
—GEORGE H. W. BUSH, Lt. USNR, 41st president of the United States

MARY PICKFORD

December
1st
1 9 4 3.

Dear Bob:

Please forgive the belated thanks which are, never the less, very sincere for your help to me.

I was scared to death of my initiation into a comedy routine but I think you would have been proud of your pupil. I was able to rehearse it before about one hundred convalescent boys in the hospital as we gave a short performance there before the main entertainment on the platform. They are the most appreciative lot and seemed so grateful for any attention. It must be a Hades up there on that desert.

Thanks again

Very cordially yours,

Mary

Mr. Bob Hope,
Cor. Moorpark and Ledge,
North Hollywood, Calif.

Letter from Mary Pickford.

William Beaumont Hospital
El Paso, Texas
June 13, 1945

Dear Bob Hope:
This acknowledgement is a wee bit tardy, but I do want to thank you for your Christmas cards of this year and of last. The first year I didn't think much of it since you had been our guest at Bizerte, but for 1944 I appreciated being remembered very much.

On March 2, I came home for a thirty day leave from the 56th Evacuation Hospital. The war in Europe ended and I did not get to rejoin my unit. I was very sad for of course I think that our unit is the best.

I think that the American soldiers are the best in the world and I love them. I have every reason to believe that you share my opinion. You did more for our fellows than anyone who entertained in our area, and I want you to know how very much I appreciate you. You can still do a lot for us, for we feel a little "lost" among those who have not shared the joys, sorrows, and fears with us overseas. I hope that you make a tour of the hospitals where the handicapped returnees are located—especially in Texas.

. . . Thanks for the happiness that you gave us and for the memory of you which we shall have in our hearts for always.

Sincerely,
Rose Craig, 1st Lt. ANC

October 29, 1945
Lt. Rose Craig ANC
William Beaumont Hospital
El Paso, Texas

Dear Lieutenant Craig:
This is a little late to acknowledge your letter of last June, but I'm always glad to hear from anyone who was attached to the 56th Evacuation Hospital.

I just returned home from a tour of camps in the European Theater about a month ago and started right in on a new picture for Paramount.

. . . I'm glad to learn that you've been returned to the States. We plan on playing quite a few hospitals during the coming season and, who knows, we may be dropping in on you at Beaumont one of these days. In the meantime, best of luck to you.

Sincerely,
Bob Hope

World War II had heroes other than the two-legged kind. Chips, a German Shepard mix, earned himself the title of "most decorated war dog of World War II." His stellar military career included being awarded the Distinguished Service Cross, the Silver Star, and the Purple Heart.

His fame was not without controversy, however. The dispute was not over the dog's heroic acts—those were well documented. It was over whether or not it was proper to award such medals to a canine when so much human life had been lost in this war. The honors were ultimately rescinded, yet Chips is still considered a World War II hero by all accounts.

This gallant canine served dutifully alongside Allied Forces in Sicily, North Africa, Italy, France, and Germany. During the invasion of Sicily on July 10, 1943, Chips and his handler Private John Rowell of the 30th Infantry, 3rd Division approached a hut with caution, and quickly came under heavy machine gun fire emanating from what they soon discovered was a grass-covered bunker. Chips took off running—not away from the danger, but directly toward it. In the midst of flying bullets, Chips attacked the gunners, dragging the first enemy combatant out of the bunker by his teeth. Three other gunners came out with their hands up. Chips suffered a scalp wound, cuts, and a few powder burns in the attack, but he was in good enough shape to assist in the capture of ten

"Chips the War Dog." US Army photo.

Italians later that same day. Chips was honorably discharged from military duties and returned home on December 10, 1945.

Chips and so many others went above and beyond the call of duty. No matter what they were faced with, they summoned the courage to complete the mission. Soldiers, sailors, pilots, marines, nurses, medics, military dogs, entertainers, news correspondents, those on the front lines and those on the sidelines, the Red Cross and chaplains, those at home and those abroad—all standing together.

And at times, standing alone.

Pfc Angelo B. Reina, 391st Inf. Regt., guards a lonely Oahu beach position. Kahuku, Oahu. Rosenberg, Hawaii, March 1945. 111-SC-221867. National Archives Identifier: 531323.

DEAR BOB . . .

WAR IS REAL

— — — — — — — — — — — — — — — — —

THE BOMBING OF PEARL HARBOR SO SHOCKED AND STIRRED THE HEARTS OF America's men and women that it seemed just about everyone stepped up to serve and protect her in whatever way they could. Business owners boarded up their stores and enlisted. Farmers left their farms behind and enlisted. Singers, actors, bandleaders, sports figures, and celebrities in every facet of entertainment weren't nearly as concerned over their next album, film, or home run as they were over the future of their country. Of the whole world, for that matter. This was everyone's war, and everyone was showing up to help end it.

> "My father, Lawrence 'Yogi' Berra, was a Seaman First Class at the Normandy Landing in 1944. Whatever he saw that day and throughout his military career, I know little about because he didn't talk much about his wartime experiences.

> "When he got drafted in 1942, he had already signed to play in the Minors for the New York Yankees. But he didn't hesitate to put his baseball career on hold and serve his country. Since his brother was already serving in the Aleutians, and Dad knew how cold it was there, he joined the US Navy in hopes of a warmer climate.

Seaman First Class Yogi Berra.
Photo courtesy of Larry Berra.

"He was scared at first because he didn't know how to swim. But his actions on D-day earned him a Purple Heart. All Dad would tell us about the Normandy Invasion was that the sky looked like the 4th of July. He was operating his machine gun and watching that sight and one of the officers yelled to him, 'Better get your head down and stop looking, or you're gonna get it blown off!'

"When the movie *Saving Private Ryan* came out, the family took him to see it. The opening scene was the battle that Dad had been in—the Normandy Invasion. After the film, he didn't say much, only that it had brought back a lot of bad memories—he remembered the feeling he had when he was pulling so many soldiers out of the water who had been shot and drowned.

"One day I asked him if he had any regrets about the war. He said, 'None. Everyone wanted to do their part to help. You did what you had to do.'

"Dad never got the chance to see Bob Hope during his time in the military, but he certainly got to know him later in life, and he admired Bob immensely, I can tell you that!"

—LARRY BERRA, son of Yogi Berra

Seaman First Class Yogi Berra.
Photo courtesy of Larry Berra.

"Well, here I am at the Great Lakes Naval Training Station. . . . Nobody paid any attention to me. I said to the Commanding Officer, 'Where's my big welcome? I'm Bob Hope.' He said, 'Well, we decided to skip it. This is the Great Lakes country. One more drip won't make any difference.'"

. . . Bob Hope

Other well-known entertainers who served in uniform in World War II (either before or after becoming celebrities) included Tony Curtis, Jackie Robinson, Ronald Reagan, Clark Gable, Glenn Miller, Joe Lewis, Mel Brooks, Don Knotts, Dick Van Dyke, Norman Lear, Johnny Carson, Bea Arthur, Jonathan Winters, Tony Bennett, Paul Newman, Forrest Tucker, and Jimmy Stewart. There were plenty more.

Audie Murphy, the most decorated American soldier in WWII, would go on to a successful film and songwriting career after the war.

Carole Lombard, wife of Clark Gable, perished in a plane crash in January 1942, while returning home from a war bonds tour. President Roosevelt declared Carole the first woman to die in the line of duty in World War II.

Following her death, Clark left his successful Hollywood career behind and, even though he was beyond draft age, joined the US Army Air Corps in her honor. He flew some combat missions, but like Hope, Gable's creative talent was put to good use in the making of recruiting films.

The entertainment industry suffered another great loss when on December 15, 1944, renowned Big Band leader Glenn Miller, who had joined the US Army Air Force and was using his musical talents for the military, went "Missing in Action." He had previously escaped one brush with death when his former London office at the BBC was bombed, killing seventy, but this time, Major Miller wasn't so lucky. It is believed his plane encountered icing problems and crashed in the English Channel while on his way to see about relocating his Glenn Miller Army Air Force Band to Paris.

"I was a Combat Engineer. Isn't that ridiculous? The two things I hate most in the world are combat and engineering."

—MEL BROOKS

Mel Brooks was in the Battle of the Bulge. When the Germans broadcast to the troops using a loudspeaker, Brooks answered with his best Al Jolson voice, singing, "Toot Toot Tootsie, good-bye."

Major Glenn Miller Army Air Force Band, National Museum of the USAF.

"My father, Don Knotts, was in the entertainment unit known as 'Special Services.' Their purpose was to entertain soldiers during the war and keep up the soldiers' morale. They performed their show under pitched tents, on stage in the rain, or on a complete stage in the instance one was available. There were 35 entertainers in all in his troupe.

"They had a long sea voyage across the Pacific and played shows on the transport. They ended up in steaming hot New Guinea and began rehearsals on April 16, 1944. Frequent cold showers and clothes washing made conditions more tolerable. Dad had a few close friends in the show. Brad Rafferty was a sax player in the pit band, and together with Joseph Damiani, the drummer, they were an irrepressible threesome. Joe practiced his drums so often they took to calling him Paradiddle. Dad performed a ventriloquist act he'd been honing since high school. He killed with the act.

"One night, Don Knotts, Joe Damiani, and Brad Rafferty were in the audience when Joe E. Brown came to perform his show. He was one of the most popular comedians and actors in the 1930s–40s. During his routine a soldier shouted out, 'Hey Joe, tell us a dirty one!'

Brown stopped his jokes, got very serious, and said, 'I will never tell a joke that I would be ashamed to tell in front of my mother.' He got a standing ovation from the thousands of hardened soldiers. Brad observed, 'If an entertainer has to resort to sexual jokes and innuendo, they are shouting that they don't have enough talent to keep your attention any other way.'

"Joe's son Richard Damiani told me that in the unit were also three professional comedians. Mickey Shaunessey, who was well known after the war for movie roles and night club work. Red Ford, from Houston Texas, was a seasoned and creative comic. Donald 'Red' Blanchard was a hillbilly comedian from the radio station WLS Barn Dance Company in Chicago. Working with these three pros was great training for Dad. They all appreciated how funny he was but Red Ford, in particular, knew Dad's performance skills were growing. He gave him a few jokes to try and it went great. Red worked Dad into his act and they got huge laughs. Rather than use a dummy, Dad preferred to play a dummy with Red Ford.

"As far off the radar as New Guinea was, show biz careers could be 'made' there. Jack Benny headlined for troops in the Pacific theater and came to see 'Stars and Gripes' on his night off. He was so impressed with Red Blanchard's comedy he came backstage and offered Red a contract to join his top-rated radio show after the war. Dad was stunned when Red turned him down, he preferred to stay in Chicago!

"Eventually Dad found a mentor of his own. Lanny Ross was a successful singer, at times compared to Rudy Vallee. During the war, Lanny was an officer in Special Services. One day he told Dad to look him up in New York City after the war. Dad was skeptical he'd remember but Lanny did, and used his influence to get him an audition on a popular radio program, 'Bobby Benson and the B-Bar-B Riders.' Dad voiced the cantankerous Old-Timer, Windy Wales, who became a well-loved character. Dad was recognizable by this distinctive voice. Had listeners met 'the real Windy,' they'd have been hard-pressed to recognize an agile 26-year-old in the part. They'd probably think the voice of Windy came from veteran actor, Gabby Hayes."
—KAREN KNOTTS, daughter of Don Knotts*

* Additional details provided by Robert Metz.

(Left) WWII army nurse lapel pin.

(Right) Lieutenant John F. Kennedy being awarded the Navy and Marine Corps Medal for heroism in rescuing members of the crew of the PT-109; original photograph taken June 11, 1944. Captain Frederick L. Conklin, commandant of Chelsea Naval Hospital; John F. Kennedy. Chelsea Naval Hospital, Chelsea, Massachusetts. Copy photo taken by Robert Knudsen from original photograph on July 6, 1961. [Original photographer unknown] Courtesy of John F. Kennedy Presidential Library.

> "One thing that was amazing about World War II was that everybody signed up for the duration plus six months. Flyers got to leave combat after 25 missions, or 35 missions, but other than that, you were in it."
> —TOM HANKS

Even Oscar did his part in the war years. The traditional 24K gold-plated statuettes were reduced to a more basic emblem of glory. Metal was in high demand for our military, so the Academy figured it would do some self-imposed rationing. Many members felt it wouldn't be right to flash their shiny gold statues, designer gowns, tuxedos, and diamonds when so many people across the country and the world were doing without. For three years, Oscar's gold-plating was traded for plaster and simply painted gold. After the war was over, the Academy gladly replaced the wartime statuettes with the gold-plated ones.

Bob Hope at 1943 Oscar ceremony.

"Welcome to the Academy Awards. Or as it's known at my house—pass over."
. . . Bob Hope

Feb. 10, 1945
Italy

Dear Bob,
Pardon me for being so familiar, but I just can't picture the title "Mr. Hope." It doesn't sound like what you really are. I even doubt very much if this letter will reach you personally, but here goes nothing.
. . . I'm living in a tent with four other boys, who also are your fans. We probably won't be able to see a show of yours, and I really envy the ones that do. . . . You might be interested to know where the boys are from, and of what descent they are. We have been all over enemy territory on our raids and the B-24 is the baby that takes us back and forth.

Lt. Edward Y. Parsegian	*Pilot*	*Armenian*
Lt. Delmar L. Brinkman	*Pilot*	*German*
Lt. Jack R. Fordyce	*Bombardier*	*English*
Lt. George A. Fuccillo	*Navigator*	*Italian*
Lt. James N. James	*Pilot*	*Scotch/Irish*

There you are, Bob, fellows whose ancestors are from all parts of the world.

We're not complaining or bragging; we're just trying to do our share to end this mess.

I know that you're swamped with sacks of mail, and if you can get around to answering one of us, it would mean that you did receive the letter.

Well, I'll stop wasting your time and sign off.

Lots of luck on your tours, and keep your feet dry.

Sincerely,
Eddie
Our address:
485 Bomb Group
829 Bomb Sqd.
APO 520 c/o Postmaster
N.Y.C., NY

(Left) US Navy pilot George Bush in the cockpit of an Avenger (1942–1945). Courtesy of George H. W. Bush Presidential Library and Museum.

(Right) Ronald Reagan, 40th president of the United States, served from 1937 through the end of the war. Courtesy Ronald Reagan Presidential Library.

Every day, every letter, every postcard, every news report, brought the reality of war a little closer to home.

> *Holland*
> *22 December 44*
>
> *Dear Bob,*
> *Though I do not hold out much chance of your remembering me or of your answering this letter personally, I am writing to fulfill a two year old promise. Maybe if I tell you that I was one of fifty-four Australian flyers who were in Chicago in December '42. Maybe you remember taking a party of us around to a number of nightclubs.*
> *. . . Am very sorry to say that of those fifty-four pilots that were in Chicago, only about fifteen remain alive . . .*
>
> *Frank A. Lang*
> *Royal Australian Air Force*

"I can't read those letters without crying. I saw their young faces, some of them were only 18 or 19 years old. I sympathize with their families. The pain and anguish never dies if you lost a loved one over there. The parents tell me whether their sons were frightened or not. Often, these boys were away from home for the first time in their lives. They say, 'Thank you for making my son laugh before he died.' They'll tell me what he was like as a

Navy chaplain holds mass for marines who lost their lives in initial landings at Saipan, June 1944. US National Archives.

child, whether he had a girl waiting for him back home, what his dreams were. I will always feel sad for those who died, but I know God hasn't forgotten them."

...Bob Hope, *Thanks for the Memories: A Celebration of His Legendary 80 Years in Show Business*, American Media, Inc.

Standing in the grassy sod bordering row upon row of white crosses in an American cemetery, two dungaree-clad Coast Guardsmen pay silent homage to the memory of a fellow Coast Guardsman who lost his life in action in the Ryukyu Islands. Benrud, ca. 1945. 26-G-4739. National Archives Identifier: 513229.

Dec. 28, 1944
Cpl. Chas. Boghorian
Co. I 3rd Bn. 5th Marines
c/o Fleet Post Office
San Francisco, California

Mr. Hope,
Rec'd the Xmas card you sent me, and thought it was swell. Thanks, old man. I appreciate it a lot. Brother, if them words would only come true. A homeward bound New Year!

...No doubt you remember the picture I have enclosed (of Harry G. Ray). He was one of my best friends in the Company. He was killed in action against the enemy on Ngesebus (a small island north of Peleliu).

Thanks again for the wonderful Xmas card.
A Marine—Cpl. Chas. Boghorian

The crew of the USS *South Dakota* stands with bowed heads, while Chaplain N. D. Lindner reads the benediction held in honor of fellow shipmates killed in the air action off Guam on June 19, 1944. National Archives, July 1, 1944. 80-G-238322. National Archives Identifier: 520649.

Harry Ray on stage in Bob Hope military show. Photo sent to Bob from Cpl. Chas. Ray KIA on Ngesebus (a small island north of Peleliu).

June 6, 1945
Cpl. Chas. Boghorian
Co. I 3rd Bn. 5th Marines
c/o Fleet Post Office
San Francisco, California

Dear Charlie:
Came across your letter the other night when I sat down to look over my G. I. Mail for the past few months.

Sorry I haven't managed to answer you before this, but I've really been on the "go" all season . . . one tour after the other.

. . . Sorry to hear about Harry Ray, he was a swell kid. Here's hoping this mess will be cleaned up before too long and you'll have "a Homeward Bound New Year" before this year is over. Good luck!

Sincerely,
Bob Hope

February 18, 1947

Thank you, Bob Hope, for your tribute to our Iwo Jima Marines. I waited all day for someone to remember the day and wondered if relatives and participants were the only ones who would.

Again, thank you. You see, my son, a Platoon Sergeant drove the first motorized unit (his tank) on the shores of Iwo Jima and three days later he was dead.

Mrs. Muriel A. Davison
San Bernardino, Calif.

"They fought together as brothers in arms; they died together, and now they sleep side by side . . . To them, we have a solemn obligation. The obligation to ensure that their sacrifice will help make this a better and safer world in which to live."
—FLEET ADMIRAL CHESTER W. NIMITZ, September 2, 1945

Max Walter Selz
Flushing, N.Y.C.

My dear Mr. Hope,
Many, many, many thanks for your mention of the dear ones of those that made the supreme sacrifice in this last unpleasantness.

Since January 20, 1945 when my 18 year old son made this sacrifice, yours has been the first mention of us left behind, so far behind.

Sincere Merry Christmas and a very Happy New Year to you and yours.

M. Walter Selz

(Left) Battle of Iwo Jima, 24th Marine Regiment. United States Marine Corps photo.

(Right) I Gave a Man! Poster. National Archives, Office of War Information, #514558.

Flag raising, Iwo Jima, February 23, 1945. Photo by Joe Rosenthal, Associated Press. Courtesy of the National Archives.

Kyusky, Japan

Hi Friend,
. . . I remember the first night I spent on Iwo Jima. I said my prayers and I imagined I could see my little girl getting into bed even though the Japanese were (hitting us) with their mortars. At this time I was dug in beside the body of a buddy of mine, Gunny Sgt. J. Basilone. But all I could think of was home. Later on in the Operation, I came across a fellow from Indianapolis. He had been hit with mortar fragments. While I was dressing his wounds, of which there were many, also giving him plasma, believe it or not, he was talking about home. When we put him aboard a trac to evacuate him, he said, "Well, at least I am headed for home."

This story is true, Bob, and I guess he is home by now. I have been transferred to the 2nd Div. now, and sure hope to get home soon.

. . . That's all for now, only I hope the people back home hold up their end of the bargain as good as we held up ours.

One of your fans,
Harry

"Among the men who fought on Iwo Jima, uncommon valor was a common virtue."
—ADMIRAL NIMITZ

" . . . we should thank God that such men lived."
—GENERAL GEORGE C. PATTON

On February 3, 1943, at 12:55 a.m., the *Dorchester*, a luxury liner repurposed as an army transport ship, found itself in the crosshairs of a German submarine's periscope. Of the three torpedoes immediately fired at them, one was a direct hit, knocking out power and radio capabilities and sending the ship's 902 passengers into utter darkness and chaos. Four chaplains, Lieutenant George L. Fox (Methodist), Lieutenant Alexander D. Goode (Jewish), Lieutenant John P. Washington (Roman Catholic), and Lieutenant Clark V. Povling (Dutch Reformed), did their best to bring a sense of calm to the troops as the ship steadily took in water, sinking some twenty-seven minutes later. These were icy waters 150 miles off the coast of Greenland, and despite Captain Hans Danielsen's warning of the waters being patrolled by German U-boats, and that it would be wise for them to sleep fully dressed with their life jackets on, many had not heeded his words.

In the midst of the confusion, these four relatively new chaplains faced the emergency with uncommon bravery. They helped the wounded, offered prayers, and handed out life jackets. When the jackets ran out, eyewitnesses said that the four chaplains took off their own jackets and handed them to the next four men in line.

Those who had made it into the lifeboats continued to watch as these four chaplains stood arm in arm and sang hymns and spoke prayers over the troops in different languages. There were Catholic prayers in Latin, Jewish prayers in

Hebrew, and English prayers heard as the four chaplains bravely went down with the ship.

Of the 902 on board, only 230 would eventually be rescued. The rest, 672, including the four chaplains, would perish in the icy waters.

> "Greater love hath no man than he lay down his life for his friends."
> —JOHN 15:13 KJV

(From top left to right) Lt. George L. Fox, Methodist; Lt. Alexander D. Goode, Jewish; Lt. John P. Washington, Roman Catholic; and Lt. Clark V. Poling, Dutch Reformed. Photos and details courtesy of The Four Chaplains Chapel. The Four Chaplains Memorial Foundation, Director MSG Bill Kaemmer.

DEAR BOB . . .

HERE'S A MEMORY FOR YOU

——————————————————————————————

ANYONE WHO SERVED OR LIVED THROUGH THE SECOND GREAT WAR WAS LEFT with memories of unbelievable courage, devastating losses, and remarkable victories. Too many of these memories are lost to the world forever because the guardian of the memory is no longer with us, or spoke little, if any, about the war.

Thankfully, for this generation and those to come, many firsthand memories have been captured in G.I. letters, videotaped testimonials, and in the soldiers' personal diaries, memoirs, newspaper clippings, and books.

> "We were whisked off to the flight line, Jimmy (Edwards) to his plane, I to mine, and the 772nd Bomb Squadron of the 463rd Bomb Group took off.
>
> "The target, we learned at altitude when Brownie opened our orders, was an aircraft plant in Regensburg, Germany. Our squadron consisted of eighteen planes flying in what was called wing formation. As radio men, Jimmy and I reported back regularly by Morse code to Central Command, informing them as to our condition and location. The radio position and accompanying top gun being close to the bomb bay, it was also our job to check the bomb bay after we'd heard 'Bombs away!' from the cockpit, to be sure all the bombs had been released and the doors could be shut. After some four hours, within thirty minutes of the target, we rendezvoused with the 8th Air Force out of London, and started on our first bomb run.
>
> "As we neared the target we were suddenly hit by German fighters soaring in from every angle and spitting three hundred rounds at us in three-second bursts. We radio men were now at our 50-caliber gun posts spitting back. Our vision was limited to what was coming at us from high angles at the side and from above, so I didn't see it happen—I just heard another crewman say 'Del Signore's been hit.'

My heart thumping, I strained to see for myself, but my vision was blurred by heavy flak and angry puffs of black bursting everywhere, a kind of deadly Rorschach in the sky. As we fought our way out of there, Del fell behind. Soon he was out of sight and my heart sank. But about twenty-five minutes after the rest of us had landed, Del—with only two engines firing—managed to get his crippled plane back to base.

"I was racing to greet them when I learned that two crewmen, the ball turret gunner and radio man Jimmy Edwards, were dead. Thick-headed and choking back a scream, I had to say goodbye to Jimmy, but by the time I got to the plane they had already removed the bodies. Sometime later, still in a stupor, the horror of something I'd witnessed at the plane returned to me. It was a member of the ground crew stoically hosing out the ball turret, and I could no longer stifle that scream. Two days afterward I accompanied Jimmy's body to Bari, Italy, where he was buried in a GI cemetery."
—NORMAN LEAR*

" . . . The month of March 1945 is etched in my mind like it was yesterday. It was still dark, and near daylight when the briefing for the day's mission took place. Our bomb group, the 391st, was stationed at Roye, France. Our assignment during the month of March was the destruction of railroad marshalling yards, big German-gun emplacements, and industrial complexes across the Rhine in the Ruhr valley area.

"The Germans were now desperately trying to stop the Allies. The Battle of the Bulge was just over and both sides had suffered great losses. The Germans found themselves with their backs to the wall and they were throwing all their reserves into trying to stop the advancement of the Allied Army. The target area was ringed with the German big-gun emplacements. It was 'Flak Alley'! By this time, the Germans were deadly accurate in knocking our bombers out of the air.

---

* Excerpted from *Even This I Get to Experience* (2014, Penguin Press). Used with permission of author.

"Tension was high. Night after night the drone of five hundred to a thousand B-17's and B-24's passed over our base, striking targets deep into Germany. What a sight! And just before daybreak, we could hear them passing over again heading across the channel to their bases in England. Mission accomplished!

" . . . On one mission I recall we had an extra-large bomb load. We barely got off the ground by the end of the runway. We almost took the roofs off some housetops as we tried to gain altitude.

" . . . Once airborne the first thing I had to do, since I was the waist gunner in addition to being the radio operator, was to open the hatch windows on each side in the waist section and swing out my 50 caliber Browning machine guns readied for action.

" . . . Suddenly, as we neared the crossing of the Rhine, all 'git out' broke loose. Puffs of black smoke and bursting shells were exploding all around us. The Germans had zeroed in on our altitude. The exploding shells nearby would make our plane leap in the air. It also made something else leap—my heart into my throat! I was just sure we were 'goners.' The flak hitting our plane sounded like hail pounding on the tin roof back on my dad's barn in Louisiana. Suddenly, the Plexiglas window just over my head shattered. One slug of red-hot flak landed in my lap. Another hit the ammunition can just to my side. My tail gunner took a hit in his arm. I still have that chunk of flak that landed in my lap and a piece of the Plexiglas window for a memento of that mission.

" . . . What in the world was a 19 year old boy who had never been hardly over 200 miles from his birthplace on a 40 acre farm at Rocky Branch doing over a German city, that he had never heard of—[and] couldn't spell or speak a word of their language? Well, I don't know, except the fact that someone had to do the job and my time had come. I only did what millions of other Americans did and our Allied comrades. We helped save the world from a tyrant named Adolph Hitler. Fortunately, I made it back home to tell my story. Many others did not, including our co-pilot, George Fisher who lies in a graveyard in Lorraine Cemetery in France along with 10,489 other comrades.

" . . . The War in Europe ended May 7, 1945 while we were at Dijon.

" . . . There is no way to explain the feelings of a [by then] 20 year old going home from the war safe and sound with a heart full of thanksgiving and a vision of home and family. . . . The voyage took about twice as long as usual because of the severe storms we encountered. . . . By the time we reached New York Harbor, our ship was listing on its side at a steep angle. The hull below the water line on one side was full of water. After about seventeen days we landed in New York, the woman with the torch in New York Harbor sure looked pretty. What a sight, thousands of soldiers loaded down with duffle bags hanging on each shoulder with a couple more tied together and slung around their neck, then a bag in each hand. I could hardly walk. But our spirits ran high as people waved and bands played.

"We boarded buses and were whisked to Camp Kilmer, New Jersey for processing. The first order of business was food, especially good ole milk. That powered stuff we had drank for years was no more. I think I must have drunk a gallon right off.

"I called home and told them I had landed. After two days, I received my paperwork and boarded a troop train headed south towards the green, green grass back home."
—ALTON HARDY HOWARD*

"In times of conflict, our citizens have always been able to rise to the challenge. Maybe no greater example of that ability is found during the onset of World War II."
—CHUCK NORRIS, father fought at the Battle of the Bulge

"At 84, I've outlived a few husbands. I've been married three times to three military men—a soldier, sailor, and a spy. Each one of them saw Bob Hope during World War II (one even saw him several times). I didn't plan my marriages with that in mind, but having a

---

* Submitted by John Howard of the Duck Dynasty family.

(Above) Alton Howard (*4th from left*) and crew. Photo courtesy of John Howard of the Duck Dynasty family.

(Right) Molten flak from German gun that smashed through the window where Alton H. Howard was stationed as waist gunner and radio operator in a B-26 bomber in 1945 over Germany. Photo courtesy of John Howard of the Duck Dynasty family.

heart for your country and also having memories of Bob Hope's wartime shows could be a good gauge of a great guy.

"My first husband, Ted Jungreis, enlisted in the US Army when he was 18. He was at the Anzio Beachhead battle, and Ted and his twin brother, Irving, served in North Africa.

"My second husband, Bill Hoest, creator of The Lockhorns cartoon strip, joined the US Navy when he was 18. Bill saw Bob Hope in the Pacific, where he served on a Yard Mine Sweeper, searching for mines. Bill couldn't believe that someone like Bob Hope would come to such remote islands and put on a show. And he always brought beautiful girls to remind them 'what they were fighting for.' But more importantly, he brought a sense of home.

"After Bill passed away, I married our good friend Doc Carpenter. Doc was a member of the O.S.S. (Office of Strategic Service, the precursor for the C.I.A.), and served in Yugoslavia, Italy, and North Africa. He had the opportunity to see Bob Hope several times in those locations. As a medical doctor, Doc worked behind enemy lines, providing medicine to the citizens, while at the same time helping Allied Forces. He was instrumental in rescuing 500 Airmen that had been shot down by the Nazis. Doc was awarded the Presidential Legion of Merit for his service.

"All three of these men, and all who served with them, had survived the Great Depression, and now they were fighting in World War II. These soldiers were strong men, even when they were only in their teens and twenties. Also, all three often commented about Bob Hope and what he did for our military. Bob brought a sense of 'We're all in this together' to the public and the soldiers alike. He kept the soldiers encouraged so they could do their job, and he urged the public to do theirs."

—BUNNY HOEST, president and CEO Hoest Enterprises, *The Lockhorns*

Even the Lockhorns are of one mind when it comes to Bob Hope.

"WE FINALLY AGREE . . . BOB HOPE IS THE BEST!"

Legion of Merit Award
presented to Doc Carpenter.

"And when we got about half way down, the pilot turned around
and said to me, 'Are you a little nervous?' I said, 'Yes, it's only my
third time up.' He said, 'You beat me. This is my first.'"
 ... Bob Hope

1st Lt. Michael Rodewryre
Baltimore, Maryland
October 29, 1945

Dear Mr. Hope:
I doubt very seriously if you will ever get to see this letter, but never-
theless I made myself a promise—and I'm fulfilling it.

It was back near Tropani in Sicily 1943 when you came to visit the
3rd Division and put on your little show. I remember at that time how
I cussed you for having to attend your show. We had just completed a
pretty rough campaign in Sicily, and were hiding away for a little rest
when we were told to get ready to march 3 miles to see your show. Of
course, the order was greeted by loud "moans and groans"—because
it had been a terrific campaign on our feet and physical bodies. And
we were pretty well shot through with malaria and diarrhea. In other
words, "we were hurting." But go we did.

To say I and the gang enjoyed the show would be putting it mildly.
It was something more than a show—it seemed to lift us spiritually. It
seemed to be the first thing we really saw that reminded us of home.

And we really needed this as we had been in Africa a year before this. So I promised myself at that time if I got through, I was going to write you a letter of appreciation. Hence, this epistle.

    Much has happened since that day. . . . San Pietro, Anzio, Rome, Southern France, Germany followed for us. But we always read where you were—all over the globe—doing the magnificent job you did.

    It's "guys" like you that makes this country "tick"—believe you me . . .

    So thanks, buddy, for a grand job.

Sincerely yours,
Michael Rodewryre
Ex- 30th Infantry—3rd Division
US Army

"My father, Private Stephen Kolada, wrote the following letter to the Rev. Walter Jendrusak, O.S.B. and editor-in-chief of the Bohemian Benedictine Press, a small newspaper where Dad had been a lino-typist before entering the army as an infantryman. Less than three weeks after writing this letter, which the paper published, he was reported missing in action on Nov. 26.

"Captured by the Germans, Dad was sent to a Prisoner of War camp in Germany, where he remained until the war ended in 1945.

"My father died on Sept. 19, 2017, at the age of 97. This newspaper clipping was among his possessions. Dad proudly served his country and was buried with full military honors."
—MARY KOLADA SCOTT, California

(Stephen Kolada's printed letter)
Somewhere in France
Nov. 9, 1944

Dear and Reverend Father,
It wasn't very long ago when I had the opportunity to see you and all

the fellows in the shop. That time I didn't even dream that in a month or so I would be on the other side of the Atlantic Ocean. But it happened that I was shipped overseas and now I am somewhere in France.

My first stop was somewhere in England, where I stayed only for a short time. From there I was sent to France, where I am stationed at the present time.

The trip to this country was a long one, but it was pretty good. While on the ship, we had Catholic service almost every day; then we had all kinds of magazines for reading, various games, and USO shows for entertainment. The time was flying fast.

France is a pretty nice country, and people are friendly to us. The weather here is very bad. It rains frequently, and it is cold. While I am writing these lines, it is snowing outside. It looks like winter will be here soon. I wish we could get the heat wave which you had in Chicago a few weeks ago. Gee, we would enjoy it here.

I am getting along fine, Father. How are the boys in the shop? I hope they are fine too. Best regards to them all. Hope this war will end soon, and I shall be back in the good old U.S.A. again.

If this should be my last letter to you before Christmas, I take the opportunity to wish you and all the personnel a Very Merry Christmas.

. . . I wish I could write you more about this place and what I am doing, but my letters are strictly censored, and I must not write everything I would like to.

With best regards,

Sincerely yours,
Steve

"When the Japanese attacked Pearl Harbor on December 7, 1941, Bob Ain was twenty years old and on his own in Los Angeles, CA. A few months later, he decided he would like to join the United States Coast Guard. He knew for sure he didn't want to be a 'ground-pounder.'

"The first time he tried to enlist, he was rejected. He was too light! They told him to eat a lot of food and come back in a week. The next time he was accepted and shipped to Portland, Oregon, where he learned to fire arms while waiting to ship out.

"His next stop was San Francisco, CA, where his duty was to patrol the beach on horseback. He had 'do-it-yourself lessons' on how to saddle and ride a horse. His first assignment was a fifteen mile ride along the beach. When he stopped to rest his weary bones, the horse ripped the reins from his hand and headed back to the barn, leaving Bob to 'hoof' it.

"While at San Francisco, he volunteered to attend Radar School in San Diego for a week. He passed the exam in the top 10% of the class, which gave him a job in the radar shack as a 3rd Class Petty Officer when he finally got a ship in 1943. The Hunter Liggett was out of Bougainville and Guadalcanal, an attack transport with landing barges (LCVP). It transported Marines and Army in training for invasions.

"There was never enough fresh water, so sometimes they'd strip and shower on deck if it rained. Tough luck if you didn't get rinsed off before it stopped. But one time, they had a Pacific typhoon for two weeks, and nobody could go on deck at all.

"Bob is proud to say, he never shot at anyone and nobody shot at him for the entire war. He says, 'They pointed me, and I marched. I did what I was told to do.'"
—DIANTHA AIN for late husband, WW2 veteran Robert A. Ain, who didn't talk about the war for over sixty years

DEAR BOB . . .

WHERE THE HECK ARE YOU?

ON JULY 4, 1944, WHILE PERFORMING IN LONDON FOR SOME TEN THOUSAND soldiers, Bob Hope opened his show with, "This is Bob 'Don't ask me where I am because I don't know and even if I did know I couldn't tell because it's a military secret' Hope . . ."

The audience howled. And fully understood. This man had indeed been just about everywhere. So much so that you never quite knew where he would turn up next.

Travelin' Man, Bob Hope.

189

Headquarters Army Base
APO 953
22 July 1944

My dear Sir:
Following you reminds me of a story once told on Mark Twain. The author had gone on an extended vacation and wished privacy so had not left his address with very many people. A friend wishing to reach him addressed a Postal Card to him in the following manner:

Mark Twain
God Knows Where

After several weeks had gone by the friend received this reply. "Well, I figured that God knew where I was, but I didn't think he would tell." Many alohas and may you return safely to our Islands.

Sincerely,
Opal H. Morris
Secretary to Colonel Farnum

For his own protection, Bob's travel plans to military bases in foreign lands were a closely guarded secret, only announced days, sometimes hours, before the shows. If it was a show at home, there was more liberty to joke around with the specific locale. Local gripes, items in the news, politics, and the weather were also prime areas for humor. Because of this, Bob always had a little fun with his opening line. It was a tradition he continued throughout his career:

This is Bob "Construction Battalion" Hope . . .
This is Bob "Election Day" Hope . . .
This is Bob "Mosquito Network" Hope . . .
This is Bob "Globetrotter" Hope . . .
This is Bob "Celebrating Navy Day at Terminal Island" Hope . . .

And on and on it would go. The troops got a kick out of it.

Another practice that Bob would often do was follow his opening line with a poetic nod to his sponsor.

"Howd'ya do, ladies and gentlemen? . . . This is Bob 'Broadcasting for the aerial gunners of the Yuma Air Field' Hope . . . telling all you men to use Pepsodent

...'cause if you meet a Yuma girl who's interested in kissing, when you pucker up your mouth, your equipment won't be missing."

Following the greeting, and/or opening poem, Bob would jump right into the one-liners.

On the wind at Yuma Air Force Field:

> **"This is the only place in the country where the hangars have more flying time than the airplanes."**
> **... Bob Hope**

Performing for troops in Las Vegas:

> **"There are about five thousand men here at the Gunnery School, and there are also about a hundred WACs. ... That's about the same odds as you get at those slot machines."**
> **... Bob Hope**

> **"And they have a lot of rattle snakes here. You know what a rattle snake is, don't you? That's an eel with a crap game going on in the back."**
> **... Bob Hope**

(Left) Bob Hope and Jerry Colonna.

(Right) Bob with Little Karl plane and crew, North Africa.

24 Aug. 1944
New Caledonia
Stanley H. Goldsmith CMMIC. C2
40 C. B. c/o Fleet P.O.
San Francisco, Calif.

Dear "Bob":
Before I leave this place, I wish to thank you for the extreme pleasure I enjoyed during your brief stay in New Caledonia. Being invited to join your troupe for a little chat, and being with you for the time we were able to enjoy such pleasure, is still deeply appreciated.

Your wonderful show, truly great, has been a treat, and to see your draw of twelve to fifteen thousand hands at a single show is a spectacle to always remember.

Also, I shall not forget the many phone calls you made until I was found and able to contact you.

For it all, "Bob," my grateful appreciation to you and to Barney, who like yourself, is always a real guy and regular.

My next "beach-head" will be Camp Parks (Stateside), and then a little rehabilitation leave around the old "diggings," about October first. So all is well, in fact, wonderful!

Best of good wishes to you and yours, and the choicest luck in bountiful measure.

Sincerely,
Always . . . Stan Goldsmith

Bob Hope performing in New Caledonia.

(Left) Where's Bob? Did anyone check the brig?

(Right) Camp Roberts military police "escorting" Bob Hope from an on-post stage, 1942. (Camp Roberts Historical Museum.)

Bob Hope learned early on that his self-deprecating style of humor worked best with these military shows. The soldiers loved it whenever this Hollywood movie star would put himself down. He didn't come into their world to talk about how many celebrity events he had been invited to, how rich he was, or how many fans were lining up for his next film. He always came across as a regular guy just like them. And he was.

> "We took his own characteristics and exaggerated them. We just put them in. He thought he was playing a character. He was playing, really, the real Bob Hope."
> —MELVILLE SHAVELSON, writer/producer

The soldiers played right along with him with their own jokes and pranks. Not every celebrity might have appreciated that, but Bob loved it. He grew up in a house full of boys, so the horseplay was nothing new to him.

He may have been riding around in limousines in Hollywood and New York, but in his heart he knew he wasn't above any soldier in his audience. In fact, to him *they* were the "stars."

Hope and troupe's arrival.

"In World War II and throughout the remainder of Bob's life, Bob and Chrysler shared many of the same values—our troops, dedication, and golf."

—CHRYSLER CORPORATION

"My game has improved . . . the officials at Lakeside let me play in the daytime now."
. . . Bob Hope

WWII Chrysler tugboat ad. Used with permission of Chrysler Corporation.

2nd Lt. M. L. Dickinson 0–2045049
749 Bomb Sqdn. 457 Bomb Gp (H)
APO 557, c/o Postmaster
New York, New York
May 24, 1944
England . . . still

Dear Mr. Hope:
You probably have 10 bags [of mail] and some hireling will get this
and answer this. I'll tell you what the story is—This is my first letter
of this type, and I am a bit green. You see, Mr. Hope, I was in the RAF
and didn't get a chance to see you over here. I was about 30 miles from
the 91st when you were there, but couldn't get over because of business.
I was a Sgt. Air Gunner, and now am a gunnery officer of the 749th
B. S. (Bomb Sqdn.) Well, here's the point—I just wanted to tell you
that if it were possible I would name the ship I flew in "Here's Hope"
or some such corny thing, not because I want a picture of you or an
autograph or anything, it's just that I have for a long while thought a
lot about what a swell, wonderful and generous man you are. This has
been my feeling, and if I could do you a favor when you are down to
your last joke, or car, or anything, I would. You say "How easy to say,"
but I mean it—you're the tops, and I'm just a wee part of your ever
admiring audience.

Very sincerely,
Dick

June 26, 1944

Dear Dick:
I was very glad to receive your letter and really did intend to an-
swer it before this.
    . . . I'm planning on making a tour of the camps and bases of
the South Pacific this summer. . . . I'm really keeping in condition
by eating the right foods. Last week I wrote to "Wheaties" and told
them I was telling all my friends I owed my present physique en-
tirely to their product. Yesterday I received a letter from that com-
pany in which they mentioned something about an "injunction."

Well, I'll have to sign off now and get back to work on this pirate picture I'm making for Goldwyn. . . . Tell the rest of the fellows "hello" . . . and good luck.

Yours for Health,
Bob Hope

Quartermaster Detachment
Camp Crowder, Missouri
February 27, 1942
Mr. Bob Hope
National Broadcasting Co.
Hollywood, California

Dear Sir:
Your program reaches our camp at nine o'clock just as our "beloved sergeant" turns off the lights and shouts, "Turn off those xxxx xxxxxx xxxxx radios."

Being obedient and well-disciplined soldiers, not a sound is thereafter heard. Somehow, the next morning all of your gags are known by the boys.

I decided to investigate this phenomenon with my camera and flashgun with the enclosed results. The radio and all the heads are under a blanket. . . . It is a bit uncomfortable and hot, but the boys hear the program.

Yours truly,
Russell Haltom
Julian L. Schermer

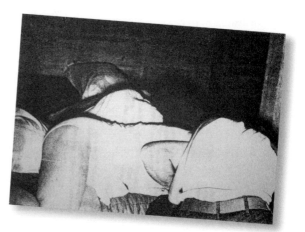

Sneaking a listen to Bob's radio program after hours. Photo by Russell Haltom and Julian L. Schermer.

Hollywood Canteen

Dear Mr. Hope:
Fun is fun, and you can make the boys and girls laugh and laugh and then some more, but there should be a limit to it . . . I think . . .
    A sailor laughed so during your show at the canteen Thanksgiving afternoon that he split his pants—the back seam from waist to——.
    I know. I am the girl who sewed it back.

Yours truly,
L. Germaine

(Top) Another popular WW2 song with lyrics written by Moe Jaffe was "Bell Bottom Trousers." The song was recorded by multiple artists, including Jerry Colonna. Published by Santley-Joy, Inc.

(Middle) Another "namesake." Courtesy of World War II Museum.

(Bottom) And another "namesake": *The Lemon Drop Kid* airplane and crew.

Private Graham P. Sitton
26 BN. M.P.R.T.C.
Co. D
Camp Custer, Michigan
Mr. Bob Hope
K.F.I.
Hollywood, Calif.
(1944)

Dear Bob:
No doubt you will never see this letter, however, I thought I would
write anyway. It makes me feel better, and if you do see it, you will
know we little fellows get a great deal of pleasure and good from your
programs.
  About four years ago you and your wife drove into my Service
Station in Burbank for ten gallons of gasoline. I have never forgotten
how nice and helpful you were to just a service station attendant who
had become confused over a minor item. However, when war was
declared, I sold my station and went to work for Airesearch Mfg. Co. in

Bob Hope on stage, North Africa, 1943.

Bob Hope and Frances Langford
at Duxford, with P47D 41-6249
"Vee Gaile."

Los Angeles, trying to do my little bit toward the war effort. However, Uncle Sam decided it would be better for me to carry a rifle; so here I am. I was inducted at Ft. MacArthur on January 8th and about a week later I was on the troop train bound for Camp Custer. I'm afraid this weather just doesn't agree with this California boy, for after working and drilling in rain, wind, and snow, I ended up in the hospital with a high fever. Our lights go out in the ward and everything must be quiet at 9 o'clock. However, the boys put up such a howl, the nurse allows us to listen to you and Bing. It is really a help to me. Besides being plenty sick, I was pretty lonesome, over 2,000 miles away from home, with a beautiful wife and boy waiting there. You keep all of that to yourself, seeing how much tougher the man alongside of you has it, or his brother, cousin, or somebody. But you can't help but think your problem is bigger to you when you're lying in a bed with strangers on both sides of you, with no loved ones anywhere near. Now, maybe you can understand that. When I heard your program I felt like I was home again, and I don't know whether you had anything to do with it or not, but I will give you the credit, after it was over I soon went to sleep, the first in several nights, and later during the night my fever broke. I feel so much better today, so just thought I would write and try to tell you how I felt. If you see this and have the time, I would be delighted just to get a line or two from you. Also, if your work ever brings you East, I know the boys of the Military Police Replacement Training Center here would be just wild if you could give a show for us . . .

Pvt. Graham P. Sitton

Jerry Colonna and Bob Hope catching some Zzzzs.

"It is impossible to see how he can do so much, can cover so much ground, can work so hard, and can be so effective. He works month after month at a pace that would kill most people."
—JOHN STEINBECK, *New York Herald Tribune*, July 26, 1943

DEAR BOB . . .

NICE OF YOU TO DROP IN

— — — — — — — — — — — — — — — — —

WHENEVER BOB HOPE WOULD WALK INTO A MILITARY HOSPITAL FILLED WITH the injured and ill who couldn't get out of bed even if they had wanted to, he would greet the patients with his signature grin, and then quip, "Don't get up, fellas . . ."

Only Bob Hope could get away with a line like that to bedridden G.I.s. The wounded appreciated how he would look beyond their injuries to see the man (or woman) bearing them. Whatever the prognosis, no matter how grim the situation, Bob's goal was to get a smile or laugh out of each of them, which wasn't always easy. For some, it was their first laugh in months.

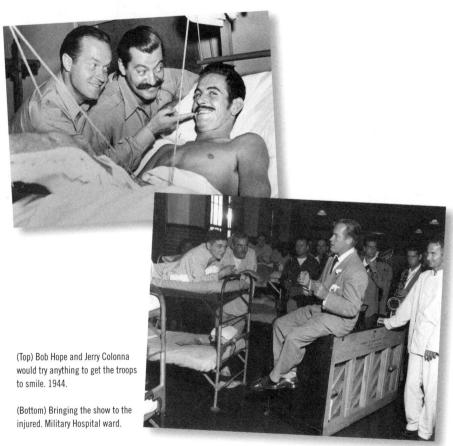

(Top) Bob Hope and Jerry Colonna would try anything to get the troops to smile. 1944.

(Bottom) Bringing the show to the injured. Military Hospital ward.

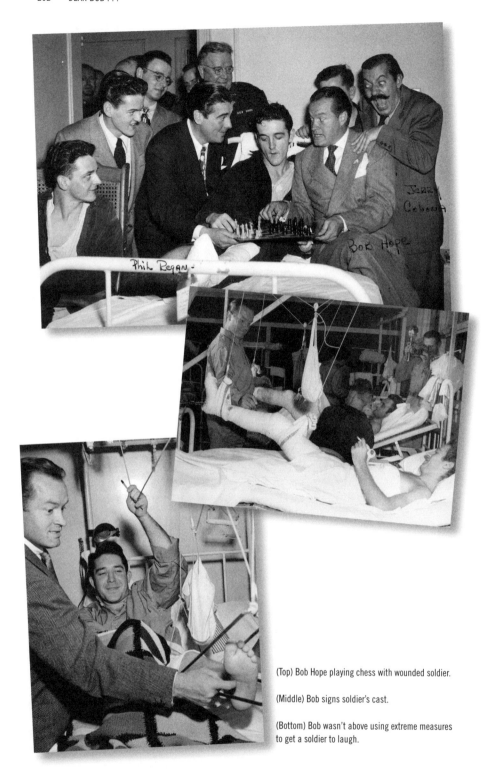

(Top) Bob Hope playing chess with wounded soldier.

(Middle) Bob signs soldier's cast.

(Bottom) Bob wasn't above using extreme measures to get a soldier to laugh.

Bob would always forewarn the celebrities joining him for these visits that they had to keep their emotions at bay. The soldiers needed news from home, some encouraging words, and as many laughs as they could handle. What they didn't need, nor want, were tears and pity.

Walking from bed to bed, the troupe did as Bob had instructed them. They laughed along with the soldiers, shared news from home, and administered the best medicine available—a double dose of hope. That's not to say tears didn't come like a flood as soon as they walked outside.

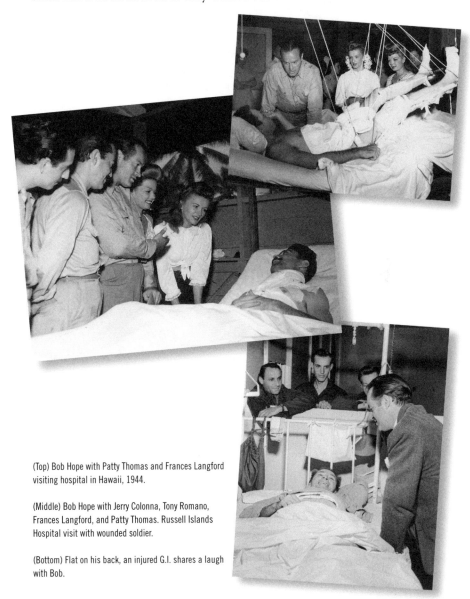

(Top) Bob Hope with Patty Thomas and Frances Langford visiting hospital in Hawaii, 1944.

(Middle) Bob Hope with Jerry Colonna, Tony Romano, Frances Langford, and Patty Thomas. Russell Islands Hospital visit with wounded soldier.

(Bottom) Flat on his back, an injured G.I. shares a laugh with Bob.

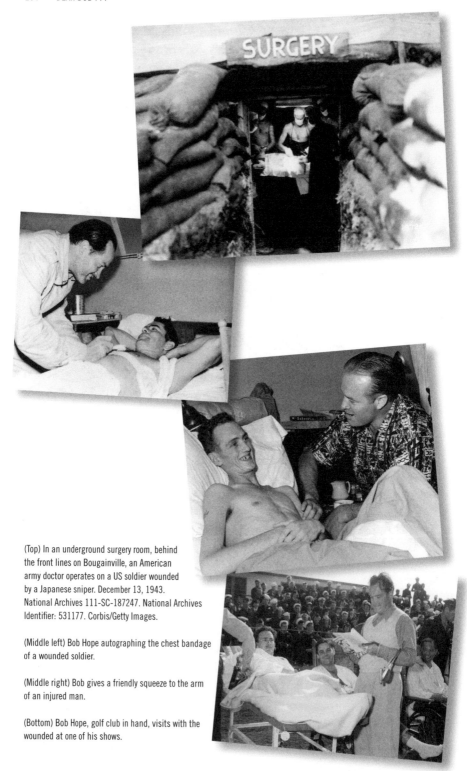

(Top) In an underground surgery room, behind
the front lines on Bougainville, an American
army doctor operates on a US soldier wounded
by a Japanese sniper. December 13, 1943.
National Archives 111-SC-187247. National Archives
Identifier: 531177. Corbis/Getty Images.

(Middle left) Bob Hope autographing the chest bandage
of a wounded soldier.

(Middle right) Bob gives a friendly squeeze to the arm
of an injured man.

(Bottom) Bob Hope, golf club in hand, visits with the
wounded at one of his shows.

"He can handle himself as well in a hospital full of suffering men as before a rough audience of 10,000 war-coarsened ones."
—ERNIE PYLE, war correspondent

Paris, France
Monday
January 15, 1945

Dear Bob,
. . . We all think you're tops in entertainment and last week while see-ing one of the Army Navy Screen Guide reels, it showed you entertain-ing with your company in the South Pacific, and I assure you that we all enjoyed seeing this in the movies as those who saw you in person. Another night we saw hundreds of our buddies with bandaged heads, arms and legs, but a happy smile on their faces . . . when the camera finally swung into the center of the group, there stood Bob Hope.

Again thanks for your personal thoughtfulness and for the pleasure you have and are bringing to us all.

Sincerely,
Bill Heenan
Sgt. W. J. "Bill" Heenan 31270319
Detachment A

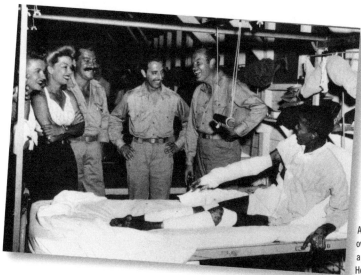

A soldier tells his own joke to Bob Hope and troupe, New Hebrides Islands.

"Believe me, I've learned one wonderful thing, talking to men in hospitals. I've learned how to listen. And I've also learned how to let myself get topped. That guy in the all-over plaster cast topped me . . . and of all people to get topped by, a guy who's plastered. For me to talk to that man at all took more than courage. It took downright gall. Fortunately, you don't stop to think of all those things when you're touring the wards. I just got a gander at this guy and said, 'How do you get a razor in there?' Nice crack, huh? He didn't mind. I guess he smiled, if I could have seen it. He must have. Because what he said was, 'I've <u>had</u> my close shave, Bob.'"
    . . . Bob Hope, excerpted from *I Never Left Home*

United States Marine Corps
May 21, 1946

Dear Bob,
This is just a few lines to you from an ex-Marine who really appreci-
ated the show you put on for us in August 1944 at Espiritu Santos, New
Hebrides, while I was in Ward #3 in Base #3 Hospital U-Sh.
    I had just came from Guam on a stretcher a couple days before you
and your troupe arrived and I mean I really appreciated the way you
acted. Some of the boys thought you looked good in that Panama hat
and the cane, so did I. The thing that I liked about you was you weren't
stuck up the way some of the actors are. You probably don't remember
me, I had got it with a grenade on D-Day, July 21st, 1944 at Guam, and
then I fought on till the 26th and then I got my right shoulder smashed
out with a 91.5 mortar. You sat on my bed and talked with me for a
while, you probably forgot me by now. You told me to write to you
when I got the time. Well, I waited long enough, I know. But I was in
the hospital 1 ½ years from July of 1944 to January 1st of this year 1946.
I was listening to your program tonight over the radio and I remem-
bered what you told me and thought I would drop you a few lines. . . .
I've been sick with malaria for [the] past week, and I'm in bed now . . .

Many thanks,
Always your friend,
Eddie E. Jolley
4 times wounded in action

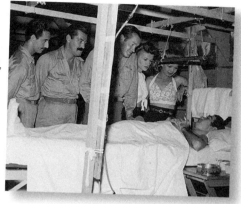

Bob Hope and his USO troupe visiting a hospital ward in the South Pacific: (*from left*) Tony Romano, Jerry Colonna, Bob Hope, Patty Thomas, and Frances Langford, 1944. Copyright. Bob Hope Collection, Motion Picture, Broadcasting and Recorded Sound Division, Library of Congress (116.00.00) [Digital ID# bhp0116].

June 11, 1946
Mr. Eddie E. Jolley

Dear Eddie:
   ...I'll never forget you fellows who were out there at Espiritu Santos in 1944...especially those in the hospital. That was surely something! Sorry to learn you're still suffering from wounds you received in action. Four times is more than enough! Here's hoping that being back home will help to speed your recovery.
   Must close now as I'm on a tour and only dropped by home to pick up my mail. Best wishes for a quick return to good health.

Sincerely,
Bob Hope

"The soldier above all others prays for peace, for it is the soldier who must suffer and bear the deepest wounds and scars of war."
—GENERAL DOUGLAS MacARTHUR

U.S. Naval Hospital
Philadelphia, PA
Dec 27

Dear Bob,
What's left of me wishes to say thanks for the greatest dose of medicine I have ever received.
   I have been following you religiously, via radio, all over the world, and it is a source of pride to be remembered by so swell a fellow.

It's swell to see your pals on top, and may you continue to be perched there always.

When last you saw me at the hospital here, I was only missing 2 legs. Now I have 6 fingers missing. In fact, I had 2 trips to the butcher shop in the past 6 weeks, but when a fellow knows that a person as busy as you are can remember, well, Bob, it still makes life worth living.

May I again say thanks a million, and hope that your star shall continue to ascend.

Your pal,
Si

Cranston 10, R. I.
June 6, 1944

Dear Bob,
I'm writing to you because my husband was one of the soldiers you brought a little of home to in Sicily. It was the only entertainment he had during his nine months of active service overseas and now he will never see any other. Yes, I mean that he was killed in action. He didn't die a hero. He never did anything spectacular. He just did his duty as best he could. His name will never go down in history as being great, and yet he was to me and I am very proud of him.

I received a letter from his Commanding Officer telling me what happened. It seems that night of March 17th they were on the front line at Anzio, waiting to be relieved. Pete, my husband, was out of his foxhole, checking on the men in his platoon, to see that they were ready to leave the minute the relieving unit arrived. Before he could get back to his foxhole, the Germans fired several rounds of artillery. One hit close to Pete and several pieces of shrapnel lodged in Pete's chest. I'm told that he died instantly . . .

Pete, or Staff Sergeant Melvin E. Petersen, was one of the finest men that ever lived, and he will always live in the minds and hearts of his friends and loved ones.

. . . My husband was like millions of others—he didn't want to leave home and go to war, but there was a job to do and he was never one to shirk, so he went cheerfully.

... I wrote to you because my husband wrote me of the show he saw with you and Miss Langford. You seem like a friend and you saw him since I did—I guess that's why I've told you all about it.

... Sincerely,
Mrs. Harriet M. Petersen

"In a lot of ways that was probably the last performance those guys ever saw. In that regard, that speaks volumes about the man."
—DENZEL WASHINGTON on Bob Hope, National Archives video

Jan. 8, 1945

Dear Bob,
It is 2100 [hours] and your program on Lux Theater just went off the air, so some of my buddies and I drew straws to have the privilege of thanking you for that show and a lot of other ones.

I am writing from the Officers' Quarters in the Percy Jones Convalescent Hospital. All the boys here are veterans and all have a scar or two to help them remember this period of history.

In your programs you [mention] a lot of the spots the boys had been ... I could see the boys settle back in their chairs and you could tell by their faces they could tell a lot of things about those particular places you had mentioned.

We are from every known theater of operations in the war today and a lot of the officers here have seen your show, and some have met you personally. Major Custer, a patient soon to return to active duty, met you in the South Pacific.

You had one of the best compliments you could be paid. One Lt. (Silver Star and three stars on his campaign ribbons) said, "He is a great guy that Hope." And he meant it. And we all mean it.

That program before Christmas of yours (and Crosby's) was great. We have learned to be pretty hard boiled, but there were unashamed tears in a lot of eyes as we remembered our boys who were spending Christmas in hospitals and fox holes.

We don't want praise and a lot of slaps on the back, but when we know of the regular guys appreciating us, it makes a fellow feel a little better when he thinks about bucking a world with one arm or a lung missing.

I have never seen you except in a show, as I was in France. And believe me, brother, after seven months in a hospital, a fellow needs a pat on the back.

Sincerely,
"A doughboy of the Purple Heart Club."
H. Johnnie Corless
Percy Jones Gen. Hospital
Battle Creek, Mich.

February 14, 1945
Lt. Johnnie Corless
Percy Jones General Hospital
Battle Creek, Michigan

Dear Johnnie:
I'm glad you and the boys enjoyed the Lux presentations of "I Never Left Home." I guess it brought back memories to a lot of you . . . I know I'll never forget the things I've seen and heard while visiting our camps overseas.

The "troupe" is still on the march . . . from camp to camp here in the States. Just returned from a tour in the East and am due to M.C. a short picture for the Canadian 8th War Loan Drive.

. . . I'll have to close now. Good luck to you members of the "Purple Heart Club."

My best,
Bob Hope

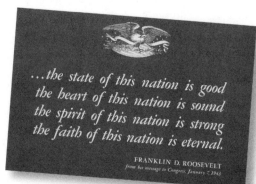

. . . the state of this nation is good
the heart of this nation is sound
the spirit of this nation is strong
the faith of this nation is eternal.

FRANKLIN D. ROOSEVELT
from his message to Congress, January 7, 1943

WWII poster citing from President Roosevelt's message to Congress, 1943.

Inscription on cross: "HERE LIES IN HONORED GLORY AN AMERICAN HERO KNOWN ONLY TO GOD."

54 Lamrock Ave
Bondi Beach, Sydney
(Australia)
Wed. 23-4-47

Dear Dr. Bob Hope,
Which is it now—Major, Dr. or just plain old Bob? I like Bob much
better, do you mind? I'm just bubbling over with news to tell you,
especially now that I'm out of the hospital.

You see, you were the first person to give me hope regarding a skin
graft on my leg, remember? . . . way back in Southport hospital during
the battle of Brisbane? Well, ever since, I've been . . . on the hunt for a
doctor to do the job, but with no luck at all. Some said it couldn't be
done, but I didn't give up hope. I remember you saying if I got to the
States, you could put me onto a good man. That was out of the ques-
tion, too, but in January this year I heard of this doctor [who] spent
5 years with the Army and still does most of his magnificent work at

Uralla Military Hospital building new faces, etc. He's a marvelous plastic surgeon. Needless to say, I lost no time . . . After seeing my leg, he said the last case he'd operated on before going into the army was the same as mine. Well, I really cried with joy when he said he'd do it. So after waiting a fortnight for a bed, off I went to Glouster House (Royal Prince Alfred) and spent 3 months.

. . . Thank God—it aches now, but at least I can feel it. . . . I certainly got my dream man in Dr. D. Officer Brown, and you too gave me the faith . . . everyone else thought I was mad for wanting it done, but I do wish you could see it. Well, Bob, all the best to those at home and hope to hear from you.

Your sincere pal,
Al

Dear Bob,
Just finished reading your book, I Never Left Home, and I'll assure [you], I enjoyed it very much. Seemed as if I was attending one of your shows. There were places where I would laugh, [and] places that I felt like crying.

. . . As for myself and lots of other boys, we have no father and mother to return to. And we've gotta make the best of everything. I saw your show in New Guinea. By my address you'll probably remember where I was at. That day was like some of the days you mentioned in your book—was raining cats and dogs. And while reading your book, you spoke of an Evac Hospital that I use to be a member of—the 56th E.H. That was the best darn unit I've been with. . . . I have read about their bad luck. If I understand it right, you were there when that happened, was you not?

. . . Bob, excuse this writing. I'm about half asleep.
. . . A regular fan of yours,

Nate Reedy

June 6, 1945
PFC Nate Reedy
43rd Field Hospital

Dear Nate:
  . . . Glad you liked my book. You're right, that 56th Evacuation
Hospital outfit is a grand bunch of fellows . . . I know a lot of
them personally. But I guess it's even tougher going out where
you are now . . . looked that way to me from the little I saw last
summer. Well, we're hoping this mess won't last too much longer.
In the meantime, best of luck to you.

Sincerely,
Bob Hope

"Never in the field of human conflict has so much been owed by so
many to so few."
—WINSTON CHURCHHILL

DEAR BOB . . .

WE WON'T BE HOME FOR CHRISTMAS

SHORTLY AFTER THE BOMBING OF PEARL HARBOR, THE SONG "WHITE CHRIST-mas" aired on the Bing Crosby radio show. The date was December 24, 1941—Christmas eve. Not knowing what was ahead for the thousands of soldiers who were enlisting and their families who were saying good-bye to them, the words of the song were especially meaningful. They spoke of the familiar at a time of drastic change, of simplicity at a time of worldwide confusion, and of peace at a time of devastating war.

Irving Berlin, a Russian-Jewish immigrant, wrote the song, not only as a trib-ute to the spirit of Christmas, but also quite possibly as a memorial to his only son who passed away at three weeks of age on Christmas 1928. Irving and his wife visited the child's grave every Christmas, no doubt with some Christmas wishes and dreams of their own.

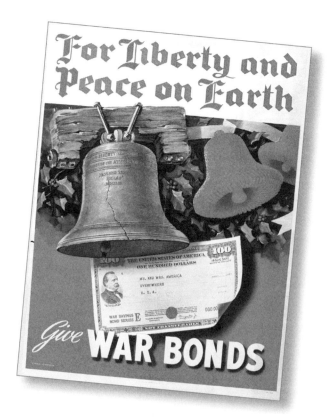

Christmas War Bonds poster,
artist Lyman Simpson.

Striking a chord with lonely soldiers all over the world, as well as their families back home, Irving Berlin's dreamy "White Christmas" quickly became the best-selling Christmas song of all time.

"I'm dreaming of a white Christmas with every Christmas card I write . . ."
V-mail, Christmas cards, love letters—the holidays propelled them all.

And nothing gave Bob Hope more pleasure than spending his holidays with the dedicated and exceptional men and women of the armed forces.

As soon as an official request for his help came in, often from the president himself, Bob would start planning his next military tour. He'd hand out the writing assignments to his writing staff, then he'd start making phone calls to celebrity friends to see who he'd be bringing along with him on these trips abroad. These were the top stars of the day, but they would drop what they were doing and would agree to go. Bob's wife, Dolores, would sometimes join him (maybe she figured that was the best way to ensure she could see Bob on Christmas). She also donated her time and skills to work with the American Women's Voluntary Services.

Dolores Hope, a devoted member of the American Women's Voluntary Services and head of the local Southern California chapter, gave freely of her time to help the war effort. This included helping Bob with bond sales, volunteering for canteen work, and even driving ambulances.

Imagine Bob Hope...

on TELEVISION

brought to you by **NBC**

Think how, on NBC Television, the amusing antics of America's greatest comedians . . . the tasty adventures of Bob Hope, for example . . . could take place before your eyes in hilarious visual action.

Just picture how television programs from the studios of the National Broadcasting Company . . . where the nation's most popular sound radio programs now originate . . . are going to up the excitement of home entertainment.

At the present time, NBC has extensive television plans under way. With the co-operation of business and government these plans, after the war, will bring about vast NBC Television networks . . . networks

gradually sprouting from Eastern, Mid-Western and Western centers and finally grouping together . . . forming coast-to-coast links to provide television for the whole nation's post-war enjoyment.

Popular-priced television receivers will bring to your home sight and sound programs up to the highest standards of NBC . . . television programs of the finest shows in this fascinating and improved field of entertainment.

Depend on NBC to lead in new branches of broadcasting by the same wide margin that now makes it "The Network Most People Listen to Most."

National Broadcasting Company
America's No. 1 Network

In Bob's spare time, he started wondering about this new idea called "television."

Bob Hope's Command Performance radio show was breaking records. Once television began to dominate the media scene, his televised military Christmas shows drew some of the highest ratings ever in television history. A record that he held for decades.

By the end of his career, Bob Hope had starred in nearly three hundred television specials, including forty-five Christmas specials, airing every holiday season beginning in 1950 and ending in 1995.

> **"I want to thank the thousands who wrote letters about my last show . . . and the three who mailed them. Seriously, I did get about 5,000 letters. The FBI is going over them now."**
> **. . . Bob Hope**

Bob had a longstanding tradition of closing his holiday shows with the cast and troops singing "Silent Night." The soldiers may have physically been in faraway lands, but their minds were at home with their families, holding their sweetheart in their arms, or kissing that new baby they hadn't even met yet.

It might have seemed ironic for the soldiers to be singing of a silent and peaceful night when so many of their nights were far from silent and offered very little peace. And yet, they sang. Show after show, these war-weary guys and gals joined Bob and his troupe in making one lasting memory together.

Whenever Bob Hope, their brother, their buddy, their dad, their pal was around, Christmas didn't seem quite so lonely.

March 23, 1945
"Germany"

Dear Bob,
I just received your Christmas card yesterday and really appreciated
it. It took exactly four months to the day to catch up to me.

You sent the card to my old outfit which I left June 17, 1944. I
landed in Normandy on D-Day and got pretty well shot up on the
17th. I got your letter while in the hospital in England . . .

Your card followed me through England, France, Belgium, Holland,
and finally caught up to me here in Germany. The envelope that it was
in was really beat up. It went through the battle of the hospitals and
replacement depots.

I guess I've bored you enough so I'll close this letter. . . . If there's any
type of souvenirs that you'd like to have from the Germans, I'll try and
get it. We're at the front and get first call on souvenirs.

So long. As ever,
Howie

Cpl. Howard Manoian 31285089
Co A 92nd Chem. Mortar Bn.

Dear "Howie":
Ever so often I spend a few days at home . . . have to do that or the
children forget what I look like and have to start all over again.
This time I ran into a stack of G.I. mail which included your letter.

Just got back from a tour East. It surely was great to be back
on California soil . . . when I stepped off the train, I kissed the
ground. . . . I never did find out who pushed me!

. . . I'm getting set to drop in on some of the boys over your
way, so maybe I'll be seeing you. Anyway, best of luck to you.

Sincerely,
Bob Hope

Christmas greetings from the Australian 450 Squadron.

Dec 29, 1944
Italy

Dear Bob:
I had a very pleasant surprise today when I came in from work. Your Christmas Greeting was received with the greatest joy. Thanks for the nice thought. I surely am sweating out this coming New Year.

[Nearly] the whole company followed me to my tent tonight. You would think they were hounding me because it is so near payday. But no! They knew I had mail from you, and nothing short of a Mark IV tank could have protected me from the mob.

Keep the letters coming, Bob, and soon I will be able to trade six of your autographs and two pictures for a picture of Sinatra. (You can pause for a second to say it stinks.)

Your M.C. on Command Performance for Christmas Day was tops. I am grateful to you for the laughs you can create to take my mind from thinking of home. I'm sure eleven million other G.I.s feel the same about it. Your Christmas Performance was on air from 6:30 until 8:45 p.m. I kept my ear to the radio, not daring to miss a line. You must have the time of your life with your programs.

Things are pretty quiet over on my side of the world. We expect something to pop soon though. So stay away from here. I remember my most exciting experience concerning you. I had been told to dig a fox hole, but being optimistic as any G.I., I flatly refused. Pretty soon someone mentioned about you being in the area. So I dug. As the story goes, I dug so deep the first Sgt. was pressing desertion charges against me. . . . I was in Africa at the time. I will soon have a year here in Italy.

Well, Bob, keep up the good work. Again, let me thank you for the hours of comfort your program has brought me.

Good luck and thank you for the memory.
Cpl. R. McClare

"I arrived at camp by airplane. And what a cheer went up when I stepped out of that plane.... I wonder if they would've cheered so hard if I had waited 'til the plane landed."
...Bob Hope

Christmas Eve, 1942
Cpl. Edward Erickson
Det. Med. Dept.
Army Airbase
Ardmore, Okla.

Dear Bob,
I'm never away from my wife, but I know that tonight she's listening to Command Performance the same as I am. It's a great country where we have men and women who take their own time to make our Christmas Eve away from our loved ones as you and the rest are doing. Please keep it up. It's cheered more than you'll ever guess.

As ever,
Cpl Edward Erickson

P.S. It's my first fan letter. Anyway, this is one fan letter you can claim. You won't have to send all those cards to yourself.

January 7, 1945

Dear Bob:
Have just returned to the States for some of that stuff called "Rehabilitation," but I have another name for it, believe me.
*   Shortly after your visit to Puerto Rico, I landed in a foreign hospital where you and your swell troupe had visited. Just my luck to be injured three weeks too late, however, while there, I received your gift of assorted toilet articles, and I take this means in offering you a belated word of thanks. Bob, you're 4.0, and your work and efforts to build up the morale of this guy's Navy is most commendable.*

I was at sea during the past holiday and upon return, again I was pleasantly surprised to receive your Xmas card (after it had followed me half way around the globe) . . . I ask for no better repayment out of this war than meeting a fellow like you. Not because you are Bob Hope, but because you are you. I sincerely wish the day is not too far distant when I can again shake the hand of a guy who, in my mind, is beyond being human.

. . . My sincerest regards to Vera, Francis, Jerry, and the rest of the swellest gang that is, including those behind the scene . . .

Most sincerely,
Jesse P. Thompson
Chief Warrant Bos'n, USNR

June 6, 1945
Jesse P. Thompson
Chief Warrant Bos'n, USNR

Dear Jesse:
Came across your letter the other night when I sat down to look over my G.I. Mail for the past few months. Sorry I haven't managed to answer you before this, but I've really been on the "go" all season . . . one tour after the other.
. . . Glad you received the package of toilet articles and the Christmas card okay. By this time, you should be on the move again . . . so, maybe this letter will also follow you around the globe. Anyway, here's wishing you the best of luck.

Sincerely,
Bob Hope

Desert Harrassers, checking in with "Dad."

Italy

December 25th, 1944

Dear Bob Hope:
I am one of the many, many soldiers overseas who was lucky enough to have been able to hear your special Christmas "Command Performance." It was really swell! I would like to be able to thank all of the stars for the swell job they did tonight! We all appreciated it because it brought us smiles and did a wonderful job of lightening our Christmas. Thanks a million, Bob Hope, Xaviar Cugot, Jerry Colonna, Dinah Shore, Jack Benny, Fred Allen, Jimmy Durante, Virginia O'Brien, Frances Langford, Ginny Simms, Kay Kyser, Dorothy Lamour, Johnny Mercer, Danny Kaye, W. C. Fields, Judy Garland, Spike Jones, Spencer Tracy. I hope that I didn't leave anybody out! It is a little late, but I would like to wish you all a Merry Christmas and a Happy New Year.

Pvt. Charley W. Dickler

Somewhere in Italy
December 25th

Dear Bob,
. . . Just two minutes ago we turned off the radio with the Christmas carols from your special Command Performance ringing in our ears and possibly a tear or two in our eyes. The two hours of fun that you and the rest of the swell group of artists cooked up brought us closer to home than anything we've heard in 2 ½ years overseas. All we want to say is thanks to you and to all the rest, pass the word along for us and best of luck in the New Year.

Captain John Callahan AC
Special Service Section
XXII Tactical Air Comd.

"I asked one of these cadets what he wanted for Christmas, but I couldn't afford it. You'd be surprised what a taxidermist charges to stuff a second Lieutenant."
. . . Bob Hope

From Sergeant E. G. Smith.

Cockspur Island Section Base
Savannah, Ga.
December 26, 1942

Dear Bob
When you finish reading this letter, you probably will not either remember me or my name, it has been quite some time since the last time I saw you. I believe it was in 1939, I used to work at Columbia Pictures and at NBC . . . I was in the sound department then, but the reason for this letter is just to tell you how it feels to be listening to your Command Performances that you put on the air.

About four months ago I was stationed in Trinidad British West Indies, and I can truthfully tell you that your audience was great. I recall that when the time came for your broadcasts, everyone that could get next to the radio would gather around and listen, and as usual you were terrific, and the show went over with a bang. The fellows who were on Watch were the most disappointed of the lot. I recall one in-

cident where one lad paid another lad two dollars to stand his watch just so he could listen to your program. How much your broadcast meant to us fellows down there, words cannot describe. . . . It helps pass the day, and makes a lot of us forget that we are not at home for the holidays, and makes us feel better.

Lieut. J. E. Schechter

(Left) The Third Marines dreaming of a White Christmas.

(Right) Christmas V-mail from the seabees.

" . . . Everywhere throughout the world, through this war that covers the world, there is a special spirit that has warmed our hearts since our earliest childhood. A spirit that brings us close to our homes, our families, our friends and neighbors, the Christmas spirit of peace on earth, good will toward men. It is an unquenchable spirit. During the past years of international gangsterism and brutal aggression in Europe and in Asia, our Christmas celebrations have been darkened with apprehension for the future. We have said 'Merry Christmas' and 'Happy New Year,' but we have known in our hearts that the clouds which have hung over our world have prevented us from saying it with full sincerity and conviction. . . . But on Christmas Eve this year, I can say to you that at last we may

look forward into the future with real substantial confidence that however great the cost, peace on earth and good will toward men can be and will be realized and ensured."
—PRESIDENT FRANKLIN DELANO ROOSEVELT from *Bob Hope's Christmas Eve at the Front*, 12-24-43

At Bob's military shows, as the first notes to "Silent Night" began, a solemn-ness would fall over the audience. The soldiers knew they would soon be leaving the staging area and walking back to their barracks, their foxholes, and for some, they would be carried back to their hospital beds. Bob's show and all its fun was over. It was time for reality to set back in. The jokes and romantic ballads would now have to live in their memories, letters to home, camp conversations, and radio archives.

But for this short while, every lonely and homesick soldier who was either at the show or listening to it over the airwaves knew Christmas had arrived.

Silent night, holy night
All is calm, all is bright,
Round yon virgin, Mother and Child,
Holy infant, so tender and mild,
Sleep in heavenly peace . . .
Sleep in heavenly peace.

"I would rather have peace in the world than be president."
—HARRY S. TRUMAN, 33rd president of the United States

And for some lucky soldiers, Christmas meant a long-awaited visit home.

A youngster, clutching his soldier father, gazes upward while the latter lifts his wife from the ground to wish her a "Merry Christmas." The serviceman is one of those fortunate enough to be able to get home for the holidays. December 1944. 208-AA-2F-20. National Archives Identifier: 535527.

DEAR BOB . . .

THANKS FOR BEING THERE

— — — — — — — — — — — — — — — — —

ON THE BASES, THE SHIPS, IN THE HOSPITALS, AND IN THE AIR, BOB HOPE WAS there for the soldiers. He ate with them, slept in their camps, and in some cases, even took cover from the same "incoming" as quickly as they did. Maybe even quicker.

He didn't only do it for one tour of duty either. He did it for decades. Five of them, to be exact. He would have kept on going, too, if it were up to him. But health and age ultimately brought an end to his military travels. As it was, his last tour of combat zones was in December 1990 (the show aired in 1991) when he was eighty-seven years old! (That's only twenty-five in Bob Hope years.) How many eighty-seven-year-olds do you know who would keep that kind of schedule, take that kind of risk, and meet the physical requirements for that kind of journey? While others his age and even younger were taking cruises down to Rio, or golfing, or playing board games in a retirement village, Bob Hope was flying halfway around the world to entertain our troops just one last time.

"The audiences are my best friends. You never tire of talking with your best friends."
. . . Bob Hope

Rain, snow, sleet, or heat, if the troops were there, so was Bob Hope.

He didn't have to go. Not for any of the wars. He could have mailed the fruitcakes and harmonicas (which he did) or celebrity photos (which he did). He could have called their mothers and fathers (he did that, too). He could have wished the troops a Merry Christmas over the airwaves and not sent out thousands of personal holiday greetings. He could have supported the troops from the comfort of his own home.

But that wasn't Bob Hope. Bob went above and beyond all of that, as these letters reveal. Nothing was going to deter him from showing up and doing whatever he could for the men and women in uniform that he had grown to love and respect.

Over his lifetime Bob Hope met and interacted with more soldiers than many four-star generals. From making sure the troops got the best seats at his shows to donating his time and money to their causes, Bob genuinely cared about this Greatest Generation. And every G.I. since. And the feeling was mutual.

December 21st, 1943

Hello Bob,
I sure hope you don't mind me calling you Bob 'cause all I've read about you makes me feel as if you're one of my best buddies.
*   What inspired this letter is what I read in Screen Guide and lots of other magazines about you and your trip to our boys over there. I'm really not the writing kind and I dislike writing big shots, but Bob in my book you're 4–0. In the Navy that's the best you can get, and you're the best in my mind. I'm back here in the States and still able to have fun, but soon I'm shipping out, and as long as I know you're still joking and there's guys like you trying to keep the boys happy, I'll gladly fight.*
*   This is just a letter I thought I should write, so I wrote it.*

Sincerely,
Harry T. Lichtenberger S 1/c
U.S. Navy

A sea of sailors and one Bob Hope.

Commander John S. Thach pins "Honorary Aircrewman" wings on Bob, March 1944. Associated Press photo from US Navy.

Nov. 23, 1944
U.S.S. Stevens
1st Div.
Postmaster
San Fran., Calif

Dear Mr. Hope,
I just don't [know] how to start this here letter. But here goes. When you was in New Guinea, you put on a show, which was a very, very good show. I remember when you asked for six men for a contest, you said the winner will get a prize. Well, I did the Hula Hula with Miss Patty Thomas, and I had my picture taken with Miss Thomas. I never did see the picture. I was wondering if you could help me out. Most of the sailors on this ship would like to see the picture.

Mr. Hope, you are a swell person. I really mean it. I am not saying this because I am banging ears, as they say in the Navy. We sailors on this ship say you are the best, well-liked comedian. I myself never seen anyone like you. You talk to guys like you knew them all your life and have pictures taken with them. As long [as] there are Americans like you, the sailors on this ship feel people like you are worth fighting for. Mr. Hope, I hope you don't think I am waving a flag when I say you are a swell person. All the sailors on this ship like you. If anyone said anything against you, and if we was to hear it, the guy would have to go to the dentist to get a set of false teeth.

The time right now is 11:20 so I better end this letter, and get some turkey. I hope you enjoy your Thanksgiving.

God bless you.

Sincerely yours,
James LaValley, Sea 1/c

June 6, 1945
James LaValley, S 1/c
USS Stevens C 4791 1st Div.
c/o Fleet Post Office
San Francisco, California

Dear James:
Really meant to send you a note a long time ago, but I've been on one tour after the other since last fall . . . and that doesn't leave much time for correspondence.

Stayed in Washington D.C. for a couple of days on this last tour. . . . there are a lot of very interesting buildings there . . . especially the Pentagon Building. I visited it one afternoon . . . and it really is a large place. While I was standing in one hall, a fellow walked up to me and said, "I've been looking for General Marshall's office for the last two hours!" I said, "So what? I've been looking for it for five hours!" He said, "I know, but I'm General Marshall!"

Under separate cover I'm mailing you a couple of pictures . . . maybe the one will be right. Anyway, I'm sure you'll enjoy the other. So-long for now . . . and good luck.

Sincerely,
Bob Hope

(Left) A WW2 student pass permitting a
private to be absent from his station at
Amarillo Air Field for stated purposes.

(Right) Bob Hope and Tony Romano,
March 1944, Caribbean.

Feb. 15, 1944
Mr. 'Bob' Hope:
Hollywood, CA

Dear Bob:
*... This letter is written to you with the thought that its message might
bring to you some measure of payment for the time, effort, and tireless
energy you are expending in personally contacting and carrying a little
laughter and mental sustenance to our glorious boys who are fighting our battles on far flung fields of this terrible World conflict. I have
always felt, after having had the pleasure of following you and your
friend, Bing, around one of the local golf courses, that you were both
'tops' and truly fine examples, and who, being in the public eye, were
worthy of the adoration of the present younger generation. This incident, which I wish to convey to you, brings out this fact more forcefully.*
*   At a recent Methodist Church meeting for ladies, at which my wife
was present, the topic for discussion was the ever-present manifestation
of God in daily walks. One of the ladies present, the wife of a retired
Minister, Mrs. F. B. Buchanan, rose and made the following statement:*
*   "As an example of this fact let me offer the following illustration:
When the average person hears the name of Bob Hope, his thoughts*

naturally turn to pleasure and laughter and frivolity. Just the same as the turning of the thought to music and lyrics at the mention of the name of Frances Langford. But in my case, when I think of Bob Hope or Frances Langford, I think of God, for in them I see just a little bit of God. I see God manifesting Himself through them to those poor boys on strange soil, helping to sustain them by building up their courage and morale, and conveying to them personally a message from those at home; keeping them in contact with their homeland. And in the maintenance of home ties, there will also remain those everlasting ties with God, which are so thoroughly essential today as never before. Frances has also doubly endeared herself to us all when, although ill, she refused to by-pass a performance, stating that those boys could risk their lives for us, so certainly she could afford to risk something to bring them a little happiness. Yes, truly this is God manifesting Himself."

My thought is, Bob . . . that you could add this to your "paycheck" of remuneration for a wonderful job, wonderfully done.

Sincerely,
C. B. Howze

. . . Tell Bing to keep up his good work also—creating the Army of the future so that you will have someone to entertain in later years.

"I was offering time and laughs—the men and women fighting the war were offering up their lives. They taught me what sacrifice was all about."
. . . Bob Hope, *Bob Hope, My Life in Jokes*

March 17, 1944
Army Air Forces Central Instructors School
Randolph Field, Texas
Basic Training Squadron 11
Office of the Squadron Commander

Dear Mr. Hope,
I am not a Major or Captain or a General. Just a plain Pvt.

I also am not very good at writing and I don't expect you will get this personally. But anyway, here goes. I have just got to thank you for all you have done for the members of the armed forces. I have followed your trip around the world in the papers and wish I could have been at every place you visited. Your sense of humor has done much to keep us entertained here at camp. I have seen every one of your pictures and want to say you have done more toward keeping our morale up than all the lectures and all the articles I have ever had the occasion to read. After the war is over I have two ambitions—first I want to meet you and shake your hand. Then I am going to buy a cabin near a lake and I am going to sleep one month and just get up to listen to your program and then go back to bed . . .

Respectfully yours,
Elias Tarr
46.B.F.T.S.
Randolph Field
Texas

"How do you do, ladies and gentlemen. This is Bob 'Command Performance' Hope telling all you soldiers, sailors and Marines that, although Johnny Doughboy found a rose in Ireland, what he really wants is that stinkweed in Berlin."
. . . Bob Hope, *Bob Hope, My Life in Jokes*

"The Philippine Islands"
April 13, 1945
THE BATS OUT'A HELL SQUADRON
499th Bomb Sq.
345th Bomb Gp.
APO 73

Dear Bob,
The fact that I am Public Relations man in this outfit has nothing to do with the fact that I am adding this letter to your mile high pile of praise.

Saw one of your Command Performance shorts last night, and it was the enjoyment that everyone in the unit derived from that short which made me decide to thank you personally for all the mirth you have spread over the fighting fronts all over the world. I saw your program back at APO 920. Benny came within 12,000 miles of us, you came right up to territory that was too hot for Benny, and gave the men a show that they still talk about. Of course, Langford and little Patty Thomas didn't detract a bit from the show, and Collonnnnnnna has his points, but it was Bob Hope they all turned out to see, and see you we did.

Your humor leaves a wake behind you which lasts a lot longer than the wake behind a ship. In addition to being Good Humor Man of every G.I. you've ever seen, you have the facility for winning friends wherever you go, and I believe that there is nothing you could ask a G.I. to do for you that you couldn't ask your best friend. My only gripe is that we don't have enough of you, in person, films or on the air.
THANKS A MILLION.

Sincerely,
Ed Hasif

Letter from a soldier to his parents . . .
Pfc. Robert Buckman
July 17, 1945
France

Dear Folks:
Another blistering day (98-degrees) with very little to do and almost too hot to do that.
. . . Things have become more civilized around here lately . . . The other night we really had a swell show—Bob Hope, Colonna, and five others in the best thing I've seen since we left the states. His (Hope's, of course) ad-libbing had the cast and audience both in convulsions. Talking about audience, there were at least ten thousand at the performance I saw and he gave four others in our camp. Two of us made lunches out of our boxes and went down at 5:00 with cokes and cards to wait for the performance, which by the way, wasn't till 7:30, and still were a hundred yards away from the stage. I understand that at

his last performance . . . some guys were down five hours early to get seats. The boys really love that Hope guy, and his contribution to their morale was terrific.

. . . Love, Robert

February 1945

Dear Mr. Hope,
I am merely a lonely Private in the United States Army, but I thought you might appreciate my writing and thanking you for something you did for me. I am only one of many millions that should thank you for what you are doing in this war. Your part is more important to us than any actual fighting you could possibly do.

I am an Infantry man and was in my fifth week of an Advanced Training cycle before I was admitted to the Station Hospital here at Camp Livingston. Through luck and an act of God, it was the Hospital instead of an undertaker's establishment.

I had the unfortunate experience of having a live hand-grenade explode about one foot from my face. The result was an injury to both eyes which required an operation, and a shattered ear drum. How I was spared any more serious injury, or possibly my own life, will always be a mystery to both me and all concerned.

There were a number of days during which I could neither see nor hear anything. Until one experiences blindness, either temporary or permanent, they have no idea how very uncomfortable it can be. It was quite impossible to read, with or without the bandages that happened to be on my eyes. I had nothing whatsoever to do except lie upon my back and think. As you probably know, the act of any seriousness of thought can readily lead to sadness and discontentment to a soldier. As long as we are busy, we have no time for being blue.

In our rooms here at the hospital, we have ear-phones connected to a radio-room, and through these I derived my only pleasure during my blindness. Most of the programs meant very little to me, because the best stations are not tuned in due to faulty reception.

I was extremely worried as to how I could go about arranging to hear your program the first Tuesday night of my stay here. Radios of our own are not allowed. The hospital radios are all turned off at nine o'clock each night, at which time we are supposed to go to sleep.

I was very lonely and blue on this particular Tuesday night, and I didn't care for the program being received on the headset on my bed

. . .

I was very surprised when 9 P.M. finally arrived and I heard the familiar theme song of your radio program very faintly. I took down the earphones and was pleased to discover that out of all the nights for the radio to continue playing after nine o'clock, it was on the night of your program.

I hadn't felt very much like laughter for quite some time, but before that short half-hour was over, I nearly shook the bed down. Even after the completion of the program, I continued laughing.

That's what I have to thank you for. It only took you and your co-workers to bring me out of the dumps, and it's hard to explain how very low I felt at the time. As long as you can do for the rest of the boys in service just what you did for me, you are to be praised highly. In my opinion, you and your show are the best morale-builders the soldiers have. And I believe my feelings are shared by most of the Armed Services. Next to letters from home, you bring me more enjoyment and happiness than anything else. I don't believe one can be unhappy when they are laughing heartily, and anyone who listens to your weekly program has no sense of humor at all if they aren't aching from laughter when you sign off.

I have never missed seeing one of your pictures, nor have I failed to read your two books. To me, they were all a scream. No one can make a joke seem as funny as you . . .

I only hope that you can understand my appreciation for making me feel like smiling and helping me to realize that there is still some joy in life, no matter what the circumstances may be.

. . . This letter comes to you a little late, but I had to wait until I had my bandages off and could see well enough to write to you.

You are doing a wonderful job in helping our morale, and I hope that sometime soon we may laugh with you in a peaceful world.

Thanking you again, I remain . . .

A favorite fan,
Pvt. O. M. Teate
Ward No. 9
Camp Livingston, LA

(Left) Bob Hope entertaining troops. England. Photo provided by Michael Pocock, MaritimeQuest, US Navy photo.

(Right) Bob's 1943 visit to army base in England.

"The most wonderful thing about England right now is Bob Hope ... He is tireless and funny, and full of responsibility, too, although he carries it lightly and gaily. There isn't a hospital ward that he hasn't dropped into and given a show; there isn't a small unit any-where that isn't either talking about his jokes or anticipating them. What a gift laughter is!"

—BURGESS MEREDITH, actor, summer of 1943

"Bob Hope, like Mark Twain, had a sense of humor that was uniquely American, and like Twain, we'll likely not see another like him."

—DICK VAN DYKE

(Left) "The White Cliffs of Dover," written by Walter Kent and Nat Burton, became a classic thanks to Vera Lynn's recording of it. The song spoke of a time when birds would return to the Dover area, instead of what had become an all-too-familiar sight—enemy planes.

(Right) Written by Ross Parker and Hughie Charles, and also recorded by Vera Lynn, was a reminder to all that England would survive no matter what.

September 8, 1944

Dear Mr. Hope:
You don't know me. I'm just another G.I. I'm one of the unfortunate GI's that has to be unfit for overseas duty.

I'm writing this letter on behalf of some of my very good friends that are overseas. These boys have written to me and told me of the splendid way that you and your troupe entertained them overseas. If you only knew how much you are doing for the war effort. You have always been our favorite comedy star, but now you are more to us than just a comedy star. You are an ideal American. You have brought to my friends overseas the things that they dream about. The things that to them were just memories, you took back to them and made them real once again.

You have a saying in show business, "The show must go on." Well, that saying is also used in the Armed Forces. Here is an incident that *happened to one of my buddies. You gave a show for some men on an island, I know not where. Among those men sat my friend. A kid of only 19. He was afraid of what was to come two days later when he was to board his ship and go into a combat area. He had intentions of missing that ship before he saw your show. This was the first time that he had ever been away from home. That kid was scared, Mr. Hope, as he was never scared before in his life . . .*

. . . I saw that boy when I went home on furlough not long ago. He had just gotten out of the hospital. He got on that ship, Mr. Hope, and he went into the combat area. He knocked out an enemy aircraft that day and he also saved the life of one of the men in his gun crew. When I asked him what he was thinking of during the battle, this is what he told me, "I was thinking of Bob Hope and Frances Langford, and the show that they put on for us before we shoved off." Those were his words, Mr. Hope. He was given the Purple Heart and the Presidential Citation for Bravery.

Here where I am stationed, we call civilians, "Feather Merchants." I use the same expression, but that expression only pertains to civilians in general. To you and your troupe, I have another expression, Mr. Hope. "Faith Givers."

. . . Thanks, Mr. Hope, Jerry Colona, Frances Langford, and the rest of your troupe. You are all soldiers in your own way, and I think that you are doing a lot more towards winning the war than are a lot of soldiers like me.

My friends and I could never find the words to express our feelings for the things that you have done to bring victory and peace. So in behalf of my friends and all the boys, I give you my humble, "Thanks and God bless you."

Sincerely,
GI Joe

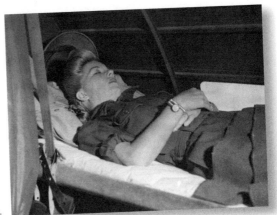

Frances Langford grabbing
a few winks between shows.

8 January 1945

Dear Bob,

*You've never heard of me, and have never seen me except as one in
a group, but I'm writing this nevertheless in hope that you yourself
may actually read it. I know all this stuff about how many letters you
people receive, and know you must be darned tired of it. However, this
is a fan letter, too. A fan letter not to gush over how magnificent you
were in some picture or how clever you sound on the radio; but to try
my best to express the very, very deep appreciation we fellows have
for your swell job. You were with us. You know how . . . lonely we can
get . . . starved for a couple of words from a guy who knows what the
latest is because he's just come from the old country. The fellows and I
saw you put on your shows—one in Tunis . . . and one at our outfit—
the 97th Bomb Group.*

*. . . When we left that show, Bob, we went back to our tents and
were fortunate that no two lived in the same tent. I sat down on my
sack and let 'em come—and I'm . . . not ashamed of it. Do you think
I was alone? I know at least 200 guys didn't get dust in their eyes at
once. It felt great, too, to be able to have a vent for the stored up feelings we had had for darned near two years.*

*. . . I don't want to make this too long and boresome, Bob, but I
could go on and on like this for fifteen pages. . . . sure, we like your
pictures, but the other you, too, hits us where it counts. And this isn't
entirely to you. Bob, this type of letter is the same really sincere letter
that almost any G.I. would write to Bing Crosby, Betty Hutton, Jack
Haley, Frances Langford, and a couple thousand others who get in
and bring the chins up off the belt buckles.*

*You, chances are, will never read this personally, Bob, and maybe
no one ever will; but it helps me to write it because I'm saying, for the
rest of the guys and myself . . . we appreciate it more than you can
think.*

*I'd like to close by saying something that isn't exactly the thing for
me to say, but well-wished—that is . . .*

*God bless you, Bob, and may you and your family gather in some
of the reward you deserve for your part.*

L. G. Pieplow

The Military Air Attache
Legation of the United States of America
Bern, Switzerland
20 Feb. 1945

H'allow, Bob:
. . . Last week I made a trip over to E-----land, and enjoyed dining
with Lt. Gen. Jimmy Doolittle, and 6 other beeg-star men, and during
our dinner considerable mention was made of the fine job Bing and
yourself are doing, which pleased me to no end.

Hoping this thing will soon be over enabling us to all get back home,
and enjoy our loved ones, friends, and world peace again . . .

Peter De Paolo
Lt. Col. A. C.
Commanding

"Well, that sort of squeezes the last program of the season out
of the old Pepsodent tube. I suppose we should come up with
something special to fit the occasion, but the memories of week
after week with our Armed Forces are a lot bigger than a few sec-
onds of parting words could describe. You know, when a mother
stands behind the steel gates at Grand Central Station and her
Army son waves goodbye from the train window, there isn't much
more that either could say. Off and on during the past months
we've pinned an orchid on the chests of many branches of service,
and you know how we feel about these men. We know them as the
finest fighting machine and the finest audience in the world. So
on this closing show, we'd just like to wave a temporary goodbye
and mumble a few words to the effect that if a few fellows, who'll
soon be closing an even bigger show in Berlin and Tokyo, have
gotten a few laughs out of these Tuesday Nights, we're completely
and utterly grateful. And what's more, we'll keep on dishing it out
as long as they can take it. Thanks. Good night."
   . . . Bob Hope, closing tribute to the American G.I. from his radio
show

And thanks to the Allied Forces, real hope for an end to the war was right around the corner.

> *Headquarters*
> *Services of Supply*
> *European Theater of Operations*
> *United States Army*
> *APO 887*
> *5 August 1943*
>
> *Dear Mr. Hope:*
> *On the eve of your departure from the European Theater of Operations I want to express to you how much your splendid contribution to the entertainment and morale of the U.S. Armed Forces here has been appreciated. I know how hard and concentrated has been the work that you and the talented people with you have done. You have not spared yourselves in carrying out your mission. As your reward you have the knowledge of the gratitude of every member of the U. S. Forces who has seen your performance.*
> *I add my personal thanks for a job well done.*
>
> *Sincerely yours,*
> *John C. H. Lee*
> *Major General, U.S. Army*
> *Commander*

Even Japan knew about America's secret weapon: Bob Hope.

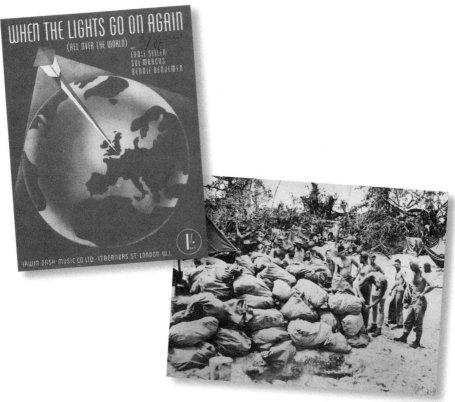

(Left) "When the Lights Go On Again" was a wartime favorite written by Bennie Benjamin, Sol Marcus, and Eddie Seiler. Vaughn Monroe was the first to record it, followed by others, including Vera Lynn. The song spoke of a day when the blackouts would be over and England could turn on their lights again without fear of enemy bombings. Publisher Campbell, Loft, and Porgie.

(Right) High Priority Shipment—Ranking in priority with shipments of food and ammunition, mail for Leathernecks on Peleliu arrives at a First Marine Division Bivouac area on the Palau Island, October 9, 1944. Marine Corps photograph.

> "I was there. I saw your sons and your husbands, your brothers and your sweethearts. I saw how they worked, played, fought, and lived. I saw some of them die. I saw more courage, more good humor in the face of discomfort, more love in an era of hate, and more devotion to duty than could exist under tyranny. . . . And then I came home to find people still living and thinking the way I lived and thought before I was given a look at the sacrifice."
> . . . Bob Hope, *I Never Left Home*

On June 6, 1944, previously scheduled radio programming was postponed for something of far greater importance. The announcer came on the air and introduced the president of the United States.

(Left) A rare break. During WWII Bob Hope would travel some 30,000 miles and perform approximately 150 shows for the troops, all while maintaining his film schedule and other personal appearances.

(Right) Written by James A. Nall, "Say a Prayer for the Boys Over There" summed up the feelings of those left behind.

As President Franklin D. Roosevelt read his announcement and called the nation to prayer, American troops, along with British and Canadian soldiers, were fighting the D-Day battle of Normandy. Before it was over, 2,500 soldiers would be killed and 8,500 wounded. The war was reaching a turning point.

"My Fellow Americans . . .

"Last night, when I spoke with you about the fall of Rome, I knew at that moment that troops of the United States and our Allies were crossing the Channel in another and greater operation. It has come to pass with success thus far. And so, in this poignant hour, I ask you to join with me in prayer:

"Almighty God: Our sons, pride of our nation, this day have set upon a mighty endeavor, a struggle to preserve our Republic, our religion, and our civilization, and to set free a suffering humanity. Lead them straight and true; give strength to their arms, stout- ness to their hearts, steadfastness in their faith. They will need Thy blessings. Their road will be long and hard for the enemy is strong.

He may hurl back our forces. Success may not come with rushing speed, but we shall return again and again; and we know that by Thy grace, and by the righteousness of our cause, our sons will triumph. They will be sore tried, by night and by day, without rest—until the victory is won. The darkness will be rent by noise and flame. Men's souls will be shaken with the violences of war. For these men are lately drawn from the ways of peace. They fight not for the lust of conquest. They fight to end conquest. They fight to liberate. They fight to let justice arise, and tolerance and goodwill among all Thy people. They yearn but for the end of battle, for their return to the haven of home. Some will never return. Embrace these, Father, and receive them, Thy heroic servants, into Thy kingdom.

"With Thy blessing, we shall prevail over the unholy forces of our enemy. Help us to conquer the apostles of greed and racial arrogances. Lead us to the saving of our country, and with our sister nations into a world unity that will spell a sure peace—a peace invulnerable to the schemings of unworthy men. And a peace that will let all men live in freedom, reaping the just rewards of their honest toil. Thy will be done, Almighty God. Amen."
—PRESIDENT FRANKLIN ROOSEVELT

Normandy, Omaha Beach, D-Day, American troops. US Coast Guard photograph.

After the president was finished, Bob Hope added some words about this largest amphibious invasion in history:

"Folks, this is Bob Hope, speaking from a P-38 Airfield, out here near Van Nuys, California . . . We looked forward to being with these men and doing our regular show here, but of course nobody feels like getting up and being funny on a night like this. But we did want to go through with our plans and visit these fellas because these are the same kind of boys that are flying those 11,000 planes in our big effort. What's happened in these last few hours, not one of us will ever forget. How could you forget? You sat up all night by the radio and heard the bulletins and the flashes, the voices coming across England, the commentators, the pilots returning from their greatest of all missions . . . newsboys yelling on the street, and it seemed that one world was ending and a new world beginning . . . that history was closing one book and opening a new one, and somehow we knew it had to be a better one. You sat there, and dawn began to sneak in, and you thought of the hundreds of thousands of kids you'd seen in the camps the past two or three years . . . the kids who'd scream and whistle when they'd hear a gag and a song. And now you could see them all again on 4,000 ships on the English Channel, tumbling out of thousands of planes over Normandy in the occupied coast, and countless landing barges crashing the Nazi gate and going out to do the job that's the job of all of us.

"The sun came up and you sat there looking at that huge black headline, that one great black word with the exclamation point, "Invasion!" The one word that the whole world has waited for, that all of us have worked for. We knew we'd wake up one morning and have to meet it face to face—the word in which America has invested everything these thirty long months. The efforts of millions of Americans building the planes and weapons, the men in the shipyards and the men who took the stuff across. Little kids buying war stamps and housewives straining bacon grease. Farmers working around the clock. Millions of young men sweating it out in camps and fighting the battles that paved the way for that headline this morning.

"And now the investment must pay for this generation and all generations to come. And folks, what a wonderful thing it is that no matter what the price, the reward will be greater than the sacrifice. We hope that thought can go along with a prayer tonight, the prayer of a whole nation. God bless those kids across the English Channel."

Then, Frances Langford sang *Ave Maria,* and in the hours that followed, Americans and all those who supported the Allied efforts held a collective breath. And prayed some more.

"I am a strong believer in Prayer. There are three ways that men get what they want; by planning, by working, and by Praying. Any great military operation takes careful planning, or thinking. Then you must have well-trained troops to carry it out: that's working. But between the plan and the operation there is always an unknown. That unknown spells defeat or victory, success or failure. It is the reaction of the actors to the ordeal when it actually comes. Some people call that getting the breaks; I call it God. God has His part, or margin in everything. That's where prayer comes in."
—GENERAL GEORGE PATTON

"The way to appreciate D-Day's importance is to contemplate what would have happened if it had failed."
—WORLD WAR II MUSEUM

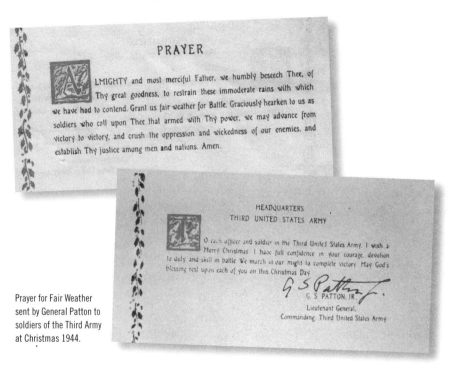

PRAYER

ALMIGHTY and most merciful Father, we humbly beseech Thee, of Thy great goodness, to restrain these immoderate rains with which we have had to contend. Grant us fair weather for Battle. Graciously hearken to us as soldiers who call upon Thee that armed with Thy power, we may advance from victory to victory, and crush the oppression and wickedness of our enemies, and establish Thy justice among men and nations. Amen.

HEADQUARTERS
THIRD UNITED STATES ARMY

To each officer and soldier in the Third United States Army, I wish a Merry Christmas. I have full confidence in your courage, devotion to duty and skill in battle. We march in our might to complete victory. May God's blessing rest upon each of you on this Christmas Day.

G. S. PATTON, JR.
Lieutenant General,
Commanding, Third United States Army

Prayer for Fair Weather sent by General Patton to soldiers of the Third Army at Christmas 1944.

DEAR BOB . . .

V-E DAY AT LAST!

— — — — — — — — — — — — — — — —

V-E DAY! PEOPLE RAN INTO THE STREETS CHEERING. AT LONG LAST IT WAS HERE.

In Bob Hope's birth country of England, as well as the United States where he grew up, and all around the world, there was great cause for celebration.

The Second World War wasn't over yet, but victory had finally been achieved in Europe. German forces had surrendered and Allied Forces were on their way to bringing about an end to the most widespread, deadliest, and costliest war in history.

> "Never give in. Never, never, never, never, in nothing—great or small, large or petty, never give in, except to convictions of honour and good sense. Never yield to force. Never yield to the apparently overwhelming might of the enemy."
> —WINSTON CHURCHILL

"On May 8, 1945 we were entertaining the servicemen and women at the U.S. Naval Training Center in Oceanside, California, when we got the news about the victory in Europe. What a celebration we had!"

. . . Bob Hope, *I Was There*

Jubilant American soldier hugs motherly English woman and victory smiles light the faces of happy servicemen and civilians at Piccadilly Circus, London, celebrating Germany's unconditional surrender. Pfc. Melvin Weiss, England, May 7, 1945. 111-SC-205398. National Archives Identifier: 531280.

"We asked our parents if we could go out and see for ourselves. I remember we were terrified of being recognized. . . . I remember lines of unknown people linking arms and walking down Whitehall, all of us just swept along on a tide of happiness and relief."
—PRINCESS ELIZABETH (future Queen of England), describing her memories of V-E Day in London

---

"My earliest childhood memory is hearing the blare of air raid sirens and running through the dark streets of London with my mother. Our destination was the local underground railroad tunnel used as a bomb shelter. It was a trip we were to make many times during those early war years. Since the trains didn't run at night, it wasn't unusual to sleep between the railroad tracks. On rare occasions, we were lucky enough to claim an empty cot.

"One night, the tunnel was hot and crowded and I had trouble sleeping. An elderly lady handed me a teddy bear and said, 'Go to sleep, child. God will take care of you.'

"Thinking God was the name of the little furry bear, I took him everywhere with me. God was my constant companion. He had soft brown fur and golden glass eyes. When I pressed his tummy, he let out a reassuring squeak that helped drown out the scary sound of overhead bombers.

"About this time, the Germans had invented a new kind of bomb called V-1. We called them buzz bombs because of the funny noise they made as they streaked across the sky. When a V-1 bomb ran out of fuel, it would stop buzzing and the silence that followed was the most frightening thing of all. For that meant it was falling to the ground. At such times, I would close my eyes and hold my breath, hoping it wouldn't fall on me. It wasn't until I heard an explosion somewhere in the distance that I could breathe again.

"One night, as we raced to the shelter beneath the flaming tails of buzzing bombs, I suddenly remembered I had forgotten my teddy bear. I insisted we go back to the house for God, but my mother said we had to keep going. When no amount of begging made her change her mind, I threw a full-blown temper tantrum right there on the sidewalk. It wasn't my proudest moment, but it worked. Against my mother's better judgment, she agreed to turn back.

"Just as we reached the house, a tremendous explosion shook the ground and lit up the end of the street. Had we not returned to the house for my teddy bear, we would have been in the direct path of a buzz bomb. My mother and I fell to our knees and wept. That elderly lady had been right. God really did take care of me.

"At five-years-old, war was the only life I had known, so when the announcement came that the Germans had surrendered and the war was over, I wasn't sure what it meant.

"Bonfires blazed, church bells rang and people literally danced in the street. For some of us, however, the end had come too late.

"My Royal Air Force father had been shot down and I'd lost my mother to an undetected bomb. I had become one of the thousands of war time orphans. While it seemed like the world was celebrating, I stoically watched the festivities with my new caretaker. Clutching my teddy bear in my arms, I wondered what would become of me."
—MARGARET BROWNLEY, author

"I have always been immensely proud of my grandmother, Valerie Glassborow, who worked at Bletchley Park during the Second World War. She and her twin sister, Mary, served with thousands of other young women as part of the great Allied effort to break enemy codes. They hardly ever talked about their wartime service, but we now know just how important the men and women of Bletchley Park were, as they tackled some of the hardest problems facing the country."
—KATE MIDDLETON, Duchess of Cambridge*

---

* From foreword to The GCHQ Book, Penguin, katemiddletonreview.com.

Bob Hope, Frances Langford, and Tony Romano, with actor Bruce Cabot, serving as a lieutenant in US Air Force. Paramount Pictures.

CEYLON

May 9, 1945

Dear Mr. Hope,
I very seldom am moved to write a letter to a radio or movie star, chiefly because I feel that they are bothered far too much anyhow. Today, however, I heard the VE Day Broadcast, which you did with Crosby. I want to express my thanks and the thanks of all of us here who enjoyed the program so much.

We were feeling rather left out of the celebrations, which we knew must be sweeping the states. Then one of the fellows happened to tune in the broadcast and that certainly changed everything in a hurry.

You and Crosby have always been sort of a personal link with the U.S.A. to me as I practically grew up listening to the two of you. Somehow you symbolize some of those wonderful evenings at home with the family. Today, then, you formed, in a wonderful way, that touch of home which we needed. When Bing began to sing "The Battle Hymn of the Republic," there were very few of us who did not have tears of emotion and who did not feel a thrill up and down our spines.

We are, after all, mostly civilians just waiting to change clothes for good and to have the worry, "Oh what shall I wear to the dance tonight?" Believe me, we appreciate the ways in which persons like yourself and Bing have gone out of your way that some of us may have a little extra enjoyment.

Thanks again for such a fitting and inspiring broadcast.
Cpl. Robert L. Croop

One envelope can sometimes say it all.

When the troops marched into Germany, they no doubt weren't prepared for what they found. They expected the usual atrocities of war—the rubble, the displaced people, the injuries and death. But what they encountered was no ordinary war carnage. Nothing could have equipped these soldiers for the barbaric scenes that were waiting for them. These men came face to face with the aftermath of an enemy whose actions were, and still are, beyond human comprehension. If there was ever any doubt that the Allied Forces in World War II were fighting to liberate the world from the aggressions of a maniac, the scenes they witnessed upon their arrival could leave no doubt.

"What hurts the victim most is not the cruelty of the oppressor, but the silence of the bystander."
—ELIE WIESEL, Holocaust survivor

A German girl is overcome as she walks past the exhumed bodies of some of the eight hundred slave workers murdered by SS guards near Namering, Germany, and laid here so that townspeople may view the work of their Nazi leaders. Corporal Edward Belfer. May 17, 1945. 111-SC-264895. National Archives Identifier: 531343.

"'Do you need any help, Little Sister?' I am lifted up, put on my feet, but I can no longer move forward my legs are shaking so. Two soldiers cross their arms and make a chair and carry me. Ambulances arrive in the village. The soldiers run. One offers to carry me, the other gives me some bread, the third one gives me his gloves. And their kindness makes me feel so good I feel like crying. The soldiers comfort me, calm me down. One of them takes out a dirty handkerchief and, like with a little girl, wipes away my tears. 'Don't cry, little sister, we won't allow anyone to harm you again.'"
—DIARY OF MACHA ROLNIKAS (14), Lithuania, *Children of the Holocaust*, Laurel Holliday

---

"The world must know what happened, and never forget."
—GENERAL EISENHOWER, 1945, upon seeing Nazi death camps

DEAR BOB . . .

V-J DAY . . . WAR'S END

THIS GREATEST GENERATION HAD A FEW MORE DETAILS TO WRAP UP BEFORE they could declare a full victory. Japan, the last holdout, had yet to surrender. The battles in the South Pacific were hard fought, and both sides suffered great casualties. But the tide was indeed turning in the Allies' favor. Bob Hope's message of hope to the troops was now one of "Hang on, the end is in sight." America and the rest of the Allied Forces were more than ready to finish this war once and for all.

On August 14, 1945, after the bombing of Hiroshima and Nagasaki, the Japanese made an unconditional surrender. In its wake, World War II had cost an estimated 50–70 million lives across the globe (some estimates count it at 70–85 million); the most widespread and deadliest war in history. One hundred million served in World War II, and that's not counting their loved ones back home who were serving in their own way.

The whole world had paid a heavy price.

American World War II generals. *Seated, left to right*: William H. Simpson, George S. Patton Jr., Carl Spaatz, Dwight D. Eisenhower, Omar Bradley, Courtney H. Hodges, and Leonard T. Gerow. *Standing, left to right*: Ralph F. Stearley, Hoyt S. Vandenberg, Walter Bedell Smith, Otto P. Weyland, and Richard E. Nugent. National Archives and Records Administration: 535983.

Allied soldiers celebrating V-J Day in Paris. US Army Photograph.

Now, the nightmare was over. At long last, the one word the world had been waiting for, five letters were finally dared to be printed in newsprint and shouted in the streets—*PEACE!*

As word spread, they ran into the streets by the thousands and celebrated in mass.

(Left) Celebration of the end of World War II in Times Square. Library of Congress, Prints and Photographs Division, NYWT&S Collection, LC-USZ62-119650.

(Right) New York City celebrating the surrender of Japan. They threw anything and kissed anybody in Times Square. National Archives and Records Administration: 520697.

Japanese foreign affairs minister Mamoru Shigemitsu signs the Japanese Instrument of Surrender on board the USS *Missouri* as General Richard K. Sutherland watches. September 2, 1945. US Navy photograph.

The surrender became official on the second day of September 1945 when papers were signed by Allied Forces and Japan aboard the USS *Missouri* in Tokyo Bay.

> "We have always held to the hope, the belief, the conviction that there is a better life, a better world, beyond the horizon."
> —FRANKLIN D. ROOSEVELT

> "I hate war as only a soldier who has lived it can, only as one who has seen its brutality, its futility, its stupidity."
> —GENERAL DWIGHT D. EISENHOWER

DEAR BOB...

GOING HOME

— — — — — — — — — — — — — — —

THE LONG-AWAITED PEACE TREATY WAS SIGNED BY ALL PARTIES AND NO ONE was happier to see an end to the war than Bob Hope. His "sons and daughters," friends and fans scattered all over the globe could finally go home.

No one knew how long peace would last, but for the time being at least, the days of foxholes and mail calls were over for the troops and for Bob. Life was returning to a new normal. They had changed, this Greatest Generation. The whole world had changed, for that matter. Everyone had been affected, some more than others, but no one was unscathed.

> "History teaches that war begins when governments believe the price of aggression is cheap."
> —PRESIDENT RONALD REAGAN

PEACE! Bob and G.I.s celebrate the end of the war. At last.

"On August 31, after some 30,000 miles, nearly 100 shows in 51 days, to an audience of 545,751 (American GIs and nurses, members of the Allied Forces, and Islanders, plus one enemy soldier) we headed for home. And what a homecoming it was. We were met with open arms by our loved ones. Coming home is the most welcomed part of going to war . . . just ask any GI."

. . . Bob Hope, describing the final summer of the war, *I Was There*

"Wars may be fought with weapons, but they are won by men."
—GENERAL GEORGE S. PATTON

The six-year nightmare was over. And the letters continued.

U.S.S. LST 492
Christmas Day—1945
At Sea—en route from Saipan to Pearl Harbor and HOME

Dear Bob:
To you, Bing Crosby, Jerry Colonna, Frances Langford, and a host of others of the motion picture and radio industries, I'd like to say "Thanks." Thanks for the fun, and cheer, and music you have sent our way. From Bizerte, Tunisia, to Nagoya, Japan, Command Performance and many other radio programs have brought to us overseas a touch of home, relaxation and fun, and perhaps most important of all, the vital knowledge that, besides our own families and friends, there were others who thought about us, too.

I hardly expect this note to come to your personal attention and I realize full well the impossibility of your answering all the correspondence that reaches you; I realize, too, that I am a very insignificant GI whose name is just a name and nothing more, but you see, you and Bing (he's old enough to have five boys yet I call him "Bing") and all the others seem like personal friends because I know your voices (and sometimes your jokes) and what you look like, and I don't suppose there's a man who doesn't feel as if you were talking to him personally at least once in a while. But in spite of all I know, I can't help voicing my appreciation for what you and people like you have

The famous British liner, *Queen Mary*, arrives in New York Harbor, June 20, 1945, with thousands of US troops from European battles. 80-GK-5645. National Archives Identifier: 521011.

done for us.

. . . I and a couple million guys like me are sincerely grateful for the kindness, support, and generous entertainment of which all of you have given so freely.

Most sincerely,
Alvin C. Yantiss

(Undated letter to Bob Hope)

Every Tuesday night at 9:00 p.m. the barracks are filled with laughing . . . because your voice is on the air. Loud shrieks fill the air—but I still leave the radio on!

Seriously, you mean more to us than being able to go thru the chow line <u>twice</u>. *Please regard this as a compliment, despite what you've heard about Uncle Sam Spam!*

My buddy in Germany mentioned seeing you and I'm sure if I had buddies practically any place in the world, they would have

*mentioned you. Yes, the atom bomb helped win the war—by blowing
things all apart. You did it by holding something together—the morale
of America's fighting men. It was a task that will always be remembered—a thankless one indeed.*

. . . Sincerely,
Joe Rogers

Bob Hope cherished these letters, and the thousands more he received during and after the end of World War II. The brave men and women, the Greatest
Generation, always held a special place in his heart. The scenes he witnessed
throughout the war, the soldiers he met and became friends with, the ones who
made it home and the ones who didn't, would last his lifetime.

Bob had fulfilled his mission to lift the morale of the troops, and to keep it
lifted throughout the duration of the war. He had not accepted this mission to
gain more notoriety. He was doing just fine in his career.

He accepted it because of what happened to him way back at March Field
in 1941, the day he realized that the men and women in uniform were *his* audience. A connection had taken place that day, and when the opportunity came
for him to do more, he accepted the assignment with everything he had in
him and purposed in his heart to stand by these men and women in uniform
no matter what.

Linz, Austria
26th Dec. 1945

Bob Hope & Bing Crosby:
*We are only two soldiers that are stationed in a Displaced Persons
camp over here in Austria and we alone want to thank the two of you
for the swell radio programs that you put on. We listened to the radio
all day and night on both the 24th and 25th of December and heard
both of you together and separate on programs, and liked all the programs very much. We also noticed that you two appeared on the radio
more times than any other Hollywood Star or Radio Star together, and
we want you to know just how much we appreciated it. I will say that
all the rest of the GI's liked your programs very much, even though
they may not be so bold as I to write about it. So we are going to write
to you and thank you for putting so much out to all the soldiers that
are stationed over in this country.*
This is my fourth Christmas spent in the Army and away from

home, and the second one for my soldier friend, so we will really say that your programs were appreciated. You two made this Christmas seem like home away from home. Bob Hope's swell jokes kept us laughing all the time and Bing Crosby and his swell songs made us realize that it was Christmas, and a peaceful one at that. So again, we want to thank you for helping us enjoy this Christmas and hope that we see you some time when we get home.

Lt. Robert E. Hughes
Pfc. Hugh Livingston
Co. "K" 330th Inf
APO 83 c/o Postmaster
New York, New York

February 19, 1946

Dear Bob and Hugh:
Glad to hear from you fellows and really very much pleased that you enjoyed the Christmas programs.

. . . We've been busy here. Bing has gone in for priest roles in his latest pictures . . . boy, he's a natural . . . and I've just finished one picture and am starting right in on another one. I did want to take a vacation, but the new Secretary of the Treasury wants to make a good impression and has asked me for a contribution.

. . . I'll have to close now because it's getting late and will be dark before I can get all my papers delivered. So long, and best of luck to you both.

Sincerely,
Bob Hope

"Bing Crosby doesn't pay a regular income tax. He just calls up the Secretary of the Treasury each year and asks: 'How much do you boys need?'"
. . . Bob Hope

Jan. 8, 1946

Bob, my Old Ship Mate:
First, I want to thank you for all the nice shows you put on over in the South Pacific. I went to one of your shows in Windy Island . . . and the theater was named after you, Bob Hope Theater . . . and Bob, I sure enjoy seeing your show. I just heard your radio program tonight and you said that you was in the poultry business. Well, Bob, you may think you lay bad eggs, but us boys think you lay golden eggs because we sure enjoyed every program you gave us boys over there. . . . If anyone tried to make us boys happy, it was you . . .

E. D. Breedlove
Twin Falls, Idaho

December 29, 1948

Dear Mr. Hope:
Approximately three and one half years ago, you and your troupe gave a performance for an army audience at Erlangen, Germany. Possibly your memory will be helped when I say that the place was—or rather, had been, a permanent German military base, and your stage was set up in the center of the drill grounds, with the buildings encompassing it.
. . . Jerry Colonna was with you, but Miss Langford was not; but we will skip any discussion regarding your wisdom or lack thereof in that choice. . . . your show was a huge success—as always, and you were called back time and again for encores.
. . . Inasmuch as I caught two of your shows overseas, the one mentioned above, and also one you gave at Maison Blanche near Algiers in 1943, I want to express my personal belated thanks; I feel safe in saying that you rate at the top of the list for all who saw and heard you . . .
May I wish you exactly what you deserve: continued success!

Very truly yours,
Robert H. Velta

April 26, 1947
Tokyo

Dear Friend Bob Hope,
Just finished reading your Coronet Condensation of "So This Is Peace."
    Being an ex-prisoner of war of 42 months with the Japanese, I
could replay with a much elaborated group of paragraphs. But all I
want to say (as I know you already understand) is that it was swell.
    An article like that makes guys like me realize that guys like you
have a lot more than just what comes out of the mouth.
    Even though a lot of so-called Americans can't appreciate the ar-
ticle, I know and want you to know that moms like mine are <u>grateful.</u>

Sincerely yours and (to use the expression of a buddy of yours) I <u>do</u>
mean sincerely,
Barney Grill

Bob didn't forget the G.I.s,
even in peacetime.

October 14, 1948

Denver, Colorado

Dear Bob Hope,
We hope this letter reaches you personally because it's a "Thank You."
Undoubtedly, the Colonel did thank you when you visited Fitzsimons
Hospital in Denver, but most of the Joes think that since you came to see
them, they want to tell you personally how swell they thought it was.
    It's a measure of the fellows' genuine liking for you that they knew
you would come to the hospital if you could find time out of the rigor-
ous schedule Denver's City Fathers dreamed up for you. One fellow in

Bob Hope, with golf club, visiting with the injured at a show.

my husband's ward wanted to hear you, but didn't because he thought he ought to give a dollar or so to the Community Chest, but he didn't have a dollar.

You gave my son your autograph when leaving the hospital and persuaded him not only to use Swan Soap, but to wash. It ought to improve his appearance.

You left behind you happiness and the conviction that "you are really a swell guy."

Great happiness to you and yours.
Vivian Gibson

Soldier's letter to his father:
24 Dec. 1949
Kodiak, Alaska

Hello, Dad:
Received your letter with razor blades today, they'll come in handy and thanks.

Our White X-mas is in the bag, about four inches on the deck. Yesterday we got the word that Bob Hope was coming up to visit the crew at Kodiak. Today he came and was swell. He had us rolling in the aisle and his coming here was greatly appreciated by all hands. He'll be at the AFB in Anchorage for the holiday. Sec'y of Air Symington got him to come . . . Bob didn't have much time to prepare the show, and what he did, adlibbing and all, was amazing. He introduced the Sec'y of Air, an AF General, and overlooked Admiral Wagner. The Admiral got on the stage and Hope said, "I'm sorry, but I didn't get your name." We all roared, and I thought old Wagner was going to place him on report. He said, "I'm Admiral F. D. Wagner," and Bob got down on his knees, took out his hankie and polished the old boy's shoes. We pretty near split our sides laughing. . . . Mrs. Hope sang some popular songs . . .

It sure makes a guy feel good when he's lost in a joint like this to have some big guy like that give up a Christmas at home to do some freezing for us. He said he'd mention us on his show Tuesday and I hope you hear it. We'll get his show in about 3 weeks, as we aren't in direct contact with the States and have to wait for the transcriptions.

Well, Dad, that's all that's now. Tomorrow is Xmas, a white one.

Bob

NOTE: Today was a bad day for him to come. Snow and 30 knot winds with temperatures around 15 degrees.

January 5, 1950

Dear Mr. Hope:
I received a letter this week from my brother in Alaska, telling of your visit to their camp at Christmas. He told me how much it meant to him and the other boys so far away from home. Here is his letter in part:

Dear Sis, you can never guess who visited us at Christmas? Bob Hope and his wife. It was the nicest Christmas present that Uncle Sam could have given us. They put on a great show, and we deeply appreciated every minute of it. Only wish more of the big names would pay us a visit. It would sure help us. (PFC Joseph White)

I am writing this letter to thank you and Mrs. Hope for giving up your holidays at home to brave 40 below zero weather in an Air Force outpost.

It must be terribly lonely for boys who have never been away from home before. I know that my brother was one of them. His praise of you and Mrs. Hope was high, and he couldn't say enough about it.

Perhaps this letter cannot repay you for your sacrifice, but I will let you know in part how the boys appreciated all that you did.

Sincerely yours,
Mrs. Lyndon Perry

Fifth Marine Division
Sasebo, Japan
19 Nov 45

Dear Mr. Hope,
. . . I am a Captain in the 5th Marine Division and haven't done a darn thing. But I've seen our 17–20 year old kids that have! It makes me sore to see them sold short! Maybe it's because you feel the same way that there isn't a guy, Army, Navy, or Marines, that will ever sell you *short. You may be a comedian . . . but Mister, you very often hit the nail on the head!*

. . . Thanks a lot for all you have done for us in the past four years, Sir. We appreciate it—believe me!

Respectfully–
Wm. H. Ingram
Captain, USMC

P.S. Have been "over" for over two years, and even "Pendleton" in California will look good to me.

February 19, 1946
Captain Wm. H. Ingram, USMC

Dear Captain,
This is rather late, but I still want to thank you for that letter you sent to me from Japan. A letter like that one surely makes a guy feel good. Sometimes you wonder if you've done the best you could; but when the "boys" say "Yes," well, I guess there's no more wondering to be done.

I'm taking it for granted that you have arrived back home. And I guess we'll all agree that there is no place like the good, old U.S.A. . . . and say a silent prayer for those boys who've kept it so.

Best of luck to you.

Sincerely,
Bob Hope

October 27, 1946

Dear Mr. Hope,
. . . There's no sense in my trying to give you a pat on the back because your back is probably sore from so many people patting it already, but I dare say that every resounding wallop across the shoulder blades in appreciation of your work was justly earned and deserved. Okay, that is enough soft soap. Now for the issue at hand. I read, sometime ago in our paper, the Youngstown Vindicator, that until you found a permanent vocalist for your show, you'd be using guests. Well, I want that job as vocalist. You came from Cleveland, Perry Como from Youngstown, so they say, so why not have a vocalist on your program from Columbiana, Ohio? Please don't say you know where Youngstown is, but not Columbiana. Columbiana is 17 miles from Youngstown, as my Ford rolls.

While I was overseas, your book "I Never Left Home" came out. My wife and several of her relatives enjoyed the book so much that they thought I should read it. So they spent a day and a (night) tearing the book apart, putting it in envelopes and mailing it to me, five pages to the envelope. That was all right, but when it got to me, it didn't come in order. I sweat it out for five weeks, until all the pages got to me and then put it together and read it. Almost a whole armored division read that book. So I think that any person that would go to all that trouble to read your book deserves at least a chance at that vocal spot on your show.

Please answer even if it's no soap.

Sincerely,
Robert Blake
Columbiana, Ohio

"I was so nervous, I said to the pilot, do you mind if I bite my nails? He said, 'No, go right ahead. Anything to make you stop biting mine.'"
 . . . Bob Hope

Springfield, Mass.
9 Jan. 1946

Dear Bob,
First of all, let me tell you to quit trying to steam the stamp off the envelope and pay attention to this letter—besides, you'll have to use your own glue, you know!!

Of course you don't remember me, but I distinctly said, "Hello, Warmer-than-me" on the sunny afternoon that you gave a show for the 1st division in Sicily. I was the 30,000th one on the left about two miles away. In fact, I was so far away from you and Frances Langford, and so near the Italian front, that I managed to send in three O.P. reports to G.H.Q. between rounds of applause. So much for the character with the inverted bathtub on his head.

As you can see by the lack of rank, serial number, etc., I have been demobilized. I've been examined, lectured, oriented, briefed, inspected, told off, paid off, and discharged. I guess I can wear a bathtub on the other end now!

. . . I felt compelled to write and thank you for your closing sentences about ex-G.I. Joe.

I think that you're helping to create the thing that we need most— appreciation. Now I don't mean sympathy (we need that as much as the Fiji Islanders need pogo sticks), or in a monetary sense either (that would be wasted and disappear as fast as my shirt in a crap game, too.)

All the ex-mudman wants is just a little common respect and decency, a small amount of time taken to help him, and maybe a priority or two to make up for the lost years. Not one of us expects a living given to him—all we hope for is just the <u>fair chance</u> to <u>make</u> that <u>living for ourselves!!</u>

Please keep up the good work, Bob, and drop that hint to the public once in a while that we shouldn't be filed under "Expendables— Case Closed!!"

A former dogface,
Paul B. Phinney

P.S. Please excuse the attempt at humor, but I'm in the poultry business, too. My latest is an egg on the end of a yo-yo string so it can be laid more than once. Think it'll sell!?!? P.B.P.

February 20, 1946
Mr. Paul B. Phinney
Springfield 8, Mass.

Dear Paul:
Thank you for your letter of last month. I'm always glad to hear that one more of those fellows who "sweat" it out in Sicily has been returned home! No place like it, is there! . . . I'm glad to hear you're back and here's wishing you the best of luck from now on.

Sincerely,
Bob Hope

"In Ike Stadium (Bremen, Germany) we did a show where 90 percent of the 8,000 combat men wore purple hearts."
. . . Bob Hope, recalling a 1945 post–V-E Day show, *World War II* magazine (September 1993 issue)

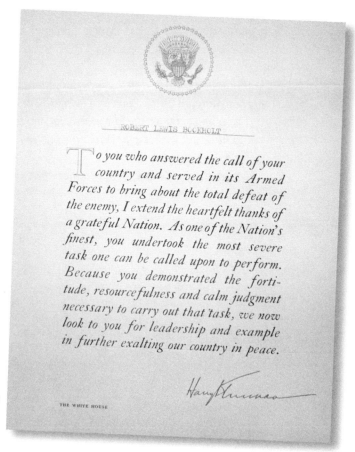

o you who answered the call of your country and served in its Armed Forces to bring about the total defeat of the enemy, I extend the heartfelt thanks of a grateful Nation. As one of the Nation's finest, you undertook the most severe task one can be called upon to perform. Because you demonstrated the fortitude, resourcefulness and calm judgment necessary to carry out that task, we now look to you for leadership and example in further exalting our country in peace.

ROBERT LEWIS BOCKHOLT

THE WHITE HOUSE

President Harry Truman expresses his heartfelt thanks to the GIs.

February 21, 1946
Cpl. A. J. Aquila
Birmingham Hospital
Van Nuys, California

Dear Corporal:
Just a short note to thank you for your kindness in sending me the package of Yanks gum some time ago. I'm surely enjoying it for I chew a lot of the stuff. In fact, Hope without gum would be like Crosby without a toupee!

I was glad to learn the boys enjoyed our show and hope it won't be too long before we can get out your way again. So long, and good luck!

Sincerely,
Bob Hope

10-9-47

Dear Mr. Hope,
. . . You have been a favorite of ours for several years on your Tuesday
shows, and I want you to know that you have been doing much for us
in what you might call "morale boosting." While my brother was in a
prison camp in Germany during the war, my mother and father were
two of your regular Tuesday evening listeners. My mother made the re-
mark one night after one of your programs that you must be a wonder-
ful person behind all your jokes and funny gags because you never for-
got to say something about the fellows, like my brother, who had given
so much and how much we had to make up to them when they came
home. Our family is one of the more fortunate ones, my brother and
my husband came back to us. It was you, Bob, who helped us through a
lot of trying evenings with your wit and humor and good advice.

. . . Sincerely,
Mrs. Maury J. Baum
Hot Springs, Ark.

"For decades, Bob Hope embodied the support Americans had for
our men and women in uniform. His countless shows around the
globe to entertain troops in wartime and peacetime were the mark
of one of our nation's great human treasures. Hope was not just his
name—it's what he gave those serving our country!"
—MIKE HUCKABEE, governor of Arkansas, 1996–2007

VETERANS ADMINISTRATION
Hospital
North Little Rock, Arkansas
April 29, 1949

Dear Mr. Hope:
The patients of this 2,095 bed Veterans Hospital have requested that I
write to you expressing their sincere appreciation for the program you
presented to them during your recent visit to this city.

*All the patients who heard and saw your show enjoyed it immense-
ly and their doctors inform me that your visit acted as a "tonic" on
many of the patients, leaving them much more alert and happy.*

*It may be of interest to you to know that the patient who came
up to the stage to play the piano for you had not spoken or laughed
during the three months prior to your visit, and that, as a result of
your program, he now laughs and talks and shows a marked general
improvement.*

*I realize that you were not aware that your audience at this hospi-
tal would be composed of neuropsychiatric patients; however, I can assure you that your program was of both therapeutic and recreational
value to all the patients who heard and saw you, and I am sure that
these mentally ill veterans enjoyed your program to the fullest extent.*

*I sincerely hope that someday your travels will again bring you into
this area and that you will come out and give a show to the hundreds
of our veteran patients who were unable to see you during your recent
visit to this station because of the space limitations of our theater.*

*I am sure that if you realize the great amount of good you did here
and also realize that few top national shows or movie celebrities come
to Little Rock, you will make every effort to revisit our hospital on
your next trip south.*

*Let me again thank you on behalf of the patients and staff of this
hospital for your excellent program and extend to you an invitation to
visit us again any time you are in this area.*

Sincerely,
H. W. Sterling, M. D.
Manager

3-28-46

Dear Bob,
*With loneliness in our hearts we sit down by our candle lit box to
write you this letter. At the present moment, we are sweating out a
treacherous williwaw (Aleutian storm to you).*

*We are on a small island east of Otter for no reason at all. We
are in the Air Corps, but the weather is so bad out here, the sea gulls
won't even fly—both of them walk every place they go. Perhaps you*

are wondering why we are writing you this letter, it is not to gripe or complain, but to thank you for many entertaining hours of your radio broadcasts.

. . . We are enclosing an article which one of our boys wrote that is very true and fitting to our case or situation. Our time will be up in Dec., then back to the good ol' U.S.A. and college for all of us.

Sincerely yours,
Pfc. John J. (name illegible), 1823367
Pfc. William F. (name illegible), 11139286
Pfc. James Hodges, 18242802
Pfc. Robert Kramer 19216114
11th Fighter Sq. APO 729
% P. M. Seattle, Wash.

Article enclosed:

REPORT FROM THE ALEUTIANS

(First name illegible) Spitzer arrived in the Aleutians Christmas 1942 in the midst of a williwaw, a cyclonic storm prevalent in the North, and spent his first night in a Quonset hut, whose floor was covered with snow. For a month it was not possible to move far from the huts without getting hopelessly lost, as the isolated snow-covered Quonset roofs were the only landmarks. Although the Islands have constantly become more livable, the lack of the vital features of normal society, plus the eternal bleakness and hostile weather, adds to the strong sense of frustration the men suffer from lack of combat. An understanding of this can help post-war adjustment for men who come home with no battle stars on their campaign ribbons.

Here is the young soldier's vivid writing:

We fight phantoms here.

Bayonet and rifle are useless.

Shells gather dew under tarpaulin hood.

Would you use a grenade

Against loneliness?

How large a cannon is necessary

To demolish monotony?

Where is the bombing plane

That can destroy a land already barren?

How many rifles, tanks, battleships

To conquer the people

Of these unpeopled lands?

How can we keep our memories from dying

When time and place murder them every day?

We fight no thundering battles,

Suffer no pity-inspiring wounds,

Are never found in the boisterous headlines

Or even the minor, modest print.

Only Unnatural Nature

To snip at our sanity.

Only the deceitful muck

Setting its traps for our feet.

Only the strangler fog

Creeping down the hills

To blind our eyes and minds,

Only the deliberate madness of the williwaw,

Shrieking, striking at each of us

With its million-pointed spears.

We whose rifles are ready, but never called

Have you forgotten us?

We only dig, build and mend

And wait;

We whose fate is not to attack,

But to hold, hold.

Say you remember us!

Say you remember the men

Who, fighting only phantoms,

Still fight for you.

Many times, after writing a column on veterans down on their luck or fighting the system, the first phone call I'd get in the morning at the paper was from Dolores Hope.

"Bob and I want to help," she'd say. "Just let us know whatever they need." Not once did the Hopes not come through for veterans in need.

My favorite Hope story is a dinner he had one night with his late publicist, Ward Grant. Hope was in his mid-80s by then, and the two men were deep in conversation when a young soldier who had just returned from serving in the first Persian Gulf War came over to their table in his dress uniform.

"I just wanted to thank you, Mr. Hope, for all you've done for our service-men and women over the years," he said. "I was wondering if you had any USO shows planned for our troops serving now?"

He hadn't, Hope said, but thank you for the compliment. The soldier shook his hand and walked back to his table. Hope called over the maître d' and told him he was picking up the soldier's check. Whatever he and his wife wanted.

Then, the comedian grew quiet, thinking. He got up and walked over to the soldier's table and asked the young man to follow him. They went to the pay phone in the lobby and Hope dialed a number he knew by heart.

The bedroom phone of the President of the United States, Ronald Reagan. "Hello, Ron, I hope I didn't wake you up," Hope said.

No, he was watching an old western on TV, Reagan told his pal. What's up?

"I've got a young soldier here who wants to know if I'm going to do any USO shows for our troops in the Gulf? What do you think, Ron?" Hope asked.

Well, it's pretty dangerous over there right now, the president said, but something could be worked out. Call him in the morning and he'd get the ball rolling.

"Thanks, Ron," Hope said, handing the phone to the young soldier to say hello and good night to the President of the United States—lying in bed watching an old western.

A month later, Bob Hope was on his way to entertain another generation of American troops fighting a war—just as he had entertained their fathers in Vietnam, and their grandfathers in WW II and Korea.

—Dennis McCarthy*

Norfolk, Virginia
February 26, 1948

Dear Bob,
You have probably received millions of letters such as this since the end of the war, however, I, too, desire to express my sincere thanks and appreciation for the wonderful service you and your most praisewor-thy troupe have so unselfishly given to us, the GIs and ex-GIs.

The fighting is over for most of us but for the thousands who are still fighting their battles from hospital beds and convalescent centers you and the troupe are still doing what medicine cannot do to speed their recovery.

---
* *Los Angeles Daily News*, June 28, 2018. Used with permission.

Into my heart as into the hearts of millions more like me, you, Jerry Colonna, Frances Langford, Vera Vague and Tony Romano have built a home fortified with gratitude and appreciation.

Please accept these <u>THANKS</u> for what you meant to me and my buddies one night in 1943 and for what you are now doing for those less fortunate than I.

Very sincerely yours,
Jimmy Hales

January 7, 1950

Dear Mr. Hope:
On the night of December 27, 1949 after you had returned from your Christmas trip to Alaska to entertain the Servicemen up there, you were relating incidents of the trip.

I was sitting relaxed, listening to what you were saying—enjoying the small Christmas tree and trimmings—the lights shining down on a picture of a nice boy of twenty who gave his life in the last war. He is my son.

Then, as you were speaking of Alaska, I thought of another boy, the son of a very dear friend, lost through an airplane accident up there.

As you were talking, I thought of all the kids who gave their young lives—the promise of the men to be—their tomorrow came and in a moment it was eternity.

For us, too, tomorrow comes and in a day is past.

Your closing remarks on that December 27th evening entered my consciousness, "some of the boys in the freezing cold in Alaska have to live in tar paper shacks and try to keep warm."

A chill gripped my soul. I pulled out my typewriter and wrote a letter to the President: "Can this be true? The money the United States spends . . . the boys in Alaska—who are there to protect us—have to freeze?" I said it just did not make sense.

I received an answer on January 3rd, 1950—a very nice letter.

They told me that last summer, the Joint Chiefs of Staff made an inspection of the Alaska area, and based on their report, legislation has been passed by the Congress which will go far to correct the conditions now existing.

I hope your words that night reached a lot of hearts—as many as your sharpshooting funny stuff—we love it. We still do not own a television—we appreciate its vast potential—but for me a radio in every room—a good movie—still carries more entertainment by far.

A very happy New Year and good luck to you.

Sincerely
Anne Kahle

Green Bay, Wisconsin
January 6, 1950

Dear Mr. Hope,
I want to thank you for your Christmas Eve visit to Alaska.

. . . When I read Christmas Eve of your visit there it took away the lonely ache. And I know all here were happier because of your sacrifice. This must have happened in other homes.

. . . Because of you, I knew what my son was doing Christmas Eve. A sort of a feeling [of] "God's in his heaven, All's right with the world."

Yours very truly,
Mrs. Clarence Bastin

R. C. Blancard Jr.
Larchmont, NY
May 15, 1946

Dear Bob,
This is just a line from one of the G. I.'s who saw you in Africa. At the time, I was with a Searchlight Battalion, sitting in a Staging area outside of Bizerte, waiting to go to Sicily when it was invaded. We were told that you and Frances Langford were putting on a show for the boys and, as a more than welcome relief . . . I went gleefully down to see your show. . . . You had been off the stage just a few minutes when that familiar dirge, the air raid siren, began to scream its nightly

tune. Believe me, I have never witnessed nor taken part in a madder scramble than that one, to get the blazes out of there.

Later on, I recall, our lights were set up outside of Bizerte, instead of going to Sicily, and we covered a good part of that invasion. Shortly after getting in position, we had a rather large-sized visit from our friend . . . and his bombers. It is with a lot of pride that I can say our outfit stopped him from reaching his target that night. [They] were after the harbor that time. It seems that there were three or four aircraft carriers in the harbors . . . That was in July and August of '43. If I remember correctly, you and the lovely Miss Langford spent a few minutes in a culvert the night of your show.

. . . Later on we went to Foggia, Italy. After being there a while, we were suddenly changed into combat engineers and put up by the front lines. We used to listen to you on the radio every time we had a chance and, naturally enough, I have listened to your program a heck of a lot since I came home. I notice that you are still in there pitching for the G.I. boys and those of us who were over there . . . Seeing your show took me completely away from all that stuff that was going on there. For that brief time, I was back in the good old U.S.A. Of course, right after you were gone, I was violently reminded as to my whereabouts.

I just want to say, "Thanks for the Memory." It is a darned nice one. And thanks for staying in there and giving a hunk of hope (and that's not a pun) to those fellows who are still on the "Purple Heart List" in the hospitals all over this country of ours. I haven't forgotten how close I came to being one of those boys . . .

Sincerely,
Rudy Blancard

June 11, 1946
R. C. Blancard
Larchmont, New York

Dear Rudy:
. . . Instead of your thanking me for what I've been able to do in entertaining the G.I.'s . . . I want to say "Thanks for the Memory" of all that you boys have meant to these United States . . . our

continued freedom and happiness. Let's hope that we can keep this a "living" memory that will not be forgotten . . .

Sincerely,
Bob Hope

1-1-46

Dear Mr. Hope,
I've got a lot to thank you for, but you don't even know why. This is sort of a long story for a fan letter. Don't know if I have the date right, but that doesn't matter to me. Saw you in late June or maybe even early July of 1943, when you put on a show for us at the Army Air Base in Boving-ton, England. We finished our operational training there, and started our raids shortly afterward. I lasted a short time cause we were shot down on Aug. 24, 1943. Was taken prisoner and found out that I wasn't the only one who thought you were a right guy. Two and a half months in a German Hosp. and the boys there often talked of you. Then, in Pris-on Camp at Krems, Austria, an old joke of yours you used in England seemed to be a standby with us. It wasn't easy, but we used you as a joke, too. "Wonder who will get here first? The Russian Army, The U. S. Army, or Bob Hope?" Thanks for all you've done for us and especially me.

Yours,
Johnny
Ex. T/Sgt. John F. Astyk
U.S. 8th A. A. F.

P. S. Excuse me, but I never wrote a fan letter before.

July 13, 1947
Pittsburgh 21, Penna.

Hi, Bob:
This letter comes under the heading of things long postponed by an ex-GI and it will also serve to explain the enclosed souvenir for your wartime keepsake department.

On that warm evening in August of 1943, while I was watching you and the rest of the crew put on your smooth show at Maison Blanche airdrome outside of Algiers, I made up my mind to join the fan-letter panic someday to extend congratulations on truly wonderful work—before, during, and since the war.

. . . I traveled a short distance from a small field the other side of Algiers along with my mates from the Air Corps' greatest fighter squadron—the 345th of the 350th Fighter Group. I worked intelligence and hence was in position to glom onto the captain's binoculars for the evening—so that the mob could use them on Frances from the 17th row! Swell girl that she seems to be, I hope she didn't mind.

Those were uncertain and secretly lonesome days, as we all remember.

The enclosed pages are part of the original file of a bulletin board daily we published for the outfit through the two-and-a-half years we spent overseas as a unit. We're trying to swing a printed history for the squadron later on and I found the enclosed in the stuff we have for research. Sorry I couldn't find the day-after story, but be assured the boys liked the show plenty. . . . Note in the issue of August 25 your show rated "play" right up alongside the Soviet smash through the Ukraine!

That's all, except to say that I've listened in while you gave the weight of your world-wide popularity to so many good causes—for the GI's included. Not many people in life are able to get the true belly laughs and the down-deep heart tugs all on the same program—and to do it as effectively as you.

For myself—and a lot of the Army gang who never got around to letters—I hope you'll never forget that what you've done, especially during the war, is of the stuff that goes on forever.

Truly yours,
Edward McCann

Enclosed excerpt from soldiers' bulletin board daily, published by Edward's outfit:

SUNTANS COMPULSORY TONIGHT—Suntans must be worn by G.I.s attending the Bob Hope-Frances Langford show tonight at Maison Blanche, Lt. Richardson, Squadron Executive Officer, announced this afternoon.

March 7, 1948
Mr. Bob Hope
Hollywood, California

Dear Sir:
A long time ago I made up my mind to write this letter, but we all have bad habits and one of mine is putting such things off. It is not intended to be a "Fan Letter," even though I suppose I am an avid fan of yours, but is more intended as a "Thank You." I have always felt that roses should be given to people while they could still smell them rather than sending them to funerals, so here goes.

During the recent war, it is well known that you made a number of trips into various theaters of action to entertain combat troops, and those ex-combat troops relegated to hospitals. During one of these trips, you and your troupe entertained the patients of a certain hospital en masse, and then, taking time from what few minutes you had to attend to personal matters, you visited many bedridden men in wards who were unable to be moved to where the original performance took place. I was one of those patients.

I am not griping or complaining, rather, I am explaining when I tell you that on the morning of the day that I saw you I had been told that I could take my choice of two things: keeping what legs I had left with the probability of never walking again, or having them amputated with the possibility of walking with artificial limbs. I'll not lie . . . I was plenty scared . . . down in the dumps . . . a young kid with what appeared to be a pretty dismal future. Understand you, I was NOT feeling sorry for myself, but I'd definitely be lying if I told you that I wasn't giving it plenty of thought.

Mr. Hope, you'll probably never remember this, but as you walked down the ward saying a few words to first one man and then another, you gave each man a new chance to regain himself by the cardinal dosage, i.e. laughter cures all ills. The thing I refer to as your not remembering is what you said when you looked at me. With your permission, I will quote your exact words as you walked up beside my sack, glancing at my legs before you spoke: "I BET YOU'RE GLAD YOU DIDN'T HAVE TO COME DOWN AND HEAR US TODAY." Didn't have *to? . . . I couldn't have moved six inches if my life depended on it! Allow me to tell you, sir, that could you possibly recall, I made no answer to the statement in quotes above, but that I broke into almost hysterical laughter. Imagine, had you said what I expected* to hear, i.e. that old soap about how are you, old man, and is there anything we can do, etc., I'd have probably been cussing yet.

That, Sir, is why I am writing this letter. I know of no other man whom I have ever encountered who could have so well lifted a lowered man's spirits than you did that day. To go further, when I commenced to laugh, you said, and again I quote, "THAT'S A BETTER LAUGH THAN I GOT DURING THAT ENTIRE THREE HOUR SHOW AND I HAVEN'T SAID ANYTHING YET!" You stayed within range of my hearing about 20 minutes that day, and if I live to be a million, I will always treasure it as the outstanding day of my life.

Mark you well, Sir, I do not write this as idle praise or in any sense of flattery, neither do I have any requests or axe to grind. This comes from the bottom of my heart in the most sincere manner I can possibly express, THANK YOU.

Yours sincerely,
Jack A Simmons
Sheriff's Department
Palm Beach County Court House
West Palm Beach, Florida

U.S.S. Barnstable (APA-93) C & R Division
c/o FPO
San Francisco, Calif
Dec. 20, 1945

Dear Bob,
I'm not sure that this letter will ever reach you, or if it does, that you will have time to read it. Nevertheless, I wanted to make some effort, even though small, to tell you how much myself and millions of other G.I.s think of what you have done for us.

I have been all over the world since entering the Navy, and from the frozen North Atlantic to the hell that is known as the South Pacific, I have never encountered a soldier, sailor, or Marine, that didn't admire and praise you.

I've heard records of your broadcasts in Africa and the Philippines, and was never closer to home in spirit than when I could hear your voice.

South Pacific USO Show.

    I know, too, of all the time you have spent doing benefit shows and the thousands of miles you spent touring camps and far flung bases.
    . . . this comes from the bottom of my heart, "Thanks for all the pleasure you have given me."

Sincerely,
"Butch"

May 26, 1946

Dear Bob:
The local papers announce that you will go on the green to raise a bit of 'green' in Houston on June 14th for the Service Men's Rehabilitation Fund. I am sure you will dig up a lot of green stuff.
    . . . I received Bing's photo Saturday so that you two inimitables now repose side by side upon the family piano. It may become necessary to separate the two of you before retiring at night because I wouldn't be surprised to be awakened in the wee hours any time with a lot of shenanigans going on.
    I'm sure our service men and women will testify that when the going was rough and their spirits lagged, they were rejuvenated by HOPE!

Sincerely yours,
W. A. Moore

New Sharon, Iowa
January 13, 1950

Dear Mr. Hope:
I want to write to you to let you know how much we appreciated you going to Alaska to entertain the service people up there and making their Christmas happier.

It was very generous of you and Mrs. Hope and your two sons to give up your "Home Christmas" to serve others. I pray that you will receive a blessing for it.

We have a son at Anchorage, Lt. C. L. Harper, one of the GCA boys you mentioned in your wonderful report upon your return to stateside.

He had written us about your plane coming in to Elmendorf on a zero visibility GCA, and it pleased him a lot that you praised the boys for work well done.

. . . We enjoy your radio programs very much and hope you will be able to continue them for many years to come.

Thanks again for taking Christmas cheer to our son and wife and the many other service people who are so far away from home and loved ones at Christmas time.

Sincerely,
Mrs. Cecil Harper

Reserve Officers Association of the United States
National Headquarters
2517 Connecticut Avenue, N. W.
Washington 8, D. C.
February 23, 1949

Dear Mr. Hope:
On behalf of the members of this Association I want to thank you for your participation in the program "A Salute to the Reserves" on Saturday, 19 February 1949.

This was not only a wonderful show, but it was also a splendid contribution to national security.

The individual citizens of this country, as a whole, do give all their efforts in case of war to help the war effort. Unfortunately, in peace time, the average citizen is inclined to forget that each citizen has his part to play in providing national security for the country.

Your program vividly brought to the attention of the public the part each individual must assume if national security is to be provided.

I want to again tell you how grateful we are for what you did.

Yours very truly,
E. A. Evans
Brigadier General, ORC
Executive Director

Tokyo, Japan
1/26/47

Dear Mr. Hope,
We are four of the thousands of GIs now fighting to keep the peace which was so gallantly won by our older brothers. Four of the boys who have now been forgotten by their fellow Americans.

Today we got hold of a December copy of a magazine in which we read your article, "So this is Peace," an article written by a man who has been fighting without a uniform ever since the bombing of Pearl Harbor. A man who has never raised a gun to kill his enemy, but has raised the morale of thousands of American soldiers 100 fold. Something far more important than firing a rifle. We have always admired you for this, Mr. Hope, and when the war was over we thought your job, a job well done, was over. But you have shown us and thousands of other Americans that you are a man who does not give up when the fighting is finished, but will go right on fighting until a <u>perfect</u> peace is won. . . . You are a good American.

Sincerely yours,
Pfc. William Christensen
PFC Joseph R. Cinelli
PFC Pete Christofferson
PFC Gianville Hardiss Jr.

Bob Hope wasn't a military medic, and yet, according to the hundreds of thousands of letters he received during World War II, his words were indeed healing. He wasn't a battlefield surgeon, but his humor was able to cut through a soldier's lonely heart and remove any blockage of hopelessness and despair. He was no psychologist licensed to treat PTSD, back before it even had a name. Still, he lifted the spirits of so many war-weary and wounded soldiers from the many battles taking place all across the globe.

Bob didn't wear a uniform. He wasn't a private or an officer. He didn't have the authority to shout out commands, or the power to issue a weekend pass. What he did hand out were endless respites of laughter and mental furloughs for soldiers who desperately needed them. And, as they say, his timing was perfect. His shows and hospital visits, letters, and phone calls home were perfectly timed medicine. No, this "soldier in greasepaint" didn't fight alongside the troops, but many soldiers felt he stood even closer than that.

There's a reason Congress named Bob Hope the first Honorary Veteran, approved by President Bill Clinton on October 30, 1997. Bob Hope had gone above and beyond any call of duty. "G.I. Bob" may not have laid down his life on the battlefield, but he lived every bit of it, from March Field until his death in 2003, giving back whatever he could to those who were giving all that they had.

PUBLIC LAW 105–67 105TH CONGRESS

Joint Resolution To confer status as an honorary veteran of the United States Armed Forces on Leslie Townes (Bob) Hope.

Whereas the United States has never before conferred status as an honorary veteran of the United States Armed Forces on an individual, and such status is and should remain an extraordinary honor not lightly conferred nor frequently granted;

Whereas the lifetime of accomplishments and service of Leslie Townes (Bob) Hope on behalf of United States military servicemembers fully justifies the conferring of such status;

Whereas Leslie Townes (Bob) Hope is himself not a veteran, having attempted to enlist in the Armed Forces to serve his country during World War II, but being informed that the greatest service he could provide the Nation was as a civilian entertainer for the troops;

Whereas during World War II, the Korean Conflict, the Vietnam War, and the Persian Gulf War and throughout the Cold War, Bob Hope traveled to visit and entertain millions of United States servicemembers in numerous countries, on ships at sea, and in combat zones ashore;

Whereas Bob Hope has been awarded the Congressional Gold Medal, the Presidential Medal of Freedom, the Distinguished Service Medal of each of the branches of the Armed Forces, and more than 100 citations and awards from national veterans service organizations and civic and humanitarian organizations; and

Whereas Bob Hope has given unselfishly of his time for over a half century to be with United States servicemembers on foreign shores, working tirelessly to bring a spirit of humor and cheer to millions of servicemembers during their loneliest moments, and thereby extending for the American people a touch of home away from home:

Now, therefore, be it Resolved by the Senate and House of Representatives of the United States of America in Congress assembled, That Congress—(1) extends its gratitude, on behalf of the American people, to Leslie Townes (Bob) Hope for his lifetime of accomplishments and service on behalf of United States military servicemembers; and (2) confers upon Leslie Townes (Bob) Hope the status of an honorary veteran of the United States Armed Forces.

Approved October 30, 1997.

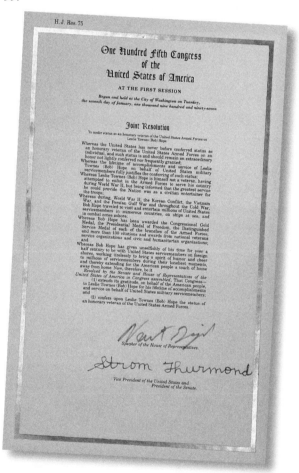

Congressional Resolution—Honorary Veteran of the United States. Never before conferred on an individual. Approved 10.30.1997. Document was approved by President Bill Clinton (William J. Clinton).

(Top) 1951—President Truman presents Bob Hope with a "Citation of Thanks" signed by an estimated 100,000 G.I.s.

(Bottom) Bob Hope and President Harry S. Truman.

"How wonderful it is that nobody need wait a single moment before starting to improve the world."
—ANNE FRANK, Holocaust victim

"I've performed for eleven presidents ... and entertained six."
... Bob Hope

(Top) Bob Hope and troupe with General George Patton.

(Bottom) Bob Hope with General Eisenhower. Bob is wearing the Medal of Merit presented to him by General Dwight Eisenhower, Chief of Staff, Pentagon in 1946 for his wartime contributions to morale on all fronts of the war. Inscription sent: "To Bob Hope with appreciation of his great work in World War II—warm regards, Dwight D. Eisenhower."

Bob Hope was friends with generals, presidents, and the everyday soldier. Winston Churchill, Jimmy Doolittle, Dwight Eisenhower, George Patton, Harry Truman, Franklin D. Roosevelt were all just a phone call—or letter—away.

He golfed with presidents, lent them jokes, and was invited to the White House so many times he referred to it as his favorite bed and breakfast.

"I love to go to Washington. If only to be near my money."
. . . Bob Hope

Bob's five decades of entertaining our troops ended with his final televised military show in 1991. There were times he was ducking the same artillery and mortar shells that the soldiers were ducking, and all he had for protection was a golf club and a sneer.

"Beginning in May 1941, and continuing for nearly fifty years, Bob Hope brought his variety show to military camps and war zones across the globe to entertain the troops and provide them a brief escape from the trials of the battlefield. Flying millions of miles, he headlined 57 USO tours from World War II, Korea, Vietnam, Desert Storm, and installations around the world, most often over Christmas."

—BOB WORK, deputy secretary of defense, Pentagon, September 28, 2016

"I can't believe it's been fifty years of playing military bases. I can close my eyes and see my life go by—on chipped beef and toast."
. . . Bob Hope

Bob Hope saw more than enough war for any human being, but he was no fan of war. He was simply unashamedly steadfast in his support of those who were willing to put their lives on the line for our freedom and peace. And that support never waned.

Yet as hard as he pushed himself, as much as he gave, he was still only human.

The Guinness Book of World Records lists Bob Hope as the "most honored and publicly praised entertainer in the history of the human race." He holds the record as the entertainer with the longest-running television contract—sixty-one years with NBC, as well as hosting the Academy Awards more than any other host (nineteen times).

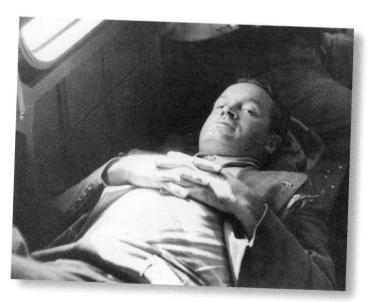

Bob Hope catching a few winks between shows, 1944.

He was given the Medal of Merit by President Dwight Eisenhower, the Presidential Medal of Freedom by President Lyndon Johnson, the Congressional Medal of Honor by President John Kennedy, the Foundation Freedom Award by President Ronald Reagan, the National Medal of Arts by President Bill Clinton, and was named the First Honorary Veteran of the United States Armed Forces by an act of Congress in 1997. Other presidents have also recognized his amazing service.

The US Navy named a ship in his honor, the USN *Bob Hope*, and the US Air Force has *The Spirit of Bob Hope*, a C-17 Globemaster III. Bob Hope was knighted and named a commander of the British Empire by Queen Elizabeth. France gave him their highest honor, the Legion d'Honeur.

His honors and awards would almost fill a book themselves. Or a museum. As it turns out his career artifacts, awards, and memories are spread out in several museums and Halls of Fame. He was given fifty-four honorary doctorates. Not bad for a high school dropout. He was an extraordinary version of the everyday man, and proof of how far someone can go with a healthy sense of humor, boundless drive, and singleness of purpose.

> **"They gave me the USO award the year I didn't leave the country. They gave me an Oscar for being a humanitarian. And the B'nai B'rith gave me an award for being a Christian. I can hardly wait to break a leg—it might mean the Nobel Prize!"**
> **. . . Bob Hope**

Bob never did receive that Nobel Peace Prize. But he dreamed of a world at peace. And now that the Great War was finally over, he was more than ready to return home to his family . . . until the day when the troops would need him again.

And without hesitation, he would go.

> **"Being active and involved keeps you going. It does me. My theme song is 'Thanks for the Memory,' and I've got some great ones. Yet when I think back, the moments I remember most vividly are not rubbing elbows with the great, or the awards I've received, much as I enjoy all that. What I remember best are quiet moments with my family, unwinding on the golf course, convivial times with old friends; or some poignant thing said by a wounded boy as I bent over his hospital bed trying to bring him a moment of cheer."**
> **. . . Bob Hope**

Bob and Dolores kiss. Was he coming or going?

"This man drives himself and is driven. It is impossible to see how he can do so much, can cover so much ground, can work so hard and be so effective. There's a man. There is really a man!"
—JOHN STEINBECK

Laughter was his ammunition. Peace was his mission. Hope was his name.

Cartoonist Michael Ramirez. Used by permission.

THE END

. . . of World War II. But not of Bob Hope's lifelong commitment to bringing humor and hope to the world and to America's brave and dedicated G.I.s.

BOB HOPE'S WORLD WAR II MILITARY APPEARANCES

A general overview of locations. Each area would feature multiple planned shows, with countless impromptu performances given in remote locales and hospitals.

1942–
Alaska

1943–
Bizerte, North Africa
Tunis, North Africa
Marrakech, Tunis
Palermo, Sicily
Polebrook Air Force Base, England
Tarawa, South Pacific
Algiers, North Africa

1944–
Guadalcanal, South Pacific
Brisbane and Sydney, Australia

1945–
Amiens and Chateau, France
Marseilles, France
Munich and Nuremberg, Germany

The following is Bob's 1944 Itinerary for USO. This is a partial list of the military shows that Bob and the troupe did that summer, according to Jerry Colonna's writings and other accounts. Many of the impromptu shows are missing, such as Pavuvu, Noemfoor, Woendi, and Sarmi. But the list clearly shows how Bob Hope and company were kept on the move, and this is besides Bob's radio shows recorded at military bases across America, his films, and personal appearances. And it only covers *one* summer of the war.

1944 Itinerary for USO
Unit #130
Bob Hope
Frances Langford
Jerry Colonna
Patty Thomas
Barney Dean
Tony Romano

PACIFIC TOUR, 1944

Date	Place	Audience
July 12	Maluhia	10,000
July 13	Aieu Naval Hospital	1,000
	Nimitz Bowl	20,000
	Pearl Harbor	20,000
	Navy Yard	20,000
July 15	Jungle Training Ctr	7,000
	Fort Hase	5,000
	Tripler Hospital	2,000
July 17	Kauai	15,000
July 20	Christmas Island	650
July 21	Canton	1,000
July 23	Tarawa	3,000
July 26	Eniwetok	10,500
July 28	Kwajalein	13,000
	Makin	5,000
July 29	Majuro	4,500
July 30	Guadalcanal	1,300
July 31	Emirau	14,000
August 1	Green Island	15,000
August 2	Bougainville	30,000
August 3	Bougainville	25,000
August 4	Treasury Island	20,000
August 5	Munda	15,000
August 7	Guadalcanal	48,000
August 8	Guadalcanal	38,000
August 9	Tulagi	10,700
August 10	Espiritu Santo	21,000

August 11	Espiritu Santo	18,000
August 12	New Caledonia	15,000
August 13	New Caledonia	45,000
August 14	Laurieton	450 of the 600 or so residents*
August 17	Sydney	2,100
August 21	Hollandia	10,000
August 24	Wadke	16,000
August 25	Owi	8,000
August 27	Aitape	30,000
August 28	Los Negros	22,000
August 29	Endila Island	8,000
	Manus	8,000
August 30	Ponam	2,500
August 31	Los Negros	5,500

*unplanned show after Bob's plane crash

ACKNOWLEDGMENTS

Our sincere thanks to the following people and organizations who helped make this book possible:

BOB & DOLORES HOPE FOUNDATION
Members:
    Linda Hope, chair / CEO
    Tony Montalto, president / CEO
    Miranda Hope
    John McDonnell, secretary

Directors and Nonmembers:
    Jack Peter, treasurer
    Kenneth J. Levy, director of marketing and public relations
    James Hardy, Bob Hope archivist
    Harlan Boll, publicity

MACKENZIE FUHRMANN, ASSISTANT TO LINDA HOPE
    Annette Siegel
    Jonathan Reichman, Esq.
    Hutton Andrews Kurth LLC
    Dixon Q. Dern, Esq.

BOB HOPE'S STAFF OF WRITERS WHO, OVER THE YEARS, SUPPLIED HIM WITH THE SPECIAL MATERIAL THAT BROUGHT HEALING LAUGHTER AT HOME AND ABROAD. A SPECIAL THANKS TO THOSE WRITERS WHO WROTE FOR HIM BETWEEN THE 1940S AND EARLY 1950S. HERE ARE JUST SOME OF THE NAMES WHO WERE ON THE TEAM:
    Melville Shavelson
    Sherwood Schwartz
    Albert Schwartz
    Fred S. Fox Sr.

Seaman Jacobs
Gig Henry
Norman Panama
Melvin Frank
Milt Josefsburg
Mort Lachman
Larry Gelbart
Bill Larkin
Charlie Lee
Norman Sullivan
Lester White
Jack Douglas
Rene Duplessis
Sam Kurtzman

BILL FAITH, BOB HOPE BIOGRAPHER

RICHARD ZOGLIN, BOB HOPE BIOGRAPHER

WARD GRANT, BOB HOPE PR/PUBLICIST

BOB HOPE LEGACY LLC AND THE BOB HOPE LEGACY PARTNERS
National World War II Museum, New Orleans
Library of Congress
Easter Seals, Southern California
Bob Hope USO
Operation Home Front
Bob Hope Theater, Eltham, England
Liberty, Ellis Island

THE BOB HOPE FAMILY

KAYLA CUEVAS, ASSISTANT ARCHIVIST, BOB & DOLORES HOPE
FOUNDATION

TRAVIS PUTERBAUGH, CURATOR, WORLD GOLF HALL OF FAME

LILY BOLTON, PHOTOGRAPHER (WW2 HISTORICAL ARTIFACTS
FROM MARTHA BOLTON'S PERSONAL COLLECTION)

UNIVERSITY PRESS OF MISSISSIPPI
  Emily Snyder Bandy, associate editor
  Todd Lape, production and design manager
  Shane Gong Stewart, project manager
  Steven B. Yates, associate director / marketing director
  Pete Halverson, senior book designer
  Courtney McCreary, publicist
  and all the staff of UPM

DEBBIE J. UPTON

LIBRARY OF CONGRESS:
  Karen Fishman, supervisor, Recorded Sound and Moving Image Research
    Centers, NAVCC
  David Jackson, archivist, National Audio Visual Conservation Center
  David Sager, reference assistant
  Frances Allshouse, cataloger, National Audio Visual Conservation Center,
    Moving Image Section

MEDAL OF HONOR MUSEUM

VETERAN'S ADMINISTRATION

UNITED STATES NAVY

UNITED STATES MARINES

UNITED STATES ARMY

UNITED STATES COAST GUARD
  Admiral Schultz
  Jay W. Guyer, CDR
  Kent R. Reinhold, CDR

UNITED STATES ARMY AIR FORCE

UNITED STATES SIGNAL CORPS

UNITED STATES NATIONAL GUARD
  John Vachon

STEPHEN J. WATSON, PRESIDENT AND CEO, NATIONAL WWII MUSEUM
> Tori Bush, grants manager, National WWII Museum
> Kim Guise, curator, Bob Hope Exhibit, National WWII Museum

JOHN F. KENNEDY PRESIDENTIAL LIBRARY AND MUSEUM
> James B. Hill, archives/reference
> Mary Rose Grossman, audiovisual reference archivist

RONALD REAGAN PRESIDENTIAL LIBRARY
> Steve Branch, audiovisual archivist

FRANKLIN D. ROOSEVELT PRESIDENTIAL LIBRARY AND MUSEUM

ELEANOR ROOSEVELT LIBRARY
> Kirsten Strigel Carter, supervisory archivist
> National Archives and Records Administration

WILLIAM J. CLINTON PRESIDENTIAL LIBRARY AND MUSEUM

GENERAL GEORGE PATTON MUSEUM OF LEADERSHIP

USO (UNITED SERVICE ORGANIZATIONS)

OFFICE OF PRESIDENT GEORGE H. W. BUSH
> Linda Casey, director of correspondence

FOUR CHAPLAINS CHAPEL
> MSG Bill Kaemmer, USA, director

DAME VERA LYNN
> Virginia Lewis-Jones
> Susan Fleet
> Carole Whorwood

LARRY BERRA
> Yogi Berra Museum
> Nikki Morton, office manager

AMERICAN RED CROSS, GAIL J. McGOVERN, PRESIDENT AND CEO

AMERICAN RED CROSS, GAIL J. McGOVERN, PRESIDENT AND CEO

GREG JOHNSON, WORDSERVE LITERARY AGENCY

RUSSELL BOLTON SR., RESEARCH ASSISTANCE

KYLE BOLTON, ASSISTANCE

PARAMOUNT STUDIOS

NATIONAL BROADCASTING COMPANY

PEPSODENT

CHRYSLER CORPORATION
    Danielle McGurk, intellectual property paralegal
    Donna L. Berry, chief trademark council
    Kim Adams House
    Paul Cohen

JOHN C. HARPER, HISTORIAN, TEXACO/CHEVRON CORPORATION

PENGUIN PUBLISHERS
    Kate Middleton quote

BLETCHLEY PARK, ENGLAND

EMMA O'CONNELL, MARKETING AND COMMUNICATIONS ASSIS-
TANT, BLETCHLEY PARK TRUST

MITCH McKAY, PHOTOGRAPHER AND AUTHOR OF *IT'S NOT HOLLY-
WOOD BUT . . .*

SCOTT SHEPPARD, PHOTOGRAPHER

MARYANN SHEPPARD

PETER DUNN, PHOTOGRAPHER

GREGORY FERGUSON, PHOTOGRAPHER

LAURIETON MUSEUM, AUSTRALIA

CAMDEN HAVEN HISTORICAL MUSEUM

OZATWAR.COM

CREW OF THE PBY-5A CATALINA AIRCRAFT IN LAURIETON
James Frank Ferguson (pilot)
Robert (Bob) Dudley Sheppard (copilot)
Robert (Bob) Scott
R. V. Babcock
William (Bill) Ward

EMIL RUGGIERO

REBECCA WELCH

LIZ LANGDALE, SENIOR JOURNALIST, *CAMDEN HAVEN COURIER*

AUSTRALIAN COMMUNITY MEDIA

DEBORAH HASTINGS, ASSOCIATED PRESS

HISTORY.COM

REBECCA MAKSEL, *AIR AND SPACE SMITHSONIAN MAGAZINE*

CAMP ROBERTS HISTORICAL MUSEUM AND FOUNDATION
Gary McMaster, chairman and curator
Daniel Sebby, SGM (CA), CMD Military Museum Enterprise

IMPERIAL WAR MUSEUMS (IWM)
Andrew Webb

NATIONAL MUSEUM OF THE U.S. ARMY

NATIONAL ARCHIVES

HOLLY REED, NATIONAL ARCHIVES AND RECORDS ADMINISTRA-
TION, STILL PICTURE REFERENCE

LEE POLLOCK, INTERNATIONAL CHURCHILL SOCIETY

MUSEUM OF HISTORY AND INDUSTRY, MOHAI, SEATTLE, WASHINGTON
  Adam Lyon
  Kathleen Knies

NORTHWESTERN UNIVERSITY, AMERICAN LEGION COLLECTION

SAN DIEGO SPACE AND AIR MUSEUM

MARK LEVY, MPL MUSIC PUBLISHING, INC.

EDWIN H. MORRIS & COMPANY, A DIVISION OF MPL MUSIC PUBLISHING, INC.

MARK HOTZ

MICHAEL RAMIREZ, CARTOONIST

JULIE STRIKER, ONLINE CONTENT DIRECTOR, *FAIRBANKS DAILY NEWS-MINER*

DENNIS McCARTHY, COLUMNIST, *LOS ANGELES DAILY NEWS*

GENE PERRET

MARY KOLADA SCOTT

DIANTHA AIN

MARGARET BROWNLEY

KAREN KNOTTS

ROBERT METZ

RON CRAWLEY, SOUTH CAROLINA HISTORY

MICHAEL W. POCOCK, MARITIMEQUEST

KIRK DOUGLAS
  Marcia Newberger
  The Bryna Company
  Grace Eboigbe, executive assistant to Mr. Kirk Douglas

NORMAN LEAR
  Cindy C. Villa, grants administrator of Lear Family Foundation

JOHN HOWARD, DUCK DYNASTY FAMILY

BUNNY HOEST, PRESIDENT AND CEO HOEST ENTERPRISES, THE LOCKHORNS

JOHN REINER, CARTOONIST, THE LOCKHORNS

ADRIAN C. SINNOTT

MPL MUSIC PUBLISHING (EDWIN H. MORRIS & COMPANY)

SANTLEY-JOY, INC.

SHAPIRO BERNSTEIN & COMPANY

PEER MUSIC

BOURNE COMPANY, MUSIC PUBLISHERS

FAMOUS MUSIC, LLC

GORDON V. THOMPSON, LIMITED

WIKIPEDIA COMMONS

SETH PARIDON, FORMER STAFF HISTORIAN, THE NATIONAL WORLD WAR II MUSEUM

ALL THE BOB HOPE SECRETARIES AND PERSONAL ASSISTANTS DURING HIS CAREER, BEGINNING WITH MARJORIE HUGHES THROUGH TO JUDITH FARKAS AND JAN MORRILL.

ALL THE ENTERTAINERS WHO TRAVELED WITH BOB HOPE, OR
APPEARED ON HIS RADIO SHOW AT HOME, INCLUDING REGULARS:
Frances Langford
Patty Thomas
Jerry Colonna
Tony Romano
Barney Dean

ACTIVE MEMBERS AND VETERANS OF THE UNITED STATES MILI-
TARY, NOTABLY THE VETERANS OF WORLD WAR 2, BOTH THE
UNITED STATES AND ALLIED FORCES, AND ALL THOSE WHO PAID
THE ULTIMATE PRICE.

AND OUR HEARTFELT THANKS TO THE WOMAN WHO STARTED
IT ALL, MARJORIE HUGHES, BOB HOPE'S SECRETARY DURING THE
WORLD WAR II YEARS AND BEYOND. WITHOUT HER CAREFUL RE-
CORDS AND INCREDIBLE DEVOTION TO PRESERVING HISTORY, THIS
BOOK WOULD NOT HAVE BEEN POSSIBLE.

Bob Hope and Marjorie Hughes, Bob Hope's secretary, WWII.

ABOUT THE AUTHORS

MARTHA BOLTON was a staff writer for Bob Hope for approximately fifteen years, writing his personal appearances and prime-time television specials, including *Bob Hope's USO Christmas from the Persian Gulf: Around the World in Eight Days* (1988), *Bob Hope's Christmas Cheer from Saudi Arabia* (1991), *Bob Hope's Yellow Ribbon Party* (1991), *Bob Hope: The First 90 Years* (1993), and *Bob Hope: Laughing with the Presidents* (1996).

Martha received an Emmy nomination for Outstanding Achievement in Music and Lyrics (1987–1988 Emmys), a Dove Award nomination, and a WGA Award nomination, and is the author of eighty-eight books of humor and inspiration, including *Josiah for President* and *Didn't My Skin Used to Fit?* She is a playwright with productions playing in Indiana, Ohio, Pennsylvania, Kentucky, and Florida, and was also a writer for Phyllis Diller, the Lockhorns, and numerous comedians.

She appeared on *Bob Hope: The First 90 Years*, the Bob Hope Writers segment (NBC, 1993), and on *The Academy of Television Arts and Sciences—50th Anniversary Celebration Tribute to Bob Hope* (1996), video/documentary.

Martha's favorite Bob Hope memory:

> Once, while dropping off a joke-writing assignment to Bob's home, his guard dog, Snowjob, bit me on the top of my foot. Bob was on his way out of town, but when his assistant informed him of the incident, he sent me a telegram the next day that read, "Dear Martha, please come back soon. I'm ready for another hors d'oeuvre. Love, Snowjob."

LINDA HOPE is the eldest daughter of Bob Hope's four children and is an Emmy-winning producer of *Bob Hope: The First 90 Years* (1993). In addition to winning the Emmy for Outstanding Variety, Music or Comedy Special, the three-hour television event also received three additional Emmy nominations. Linda produced many of Bob's television specials and ran his production company for the last twenty years of his working life. Linda's producer credits include *Bob Hope's Christmas Cheer from Saudi Arabia* (1991), *Bob Hope's Yellow Ribbon Party* (1991), *Bob Hope: Laughing with the Presidents* (1996), and *Bob Hope's 100 Years of Hope and Humor* (2003). She is the author of *My Life* *in Jokes*, a unique work that tells Bob's life, decade by decade, through his jokes. The book was released for Bob's one-hundredth birthday.

Linda's favorite Bob Hope memory:

My dad had enough frequent flyer miles to own an airline. At least that was the situation until his friend Alex Spanos made a case for him to finally get his own plane when Dad was in his eighties. Dad was delighted each time he flew in that plane.

One time we were flying across the country and he called me up to the front seat where he was sitting. I went up there and bent down to hear what he wanted to say. With a sense of wonder, he pointed to the window and said, "Look out there."

I looked and saw nothing. "Dad, it's just black out," I said.

"Keep looking ... that's going to be Chicago down there. I'll never forget when I was just starting out I almost starved to death in that city. I remember watching all the 'swells' dining in a fancy restaurant and hearing my stomach growling. I wasn't sure if I'd ever make it ... and here I am, up here, in my own plane, flying over this great country ... only in America. It makes you feel proud."

My father never did lose that sense of awe. He immigrated to this country from England when he was four years old. That restricted him from ever running for president. If he could have tossed his golf hat into the ring, many people say he might have won. But that wasn't how he chose to serve his "adopted" country. It was by promising to be there for the men and women who protected this land that he loved so much. And for fifty years, he didn't break that promise.

For additional Bob Hope World War II memories (pictures, audio, and more), visit our link: http://bobhope.org//DearBobmore.